In a career spanning more than 20 years, Je
cially and critically well-received books, ir
phies of 'Shirley' Strachan from *Skyhooks* and *Dragon*'s Marc Hunter.

He also co-wrote the recent Kasey Chambers memoir, called *A Little Bird Told Me*, and worked with Mark Evans of AC/DC on his bestseller, *Dirty Deeds*. In 2005, Jeff worked with test cricketer turned commentator Michael Slater on his book, *Slats*.

His other books include studies of Jeff Buckley (which has been adapted for a feature film), the Finn brothers and Keith Urban. Jeff was ghostwriter on a project called *In Harm's Way*, the story of a former Australian soldier and his attempts to emancipate two children in Lebanon.

His biography of Johnny O'Keefe is out through Hachette Australia. His latest book is called Up From Down Under: How Australian Music Changed the World.

Jeff lives on the NSW south coast with his wife and two children.

www.jeffapter.com.au

A NEW TOMORROW

A NEW TOMORROW

THE SILVERCHAIR STORY

JEFF APTER

Text copyright © 2014 Jeff Apter

All rights reserved.
No part of this book may be reproduced, or stored in a retrieval system, or transmitted in any form or by any means, electronic, mechanical, photocopying, recording, or otherwise, without express written permission of the publisher.

ISBN-13: 9781495365942

For the daysleepers

CONTENTS

Acknowledgements		**xi**
Prologue	WaveAid, 29 January 2005, SCG	**xiii**
Chapter 1	Innocent Criminals	**1**
Chapter 2	Frogstomping All Over the World	**32**
	Madness in the Moshpit: An interview with David Fricke	61
Chapter 3	The Freak Show	**71**
	Abuse Me: An interview with John Watson	100
Chapter 4	So Where'd That Year Go?	**107**
	Silverfan: An interview with a Silverchair obsessive	120
Chapter 5	Ballroom Blitz	**125**
	The Peacemaker: An interview with Nick Launay	168
Chapter 6	Can I Get a Hallelujah?	**177**
	Emotion Sickness: An interview with Elissa Blake	188
Chapter 7	Dramarama	**194**
	The Label Guy: An interview with Kevin "Williamson	229
Chapter 8	Free Dissociation	**236**
	The Engine Room: An interview with Ben Gillies and Chris Joannou	256
Chapter 9	A New Tomorrow	**263**
	Young Modern: An interview with Daniel Johns	275
Silverchair Discography		**284**

ACKNOWLEDGEMENTS

Firstly, many thanks to Meredith Curnow, Brandon VanOver and all at Random House – the mint juleps are on me; thanks also to Silvia Kwon, for reminding me that I could actually do this in the first place; John Watson, Melissa Chenery and all at Eleven for being way more accommodating than they had to be; Desney Shoemark (and Stephanie Holt) for making sense of it all; Diana Gonsalves for digging deep and Elizabeth Asha for being there; Elissa Blake and Darren Gover for coping with a temperamental author-under-development; David Fricke, Robert Hambling, Nick Launay, John O'Donnell, Van Dyke Parks, Craig Mathieson, Tobin Finnane, Peter McNair, David Bottrill, Gerald Casale, James Hackett, David (and Gillian) Helfgott, Luke Steele, Scott Horscroft, Andrew Humphreys, Julian Hamilton, Matt Lovell, Phil McKellar, Kevin 'Caveman' Shirley, Kevin Williamson, Paul Mac and Tracee Hutchison for going on the record (at length); Rob Hirst for giving it the once over; Guy McEwan at the State Theatre for the backstage pass; Bob Allen and Gordon Murray at www.billboard.com; the Silver-families for checking the facts; and www.chairpage.com for their bottomless archive; plus Tony Mott, Val Maclver, Fiona Simpson and Gabe Cramb; and, of course, Daniel Johns, Ben Gillies and Chris Joannou (aka Silverchair) for revisiting the past – and for making the music in the first place.

Comments and quotes that appear in the text, unless otherwise noted, were derived from interviews conducted by the author with the following people: Daniel Johns, Chris Joannou, Ben Gillies, Tobin Finnane, John Watson, John O'Donnell, Nick Launay, David Fricke, Elissa Blake,

JEFF APTER

Van Dyke Parks, Robert Hambling, Tracee Hutchison, Matt Lovell, Peter McNair, Craig Mathieson, Paul Mac, Phil McKellar, Gerald Casale, David Helfgott, Julian Hamilton, James Hackett, Kevin Williamson, Kevin Shirley, Luke Steele and David Bottrill.

Prologue
WAVEAID, 29 JANUARY 2005, SCG

> Watching Midnight Oil [at WaveAid], we figured we only had one opportunity to be a great, great band. The great ones are the bands who have been together since they were kids, sorted out their shit, and kept going and twenty years later they were still killing it. So we said, 'Right, studio time.'
>
> Daniel Johns, 2006

Daniel Johns isn't supposed to look this good. In fact, no one should be allowed to look this good. The twenty-five-year-old Johns was stripped to the waist, his pierced nipples on full and erect display, with his newly buffed and tanned torso oozing sweat and muscle, as he and his Silverchair bandmates, bassist Chris Joannou and drummer Ben Gillies, powered their way through a short yet overwhelmingly powerful set at WaveAid, a fundraiser for the many victims of the horrendous Boxing Day tsunami. And Gillies and Joannou scrubbed up equally well – both were now male-model-handsome, having shed the puppy fat, the Mohawk, the crewcut, the arse-length mane and the various other ill-chosen looks that had marked their appearance over the past ten years.

But it was Johns who looked every bit the pagan rock god, as the band commandeered the stage at the Sydney Cricket Ground. Maybe his rude health was due to the fact that he was no longer a vegan, having finally submitted to his body's basic needs and become a more 'traditional' vegetarian. 'I occasionally have to eat some form of animal protein, such as eggs, because my body isn't strictly suited to veganism,' he told me afterwards. 'But I'd never eat a cow burger or something.' Or possibly it was the glow that comes from sharing your life with someone as supermodel-stunning as Natalie Imbruglia.

Whatever the cause, it was a huge turnaround: only a couple of years earlier Johns was a physical and emotional wreck, his frail frame racked by a chronic bout of reactive arthritis. It was such an overpowering condition that during his darkest days he could only get about with the aid of a walking stick, and even then his movements were restricted to an old man's shuffle. When I checked in with Johns at his palatial Newcastle home in 2002, principally to learn the truth about the band's epic fourth LP, *Diorama*, it took him at least five minutes to reach his front door, even though he had to walk only a few metres. It would take him more than a year to fully recover from the debilitating condition, which forced Silverchair into a recess that derailed that album, and their relationship with their American record company, Atlantic.

When we spoke at length in 2002 about his ongoing physical therapy, Johns was in America seeking out alternative treatments for his crippling condition, on the advice of his then-girlfriend, now wife, Imbruglia. The description of the strenuous therapy he was undergoing was enough to bring tears to my eyes, let alone Johns's.

Yet he was surprisingly upbeat:

> There's no one who can give you sure answers that it [reactive arthritis] won't happen again in five years, but the doctor in LA is confident that she can fix all of this. I'm not going to get too depressed about it, because I can manage it. It's not too bad. But six months ago, if someone had told me this is the way it's going to be for five years, I would have killed myself.

And I don't think he was kidding.

Johns maintained a brave face during his subsequent 'resurrection' at the 2002 ARIAs, where the band briefly returned to playing live (and scooped the prize pool), but I wasn't the only person to genuinely fear for the guy's well-being. If this is what rock and roll success brought you – and

A NEW TOMORROW

part of Johns's problems were psychological, brought on by the demands of stardom – then maybe he should consider retiring to his home studio with his wife and his dog and keep the hell out of the spotlight.

But by January 2005, Johns was looking stunning, despite insisting he was no exercise junkie. In fact, when we spoke about his health, he told me that he didn't maintain any sort of exercise regimen to keep in such fine shape.

> I never go to the gym; I've gone maybe once in 18 months. This is what happens when you don't have anorexia and your bones aren't eating themselves. People got used to me being sick and then they said, when they saw me looking better, 'What are you doing?' I told them I was simply not being sick.

Now he was a totally rejuvenated and reborn man, flexing some serious muscle at WaveAid. It was the band's first public appearance for almost two years, a period in which most people – Johns amongst them – had accepted that time was up for Australia's biggest rock act of the past decade.

As he told me during that same January 2003 interview, his take on Silverchair's future was ambivalent at best.

> Every day I wake up and think, 'This is the last day I'm going to be in a band.' Then I go, 'Just one more day.' Then I write a song and go, 'This is the last fucking song I'm going to write for this band – Okay, maybe one more.'

Johns had seriously considered killing off the band at several key stages of its career: at the end of the lengthy, spirit-sapping tour for their second album, *Freak Show*, and after completing both 1999's *Neon Ballroom* album and 2002's *Diorama*.

> I don't know. It's not that I don't enjoy being in the band, I do. And I love those guys [Gillies and Joannou], because we have an amazing chemistry. But a lot of it is that attention span thing; I get bored, I want to do other things.

And Johns, for one, had moved on both personally and professionally since *Diorama* was released in March 2002. After his slow recovery from reactive arthritis, he'd married soapie-star-turned-songbird-actress-model Imbruglia in a hush-hush ceremony in tropical Queensland on New Year's Eve 2003. This meant that he now divided his time between Australia and Imbruglia's lavish home in the UK, which made it almost impossible to find time for Silverchair. And he was keeping some A-list company, a lifestyle that separated him even further from his bandmates, who moved in less elite circles. In fact, the night before the WaveAid show, Johns was busting moves on a Sydney dance floor alongside Nick Cave, Beth Orton, Rufus Wainwright and Pulp's Jarvis Cocker, to the soundtrack of electro-pop reprobates the Presets. This was hardly the kind of company, or music, that meant much to Gillies or Joannou.

And there was his life with the Dissociatives, an electro-pop outfit he formed with long-time sonic sidekick and buddy Paul Mac, a man Johns described as 'amazing ... one of my best, closest friends'. Their self-titled debut album, released in 2004, had been on the receiving end of both critical kudos and a healthy thumbs-up at the almighty cash register. Although Johns had dabbled with various side projects during his time out front of Silverchair, the Dissociatives was a far more serious enterprise; it was obvious that Johns had invested much more in this project than he had with such previous indulgences as *I Can't Believe It's Not Rock* (also recorded with Mac).

Even before the Dissociatives came into existence, Johns had been hinting at a more formal collaboration with Mac, who in previous lives had been an underground dance music hero and a teacher at Sydney's Fort Street School. (Johns has told me that there's still a little of the disciplinarian in Mac, 'especially when he goes, "Daniel, sit!" He's a very paradoxical human being.') 'Next time,' Johns told me in 2003, 'I feel it's going to be more important, more of an actual statement. Next time it's going to be an actual album. We're going to come up with a name for the group' – they eventually took their handle from the series of drugs that detach a user from everyday reality, not a bad metaphor for the surreal pop they created – 'and publicise it and let people know it exists.'

The fact that Johns then formed a Dissociatives band, and took it on the road, said plenty about his intentions: this was a real group that might just have a future beyond one album. And maybe Silverchair didn't matter that much to him anymore, despite their ready-made audience who'd sell their souls to catch another glimpse of Australia's alt-rock heroes. Johns seemed to have outgrown Silverchair; the idea of him plugging in and tearing through 'Israel's Son' one more time simply didn't seem likely. And Johns was as bored with the notion of long-term touring as he was playing the 'hits'.

As he said to me:

> The trouble with playing live is playing the same songs – no matter how much you try to change them around, you just get bored really quickly. Live can be a really amazing experience, but it ceases to be amazing after three months. It just becomes fucking boring.

Joannou and Gillies, meanwhile, also seemed to have accepted that Silverchair's time was up. Gillies had formed his own outfit, Tambalane, with Sydney-based singer/strummer Wesley Carr, and released a self-titled album of surprisingly melodic, mainstream pop-rock. Joannou, meanwhile, had picked up some freelance production gigs – his work with bloozepower duo the Mess Hall even earned him an ARIA nomination – and recorded, anonymously, with Newcastle band Atomica. And just like Johns, both were involved in long-term relationships: Joannou with former Superjesus singer, Sarah McLeod, and Gillies with Hayley Alexander, a Newcastle ballerina. (Admittedly, Joannou's relationship wasn't built to last: it came to a rather messy end at the 2005 Jack Awards, when McLeod, who'd terminated the relationship a few months earlier, spotted Joannou with a new partner and had a very public meltdown, on stage, while presenting an award.)

Some band insiders, however, felt that the trio's extracurricular adventures actually brought Silverchair closer together. Julian Hamilton, who played keyboards for the Dissociatives and for Silverchair during seventy-odd live shows, has written with Johns and is a close friend of the band, told me in early 2006 that:

> The more stuff Dan[iel] does outside the 'Chair, the more he'll appreciate coming back to it from time to time – and that's good. That goes for Ben and Chris, too. They've all been venturing out, working with different musicians and developing as artists and as people. I think

it's great that they can come back to the 'Chair and bring a whole new wealth of experiences to it every time they do.

But in 2003, after four best-selling albums and many millions of record sales, the former teen titans appeared to have moved on to the next stage of their lives. And there was an unmistakable whiff of finality to their last Australian tour, which wound down, appropriately, with a pair of hometown Newcastle shows in April 2003. What better way to bring Silverchair's award-winning, multi-platinum ride to a triumphant end than to raise the roof in the city where it all began almost a decade before? I definitely got a hint of that when I checked in with the band after the second sold-out show at Newcastle's Civic Theatre. Joannou, Johns and Gillies shared backstage space with their families and partners, while an effervescent Natalie Imbruglia recorded everything on a digital camera, as if this was her last chance to grab images of the band and their crew together. The mood was both celebratory and slightly nostalgic.

Yet the tsunami changed all that. The 2005 Boxing Day disaster was of a Hollywood-sized scale. A mammoth wall of water roared into and over unsuspecting Asian villages and towns, grasping everything in its path like a giant, angry fist. When it finally subsided, the tsunami had claimed thousands of lives. Natural disasters rarely come larger than this. It was so big, in fact, that as the relief efforts began, a new dilemma arose: how exactly do you address something of this magnitude? Admittedly, the entertainment industry has a solid track record when it comes to helping those in need – Live Aid, Farm Aid, Live 8 and many other equally large-scale events had done their bit to raise hard cash for the needy, and heighten awareness among the ignorant. In the process, these gigs had turned Bob Geldof and U2's Bono into modern-day saints.

The Australian music industry's reaction to the tsunami was swift and efficient. For once, matters of record label allegiances, chart positions and personal rivalries were shelved as a wealth of local talent, both contemporary and of a certain vintage, agreed to plug in and rock out. Current hit-makers such as Powderfinger, the Waifs and Pete Murray, and veterans Nick Cave and the Finn Brothers, all agreed to do their bit. Even Midnight Oil signed up, announcing that this would be their farewell gig, at least with the recently

A NEW TOMORROW

elected federal member for Kingsford Smith, Peter Garrett, out front of the band. And so WaveAid was born, and at the same time the event would mark the reawakening of Silverchair, the most successful Australian rock band of the past ten years, whose first three albums – 1995's *Frogstomp*, 1997's *Freak Show* and 1999's *Neon Ballroom* – had shifted more than six million copies internationally, numbers that were only bettered in the modern era by INXS and Savage Garden. Silverchair's appearance was proof that something positive could come out of dire adversity – and, unintentionally, the event proved exactly why they meant so much to so many. Yet the band came into the gig hugely under-prepared, having rehearsed for all of a week beforehand.

Johns said:

> The gig wasn't close to the best we've ever played; it felt a bit like an infomercial. We hadn't played for years, so we decided not to be stupid, not to play 'Tuna in the Brine'; we only had about five rehearsals, so we decided to just try and sound like a great rock band. And the cause was the big thing, so it wasn't about showboating or making a big artistic statement; just try and enjoy it.

Maybe the band's red-hot set had something to do with Silverchair's place on the all-star bill. They took over the stage at dusk, immediately before Powderfinger, the band currently regarded as Australia's leading homegrown rock and roll act, and the mighty Midnight Oil, who were saying farewell to the faithful. When Johns, Gillies and Joannou plugged in and tore through their brief set of signature songs, including such almighty singalongs as 'The Greatest View', 'Ana's Song (Open Fire)' and 'The Door', the response was wild. It was an even more fanatical response than they'd been given by the full houses on their 2003 Across the Night tour. Silverchair had simply out-muscled Powderfinger, reminding the huge crowd that the Brisvegas chart-toppers were little more than earnest pub rockers, packing none of Johns's starpower or Silverchair's sonic grunt. And in Midnight Oil, the Silver-trio saw a band that still had the power to unite an audience, even in the twilight of their career. Maybe, they considered quietly afterwards, as they retired to their separate corners of the globe, there was still a little life left in Silverchair.

This was certainly foremost in Johns's mind.

After it, we thought, 'Fuck, man, we didn't even try and people really responded.' So it was the crowd, and also playing together – we realised how easy it felt, it was so natural, the songs kept coming out. And then watching Midnight Oil, who were just absolutely killing it. We figured we only had one opportunity to be a great, great band. The great ones are the bands who have been together since they were kids, sorted out their shit, and kept going and twenty years later they were still killing it. So we said, 'Right, studio time.'

In an official statement just prior to WaveAid, Johns was pragmatic about the band's slight return.

Obviously, anyone with a heart wants to do whatever they can right now to try and provide some help to all the people who are suffering. So the cricketers play cricket, the TV people do a TV show and the musicians play a gig. It should be a really memorable occasion.

Afterwards, he was way more effusive. 'WaveAid was an amazing experience,' he gushed, 'and it was really the catalyst that made us want to start making music together again'. WaveAid was also a massive success, raising a touch over AUD$2 million for the victims of the tsunami.

Twelve months later, Silverchair made it formally known that they were back, with a new album and tour in the works. By February 2006, as they readied themselves for four shows over the next few weeks, specifically to raise the necessary cash to finance their fifth LP, they already had eleven new songs demoed and ready to record. And one of these tracks was so strong, according to a band source, that it resembled '[U2's] "With or Without You" meets [Coldplay's] "Clocks"'. It was a sure-fire hit.

Anyone who had witnessed the awesome sight of Daniel Johns strutting across the WaveAid stage like a man who had just rediscovered the simple pleasure of plugging in and making a hellacious noise, could see that WaveAid marked Silverchair's new tomorrow. They were back.

Chapter One
INNOCENT CRIMINALS

> They were absolutely dreadful. The music was amplified, it was loud and it was really bad.
> Letter to *Newcastle Herald* soon after the first Innocent Criminals show

Silverchair are Australia's most popular rock band of the past ten years. Each of their four albums – *Frogstomp, Freak Show, Neon Ballroom* and *Diorama* – has debuted at Number One on the Australian charts, and they have shifted, in total, more than six million copies worldwide. The band's fanbase stretches from their hometown, Newcastle, to most parts of the globe. In a golden run between 1994 and the end of 1999, they had twelve consecutive Top 40 singles in Australia, making them the most successful local chart performers of the 1990s. That purple patch continued in 2002 and 2003, when the four singles lifted from their *Diorama* album – 'The Greatest View', 'Without You', 'Luv Your Life' and 'Across the Night' – all raided the Top 40; 'The Greatest View' peaking at Number Three. They've also won enough Australian Recording Industry Association Awards (ARIAs) to fill several mantelpieces, including numerous Best Band and Best Album gongs.

They're an ambitious lot, who in this short stretch have grown from punked-up grunge-keteers to a trio that's happy to bring in an orchestra when needed. But there's more to Silverchair's success than great songs, powerful recordings, frenetic shows and a diehard following that accepts every creative step the band takes, no matter how radical. Their singer/ guitarist and key songwriter, Daniel Johns, has lived through any number of personal crises. He's endured a life-threatening eating disorder, crippling arthritis, chronic depression and the heavy emotional baggage that comes with a life lived reluctantly in the public eye. The fact that a clutch of paparazzi hired a helicopter to hover overhead, angling for a money shot, during his marriage to ex-*Neighbours* star Natalie Imbruglia in 2003 proved that his commercial worth hasn't waned. What he's drawn from these hardships is a batch of passionate, deeply felt songs that have connected with an audience that understands what it feels like to be an outsider.

More than once, the band has been a press release away from chucking it all in – as they freely admit. But the trio has endured and prospered, striking out for new musical territory with their 2002 album, *Diorama*, and regrouping in 2006 after having pursued their own solo projects. As their long-time manager and confidant John Watson admits, Silverchair is to Daniel Johns what the band Crazy Horse is to Neil Young – the group he continues to return to, no matter how far he strays between albums. Johns also accepts that this is a reasonable analogy.

> [But] it's more than the band I just come back to. I like to go out and make records and come back when I'm fresh, with my palate cleansed. Then I get back with the boys and kick out the jams.

From behind the scenes, savvy management has ensured that the trio hasn't suffered from overexposure, the kiss of death at a time in rock and roll when a band gains veteran status if they make it past their first album. The timing of Silverchair's rise was perfect, too: they surfaced as the grunge wave broke, in the wake of Nirvana's era-defining album *Nevermind* – and being all of fifteen at the time, they had an irresistible hook for the music media. And, impressively, their audience has hung about, even when the band found that grunge no longer filled any holes in their souls. It doesn't hurt, of course, that their lead singer is blond, blue-eyed and in desperate need of a hug, or that Johns, Gillies and Joannou have grown into strikingly handsome, camera-friendly young men.

Silverchair's rise followed one of rock's worst flat spots. It's no small irony that one of the world's biggest bands of the 1980s and early 1990s was named Dire Straits. Contemporary music was in a baggy-suited, headband-wearing state of transition, and Mark Knopfler's spruced-up mob of former UK pub rockers ruled the airwaves and the small screen.

A cursory run through the ten top singles of 1991 and 1992 reveals plenty about the dire state of music in that post-punk, pre-grunge, pre-Silverchair time. The 'Grease Mega-Mix' was 1991's best seller, with Daryl Braithwaite's slick 'The Horses' and Bryan Adams's even slicker '(Everything I Do) I Do It for You' not far behind. Pop diva Cher and supermodel-chaser Rod Stewart were selling large amounts of records, as was straitlaced songbird Mariah Carey. The pop charts have always been clogged with fluff, but this airbrushed, windswept time in pop history was especially fluffy.

The following twelve months weren't much better. Billy Ray Cyrus, the linedancing cowboy, sat at Number One with 'Achy Breaky Heart', while Julian Lennon's treacly 'Saltwater' also made the list of the ten best sellers. Watered-down soulsters Simply Red and the Australian cast recording of *Jesus Christ Superstar* shifted serious units. It was the worst of times.

Bored punters started looking towards England, especially Manchester, where such bands as the Happy Mondays and the Stone Roses were gulping ecstasy and doing their bit to knock down the wall that separated rock and dance. But their music was rarely heard on commercial radio in Australia – if it was played at all, it was during the graveyard shift when advertisers didn't really care about the playlist. In the main, this new British music was relegated to specialist stations such as the youth network Triple J, or community stations like Sydney's 2SER and Melbourne's 3RRR. The Internet hadn't been sufficiently developed to provide an outlet for those interested in music that fell between the cracks, while downloading wasn't even heard of yet. Mainstream Australia was being force-fed the tarted-up pub rock of the Baby Animals or the lung-straining bluster of Jimmy Barnes, whose unstoppable covers album, *Soul Deep*, was such a no-brainer that the man himself admitted 'a monkey could sing these songs and they'd still be hits.'

Yet during the 1980s, the very same Jimmy Barnes had been at the forefront of a distinctive style of Australian rock and roll – Oz rock, in shorthand – that had made an enormous impact. Cold Chisel, Rose Tattoo, the Angels and Midnight Oil had endured apprenticeships served in such sweaty bacterial barns as Sydney's Stagedoor Tavern, the Bondi Lifesaver and Melbourne's Bombay Rock. They emerged from this to make powerful, important records such as Cold Chisel's *East* and Midnight Oil's *10, 9, 8, 7, 6, 5, 4, 3, 2, 1*. Meanwhile, such second division acts as the Radiators, Swanee (led by Jimmy Barnes's brother, John Swan), the Choirboys and others helped flesh out the bills headlined by the A-list bands, and in the process made a reasonable living out of live work.

Oz rock crowds were male-dominated. They were up for big nights of drinking and sex, or fighting, if the ladies weren't keen. And these bands – the Oils, the Chisels, the Tatts – supplied the soundtrack to thousands of their gritty, beer-stained evenings. Though the bands were diverse in style, there were common threads: a blazing guitar riff and a ball-tearing vocal to keep the crowds keen, and if the lyrics could connect to Aussie themes, well, all the better. The publicans were happy, because the punters drank. The bands got work.

The introduction of Australian quotas on radio meant that local groups were receiving healthy airplay, which quickly led to record sales. In April 1981, Oz rock reached a very public early peak when Cold Chisel caused havoc at the Countdown Awards, smashing the set, nearly frightening the cowboy hat clear off Molly Meldrum's head. Within a month, their album *East* had sold more than 200,000 copies. Unlike what was to follow, Oz rock was a locally based sensation that was more about sweat and hard yards than image and good grooming. All was good.

However, Oz rock was fading by the late 1980s. Noise restrictions and revamped licensing laws meant that venues were closing, while bands were splitting or losing their crowd-pulling appeal. The Angels and Midnight Oil started looking Stateside for a larger audience, with mixed success, which meant their Australian followers started looking elsewhere for new bands to love. The credible, punk-influenced Australian underground bands that had emerged during the tail end of the Oz rock era – Brisbane's Go-Betweens and the Saints, Perth's the Triffids, the Nick Cave-led Birthday

Party – had all left town, either to develop and prosper overseas or crash and burn, citing the usual inner-band politics and toxic overindulgence.

As the 1990s began, there were ripples of change in the mainstream. Funky Californian punks the Red Hot Chili Peppers hit big – really big – in 1992 with their junkie's requiem, 'Under the Bridge', and its parent album, *Blood Sugar Sex Magik*, which reached Number One in Australia during November 1991 and hung about the charts for sixty-one weeks. American college rockers REM had crossed over into the mainstream in 1991 with their *Out of Time* album and its breakout hit single, 'Losing My Religion' – without sacrificing any of their garage-rock sensibilities or singer Michael Stipe's intriguing weirdness. And at the Number Seven spot on 1992's best-selling album chart was the album that started the musical and cultural revolution known as 'alternative': Nirvana's *Nevermind*.

So what was Australia's contribution while alternative music was starting to make an impression on the charts? Nothing much, just such safe local acts as 1927, Wendy Matthews and the Rockmelons, playing music designed, as one critic put it at the time, 'for people who don't like music'. Still stuck in the 1980s, most labels were trying to hunt down the next Noiseworks. Offering a more polished, American-influenced variation of Oz rock, this band were favourite sons of the beer barns. Noiseworks's first two albums, a self-titled effort from 1987 and 1988's *Touch*, sold almost 400,000 copies. But such new signings as Bang the Drum, Wildland, 21 Guns and Big Storm all fell flat, in part because the musical tide was shifting away from the slick, over-produced pop-rock that made Noise-works stars.

Occasionally, underground acts like punkish popsters Ratcat broke through with a hit, but their success was as brief as the songs they sang. Meanwhile, at the major record labels, Artist and Repertoire (A&R) talent-spotters such as Sony's John Watson, Polydor's Craig Kamber and Ra's Todd Wagstaff were on the lookout for Australian bands that packed the same anti-everything attitude and pure rock and roll clout as Nirvana, and the numerous other bands – Soundgarden, the Smashing Pumpkins and Hole amongst them – who had caught a little of Nirvana's slipstream.' Alternative' bands such as You Am I (signed to Ra Records) and stoner rockers Tumbleweed (who had their self-titled debut distributed by Festival Records, before signing with Polydor Records) were seen as the bands most likely to shake up the mainstream. But their sales didn't make much of an impression on the Top 40. Although You Am I's first four albums would debut at Number One on the Australian album chart, none had the staying power to shift serious units; within weeks of release they'd dropped off the chart altogether.

None of this mattered much in Merewether, the sleepy coastal suburb that is one stunning vista away from Newcastle, the second-largest city in New South Wales. Newcastle had been founded in 1804 as a colony for the First Fleet's worst convicts, and in the shadows of World War I it became home to one of BHP's major steelworks. It was a city of industry, the Australian version of British industrial cities such as Manchester, only warmer. For much of the century it flourished, a rough and tumble place where rugby league ruled and beer was the drink of choice. Its beachside neighbour, Merewether, slumbered quietly. But work in the steel town and its surrounds started to slacken off. The region was hard hit by unemployment, which ran somewhere near 30 per cent by the early 1990s. Merewether supplied its share of those out of work.

Silverchair's Daniel Johns was asked in 1996 about growing up in the area. 'One half of Newcastle is real industrial, and the other half is all beach and stuff,' he explained. 'It's a reasonably small town [Merewether]. People basically leave us alone, but some call us longhaired louts.' Those name-callers didn't know that these 'long-haired louts' would soon become Merewether's most famous exports and the answer to every A&R guy's prayers.

Daniel Johns was born in Newcastle on 22 April 1979. His Silverchair partners, Ben Gillies and Chris Joannou, were born on 24 October and 10 November 1979, respectively. Daniel was the first of three children for his parents, Greg, who ran a fruit stall in Newcastle, and Julie. Ben was the second child for David Gillies, a plumber, and his wife Annette. Chris was one of three kids; he had an older sister as well as a twin sister. David and Sue Joannou operated a dry-cleaning franchise. It was all in keeping with the blue-collar mindset of the area and its people: unpretentious, dedicated, dreaming of maybe, one day, wiping off the mortgage and not having to work so damned hard.

Gillies and Joannou first met in kindergarten. In grade three at primary school they met Daniel Johns, who soon became especially tight with Gillies. Initially, the boys' common bonds were simple and very much a product of their environment: they loved music, bodyboarding and surfing. But none of them were really soaking up the music of the 1980s. Despite the name-checking of Newcastle's Star Hotel in their immortal shouter of the same name, Cold Chisel and Oz rock meant little to the Merewether three. 'I never got into the pub rock scene, it didn't appeal to me,' Johns said in March 1999. Ben Gillies can remember hearing Cold Chisel on the radio 'but not really liking it'.

Instead, as Johns later revealed, it was their parents' record collections that got them interested in music. These were collections heavy with the type of bands – Deep Purple, Led Zeppelin et al. – that fancied loud guitars and crashing drums and wailing vocals and would have a lasting influence on the sound of Silverchair. Johns's father, in particular, was a huge hard-rock fan, with a serious collection of Deep Purple vinyl. 'Mum and Dad were really into the whole hippie thing,' Johns told *Rolling Stone*, 'so I grew up listening to Hendrix, Deep Purple, Black Sabbath, Cat Stevens and John Lennon.'

Growing up, Johns's favourite albums included *Led Zeppelin IV* ('one of the first records I heard, along with Sabbath and Deep Purple'), Midnight Oil's *10, 9, 8, 7, 6, 5, 4, 3, 2, 1* ('the first Australian album I got, when I was about 10 or 11') and *Deep Purple in Rock* ('the first rock album I ever bought'). Speaking with Craig Mathieson for his 1996 book, *Hi Fi Days,* Johns confessed his deep-felt love for Deep Purple. 'I wanted to be [guitarist] Ritchie Blackmore,' he admitted.

A lot of early Silverchair history replays the responses of fifteen-year-olds who aren't sure their time in the sun will last much longer than their first hit.' They said what they pleased and stretched the truth when required; they thought it all a bit of a laugh. The three, at least in the beginning, seemed completely unaffected by what Joni Mitchell once called 'the star-making machine'. Johns once boasted, unconvincingly, that his father was a big fan of Tool and Helmet, hard-rock bands from the 1990s that Johns junior happened to love and hoped to emulate. It's highly unlikely Greg Johns played their music in the car – but the claim did make Johns's pretty damned normal upbringing sound much cooler in the pages of the music press.

The boys' parents – especially their fathers – had dabbled in bands when they were younger. Gillies's father played rhythm guitar and his mother played piano. Joannou's father played bass, as his son was soon to do. Much later, Johns's brother, Heath, would start his own band – called the Army of Prawns, no less – with more than a little help from his successful sibling. Heath Johns would eventually score a high-flying post in the music industry; Joannou's sister also worked in the music biz. Music was definitely in all their bloodlines.

Gillies, Johns and Joannou had grown up within a few blocks of each other in Merewether. While Johns was lost in his Ritchie Blackmore dreams, Gillies – who had bought his first drum kit for $75, aged eight, after deciding the drummer in the school band was 'so cool' – was locked away in his bedroom, repeatedly playing John Bonham's memorable, monolithic drum solo from the Led Zeppelin film, *The Song Remains the Same*. Gillies was hypnotised by the awesome power and rhythmic pulse of the man they called Bonzo. (Gillies ended up selling that first kit for $300. It now resides, battered and bruised, in the music room of a Newcastle primary school.)

With a schoolfriend helping out on keyboards, Johns and Gillies, then aged nine, had formed a rap outfit, the Silly Men. Their repertoire included rhymes about such weighty issues as Welshmen and a leg of beef, with 'The Elephant Rap' being the highpoint of their set.

The pair would shout:

An elephant was walking down the street
And his feet were tapping to the beat
His ears were flapping and his toes were, too
And he was doing a rap, just for you.
Elephant Rap! Doing the Elephant Rap!

Years later, Gillies and Johns would still bust out these rhymes in the back of the bus when the tedium of touring became too much for them.

While Gillies was drumming with the school band, the 'Marching Koalas', Johns and Joannou had taken trumpet lessons, but the instrument didn't inspire them. (Johns once made a passing reference to taking violin lessons, but you can put that down to more Silverchair myth-making.) Gillies had been drumming for several years by the time Johns received his first guitar.

Johns said in February 1996:

> I got this little electric guitar for $80 or something for a birthday present. It was called the Rock Axe. It looked kind of like a [Fender] Strat[ocaster], but it was really small. And it was all white. I thought it was good at the time, because I could just turn up the amp and go 'Yeah!'

In Gillies's parents' garage, he and Johns started jamming enthusiastically. Johns had taken a year's worth of classical guitar training, so there was some finesse amidst the racket the two were making.

As he told *Guitar School* magazine in February 1996:

> This guy, he just taught me all the main chords and stuff. And after a year, I thought, I can't be bothered having lessons. So I just decided to figure out my own stuff. I never wanted to play all those fast guitar solos. T just thought, I'll be like Pete Townshend of the Who. I'll do what he does and play powerful chords and stuff.

Johns and Gillies tried out – and discarded – a variety of band names: the Witchdoctors, Nine Point Nine on the Richter Scale, Short Elvis. Short Elvis lasted all of one show – playing Elvis Presley covers, naturally (But they did make a brief comeback in 2006, when Silverchair renamed themselves Short Elvis for a one-night stand at Sydney's Gaelic Club.) Then it was back to the garage. Johns fronted for rehearsals trailing his trusty 60-watt Fender amp; Gillies pounded his tattered drum kit with all the gusto his skinny frame could muster. It was fun; they were making a noise. It was a good outlet for whatever frustrations they had at school, even though both seemed pretty well adjusted, if not overly inspired by the education system, as their average grades testified.

In 1991, the two twelve-year-olds played their debut school concert. They were now called the Innocent Criminals. Silverchair legend has it that Johns, exhibiting the same kind of diffidence then that made him question rock and roll's value many years later, spent the entire show singing while facing the back of the stage. He couldn't meet the eyes of the few students who'd gathered to check them out. Gillies, however, has a different recollection of the show. 'I think that's been over exaggerated,' he told me. 'I think he was just looking away, a bit.' What Johns didn't know was that his father, Greg, was watching proudly from the back of the hall, having been invited, on the quiet, by Newcastle High School principal Peter McNair.

Johns said in a 1996 interview:

> I never really wanted to be a singer. I just wanted to play guitar. Then one day we had a gig and we still didn't have a singer. None of us wanted to sing. But I ended up doing it, and from then on I've been the singer.

Around this time, Johns and Gillies started jamming with another schoolmate, Tobin Finnane, who also played guitar. 'I got talking with Daniel and Ben,' Finnane recalls. 'They wanted to get the band going.' The Gillies home had always been the drop-in centre for the boys, including Joannou, who was yet to join the band. It was on the way to school, so they always stopped in. 'You'd eat all the biscuits and keep going,' Joannou remembers, laughing. Now the band gathered there not just to eat biscuits but to jam, first in the lounge room, then in Gillies's bedroom and, finally, in the garage (aka The Loft, which would become a ground zero, of sorts, in Silverchair history). Gillies's parents were supportive, although his mother would occasionally poke her head in and tell them to turn the volume down.

One day, a Gillies family friend dropped in, at the request of Annette Gillies, to show the boys how a bass worked. As Gillies recalls, the family friend, whose name has been long forgotten, played along with the band, using the most simple bass lines possible. Johns, Gillies and Finnane were thrilled. 'We went "Wow! How cool did that sound?" Then we went on a mission to find a bass player.' Johns and Gillies asked a few schoolmates, but most were keener on playing drums or guitar, the standard instruments of choice for any budding teen rocker. But they knew that the father of their buddy Chris Joannou owned a bass – a copy of a Hofner, just like Paul McCartney played when the Beatles took over the world. Surely the bass couldn't be that hard to master? After all, it had two less strings than their own guitars. They approached their friend, encouraging him to learn how to play. Within days Joannou started jamming with them at the Gillies home.

If volume is any indication of quality, by 1992 the four-piece Innocent Criminals were on their way; Gillies recalls how 'it just seemed to get louder and louder. 'They entered a few local talent comps, playing Black Sabbath and Pearl Jam covers plus a few originals that Gillies, Finnane and Johns were thrashing out in The Loft. But then Finnane made a shock announcement: his parents were leaving Merewether to live in England for a year. Keen to keep the band together, the Finnane and Joannou families struck up a deal: Tobin could live at Chris's house for a year, while the rest of his family were in the UK. But at the last minute, Finnane changed his mind. 'I didn't think I'd get the experience again of travelling overseas,' he said when we spoke in 2003. It would prove to be a decision that would have an impact on the rest of his life, not that he knew the gravity of it at the time, of course.

At this stage, the Innocent Criminals were two pairs of tight buddies: Johns and Gillies; Finnane and Joannou. When Finnane left, the remaining three were unsure what to do next – split the band or kick on as a trio? Were they being disloyal to Finnane? But they soon realised that they'd gotten this far, so why not keep going? When Gillies and Johns made the proposal to their fast-improving bassman that they play as a trio, Joannou was all for it.

While overseas, Finnane got in touch with his friends and asked if he could rejoin them on his return to Australia. They wrote Finnane a letter telling him of their plans to continue as a trio. 'They made it clear it wasn't going to happen,' he told me, of his hopes to rejoin the band. 'I was a bit pissed off by the way it was handled.' Given the band's rapid rise, it's not surprising that by January 1996 Finnane was downplaying their first album – on which he received a thank you – and telling the Australian tabloids that 'I just don't like the music. It's not very good.' Gillies figured that Finnane was still holding 'an eight-year grudge'. Finnane, who went on to complete an Honours degree in music at the Newcastle Conservatorium and now teaches and plays guitar for a living, still felt slighted by his one-time bandmates when we spoke in 2003: 'I see them around but we don't talk to each other. The vibe's not the greatest.' Many successful bands have their Pete Best – the last man to leave the Beatles before they went supernova – and that's exactly what Tobin Finnane is to Silverchair.

Soon after the trio formed, the Innocent Criminals played their first professional show at a Newcastle street fair.

Johns recalled, with a fair dash of teen spirit:

> We got ten dollars each to play. We got up there and played Deep Purple, Led Zeppelin and Black Sabbath songs. Actually, we ended up getting bounced. This old guy complained because it was too loud. He came over and said, 'If you don't stop playing, I'm calling the cops.' So we had to stop playing. But we didn't care, we still got paid.

'They were absolutely dreadful,' the grumbling resident told the *Newcastle Herald*. 'The music was amplified, it was loud and it was really bad.'

Gradually, the three were expanding their repertoire beyond the rock albums that littered their parents' collections, even if the public response lacked enthusiasm. Meanwhile, in America, a change had come. The unlikely rock and roll epicentre was now Washington State, a north-western outpost better known for its logging. Its capital, Seattle, was the new rock heartland. Here, bands such as Mother Love Bone (soon to morph into Pearl Jam), Tad (fronted by a 136-kilo crowd-surfing lunatic going by the name of Tad Doyle), Mudhoney, Sound-garden, Alice in Chains and, crucially, Nirvana, were annexing sludgy post-Sabbath riffs to lyrics that howled with disgust at how music had lost its way and its meaning, and had become all spandex, no spleen.

Unlike their party-hearty, coke-sniffing predecessors from the 1980s, many of these grunge bands favoured heroin as their drug of choice (heroin would eventually kill Love Bone's singer, Andrew Wood, Alice in Chains's Layne Staley and, indirectly, Nirvana's Kurt Cobain). Hence their inward-looking lyrics about dysfunctional lives, encapsulated in such anthems as Nirvana's 'Smells Like Teen Spirit', Pearl Jam's 'Alive' and the entire *Dirt* album from Alice in Chains. The greed-is-good ethos of the Reagan era simply contributed to their feelings of alienation. Girl-hungry Mötley Crüe they weren't.

Collectively, this surly, seemingly anti-commercial style of rock was labelled 'grunge', a term first used in the catalogue of Seattle label Sub

A NEW TOMORROW

Pop, who would release discs from many key bands of the era, Nirvana included. Unlike such 1980s rock heroes as Van Halen's 'Diamond' David Lee Roth, Pearl Jam's Eddie Vedder sang to the floor (others sang to their shoes) and wore flannel, not spandex. Guitar solos were a no-go zone. 'Selling out' to the mainstream ranked with speaking ill of Iggy Pop and the Stooges, the godparents of punk rock, whose furious riffology had left an indelible mark on grunge. The links between grunge and the 1970s punk rock of such UK stars as the Clash and the Sex Pistols was also strong. Authority figures were there to be spat upon, and their energy was fuelled by an indefinable rage, rather than the chemicals running riot in their bloodstream, or the fire in their too-tight trousers. When rock biographer Victor Bockris wrote that punk rock 'nurtured the seeds of working-class rebellion, with a punk philosophy that was anti-superstar and anti-establishment', he may as well have been writing the blueprint for grunge.

By 1991, Pearl Jam's *Ten* and Nirvana's epochal *Nevermind*, led by the smash hit single 'Smells Like Teen Spirit', were unavoidable. Nirvana's blitzkrieg of a set at the 1992 Big Day Out, the debut of what would become Australia's annual summer rockfest, inspired thousands to pick up a guitar and scream at the world. Among them was a geeky Jewish kid from Bondi with a big mouth, Ben Lee, who formed his wisecracking band of teen punks, Noise Addict, the following day.

But it was the Eddie Vedder-led Pearl Jam that excited Daniel Johns the most. In a November 1995 interview with *Request* magazine, he admitted that his own bottomless vocal growl, a signature sound that made his band's breakthrough hit, 'Tomorrow', so distinctive, was hugely inspired by Vedder. 'He was, like, my hero,' Johns admitted in a rare moment of teen candour. 'And I was going, "Yes, I'm going to try and be like Eddie Vedder."' Johns would find himself downplaying that statement many times over the next few years, as he searched for a voice to call his own.

Just like the Beatles, Silverchair came from working-class stock, where expectations weren't high. But they were possibly the luckiest teenagers on the planet. Despite the familiar rock mythology in which bands rise up in spite of repression and the pressure to study hard and get regular jobs, the trio's principal at Newcastle High, Peter McNair, actually gave the band more rhythm than they could ever have imagined. Clearly, he recognised the trio's potential. The school prided itself on tolerance and diversity; unlike at many high schools, piercings and coloured hair weren't frowned on, and creativity was encouraged. According to McNair – who took up his post the year Johns, Gillies, Finnane and Joannou started high school – the unofficial school motto among the 1300 students was: 'It's cool to be different.' McNair encouraged them, and other school bands, to play at lunchtime for their schoolmates. (When Silverchair's success escalated, especially around the time of their second album, *Freak Show*, McNair and the band's parents developed a flexible study program for the trio to ensure they could tour overseas and still gain respectable Higher School Certificate results.)

'I was new,' says the now-retired McNair, who good-humouredly boasts of being an early Silverchair adviser-cum-roadie. 'I wanted to get the kids involved.' By charging two dollars admission (which wasn't quite in keeping with Board of Education guidelines), the band raised enough cash to rent some lights and a PA and buy a new amp. The lunchtime shows were a roaring success.' I knew there was something special,' McNair recalls of the Innocent Criminals. 'They had a sound that was so raw, so honest. The older kids were jumping around in excitement. Teachers still remember it today.'

Despite their obvious intelligence, the band members weren't finding school all that inspiring. Johns admitted he was 'shit in maths and science' and took art as an elective principally because 'it's a bludge'. (In 1997, as their Higher School Certificate exam approached, Johns revealed that he chose Marine Studies 'because I thought I'd go to the beach'; later that year he figured that 'English was my best subject because I was crap at everything else'.) A lot of Johns's and Gillies's time was soaked up writing songs, which the three mixed with cover versions in their lunchtime sets and garage jams.

Word of these Innocent Criminals made its way to the local newspaper. In late 1993 it featured a small item on the band, an article that was noticed by Terry Farrelly, who ran Platinum Studios, located in the Newcastle suburb of Cardiff. He contacted the band and offered them some studio time, at a bargain rate. Farrelly claimed to be the former drum technician for British rock giants Led Zeppelin, a band much loved by Johns, Joannou and especially Gillies. (Years later, however, Joannou wasn't so sure of the guy's history: 'Well, he had a Pommie accent,' he laughs.' He certainly sucked us in.')

It was their second time in a studio. When Finnane was still in the picture, they'd recorded originals 'How Do You Know?' (sample lyric: 'How do you know where you're going / When you don't know where you are?') and 'I Felt Like It', plus a cover of 'Twist and Shout', in a studio in suburban Mayfield. Farrelly's offer was generous: not only did it let them familiarise themselves with the workings of the studio, but they were able to record basic versions of four songs, including a six-and-a-half-minute long version of 'Tomorrow', which became their first single and the hit that launched the Silverchair juggernaut.

Johns figured the session 'cost about $75. We weren't in there for more than an hour.' In a historical footnote, ever since these Silverchair recordings, bands have been hiring Platinum Studios hoping some of the magic will rub off on them. As their manager, John Watson, told me, 'We've heard of young bands recording there, in the false belief that it's where the band recorded [their debut album] *Frogstomp*.'

Of the four demo tracks, 'Tomorrow' was the obvious standout. The band quickly discarded the other three – which included 'Never Knew Your Powers' and 'Won't You Be Mine', plus a take on the Cult's hit, 'Wild Flower'. Watson describes them as 'much more Guns 'n' Roses-influenced' songs, which 'didn't really fit alongside the alterna-rock/Sabbath influenced stuff'.

'Tomorrow' had started to come together in a Gillies bedroom jam. This was a time when a session consisted of the three playing their favourite records, jamming on a riff that they heard and liked, and seeing where their song went from there.

As Gillies recalls:

We were jamming and Daniel sang the line 'You wait 'til tomorrow' and I went 'Man, that's a cool line.' He didn't really like it, but I managed to convince him. Then we sat down with a couple of acoustic guitars and wrote the verse and the chorus and the pre-chorus.

Johns remembers it this way:

> We just had a jam, and I came up with the riff to the chorus. Ben liked it but I didn't really like it. He kept ringing me, saying, 'We should make something out of this.' I was saying, 'Nah, nah.' But finally we made it into a song.

It was a smart career-maker of a move. While the song would provide its share of nightmares in the years to follow, without 'Tomorrow', these Innocent Criminals might still be jamming in the Gillies's garage.

In early 1994, a neighbour of the Johns family, Sarah Lawson, noticed that *nomad*, the music program on multicultural TV network SBS, was promoting a music competition called 'Pick Me'. Lawson had a big influence on Johns's musical taste: 'Every band I get into is from her,' Johns said in 1996. 'If I like it I would just go and find the CD or steal her CD.' The competition's organisers were in search of the best demo recording by an unsigned Australian band, and one of the prizes was a day's recording at Triple J's Sydney studio, as well as the chance to film a video for the song.

Lawson told the band, who got about as excited as diffident fifteen-year-olds can become. They submitted the tape of their Platinum Studio session accompanied by a statement – in twenty-five words or less, as the rules insisted – as to what made the band so special: 'We're not hip-hop or rap,' the three wrote. 'We're rock!'

Out of the 800 entries, 'Tomorrow' was the song that caught the ear of one of the competition judges, Robert Hambling, an SBS freelancer and expatriate British video director who'd moved to Australia in 1988, after having worked on films including *Greystoke: The Legend of Tarzan* and *Pink Floyd's The Wall*. Hambling was destined for a long history with the band, as an archivist, video maker and insider. 'I sat at home listening to demo after demo after demo,' he told me. 'Basically, I came up with Silverchair, or the Innocent Criminals as they were then, which hit me like a brick.'

Among the entries Hambling was sorting through were such eccentricities as the Von Trapp Family Crisis, who were a favourite of *nomad*'s producer, Tracee Hutchison, a former Triple J DJ. Hutchison was torn. She knew that 'Tomorrow' was a strong song, but she was keenly aware of the need to select an act in keeping with the SBS multicultural charter. And she also knew that the program was in line for the axe. 'I was merely being mindful of what I hoped "Pick Me" might achieve for the longevity of a popular music program on SBS TV,' she reflects, adding, 'You know, keep it on air.' Hambling described the Von Trapps as 'a Melbourne-based goof band; good but wild and wacky'. Another entrant was a solo artist calling himself Fishhead, who cut up samples from TV shows *The Fugitive* and *Star Trek*. Much of the rest was, well, unremarkable.

No wonder Hambling was sold 011 the Innocent Criminals. He told me:

> 'Tomorrow' had all those things you want out of a great song. Memorable lyrics, a really good hook. And there was no denying their connection to the Seattle sound. But it never went through my head that they were borrowing; it was just what they were listening to. And my point at the time was that if you're going to pick a competition based on the best entry, this is it; it doesn't get any better than this. Three very young kids, living in Newcastle, playing out of their bedroom – what else do you want?

In reply, Hutchison said:

> If anything, it was the fact that 'Tomorrow' was much more musically accessible than where *nomad* sat most weeks that made me think hard about making it the winner. It was destined to be a mainstream hit and there was nothing mainstream about *nomad*.

Yet Hambling persevered.

> They still weren't convinced. I thought I was going nuts. So I went around to Nick Launay's [Hambling's record-producer neighbour and friend]. He thought it was good, so I asked him to do one of his magic edits on it. By then he thought it was brilliant, so I knew I wasn't mad.

Finally, a consensus was reached, common sense prevailed, and 'Tomorrow' was declared the winner.

During the competition judging, Hambling had called the number supplied with the Innocent Criminals entry to advise them they were on the shortlist. Unaware, at the time, of their ages, he spoke with Johns's mother. Even though she told him Daniel was at school, he was convinced she was the singer's wife or girlfriend, because the song sounded so damned mature. Surely that wasn't a kid growling those pissed-off lyrics. Soon after, Hamblmg called the Johns household again, to announce that the Innocent Criminals were the winners. This time his call was answered by Daniel, who was told they'd won the right to record 'Tomorrow' at Triple J and have *nomad* direct their video. 'We didn't, like, go spastic or anything,' Johns recalled of the news, 'but we were pretty happy.'

When the band convened in Gillies's garage, however, they could barely contain their excitement.

According to Joannou:

Daniel was over at my house – after school, we'd go past my house and we'd always come in, have a drink, and then go home – and, like, Daniel's mum was at my house and she ran out and said, 'They won! They won!' We were just crazy, running around, going so berserk. It was so exciting.

Gillies remembers 'running around my house and yelling at the top of my voice. Then I remember thinking, "Fuck, how long is this going to last?"'

This wasn't the last competition they would win. Three weeks after their *nomad* video screened, the band cleaned up at the annual Youthrock awards, a school band competition held at Campsie in western Sydney. They were the pick of forty bands, winning a day's recording at a Sydney studio and $1500 worth of musical gear for their school. In the audience was John Woodruff – who would later guide Savage Garden to huge international success – who was keen to manage the band. The year before, when Finnane was still in the Innocent Criminals, they had won the Encouragement Award at the same event. But whereas Youthrock was a small-scale, teen-band comp, *nomad* would bring the band national attention.

Hutchison subsequently called Johns, asking him if the song could be cut down from six to a more serviceable four minutes. She was hoping that her then husband, producer Tim Whitten, could do the edit, although that ultimately didn't happen, and she asked Launay (who had done a rough edit on the demo version on his home equipment) to produce the song. (Hutchison had also tried, and failed, to encourage the Silverparents to hire John Needham, the manager of indie-rock band Died Pretty.)

Launay was excited to be asked, even though he and Hambling had already played their rough edit of 'Tomorrow' to their many record company contacts and none seemed too impressed. 'We got an amazing "So what?"' Hambling recalls, still shaking his head many years after the event. They had started nurturing plans to release the song themselves if they couldn't get a label interested in the band. But one label it seems Launay and Hambling didn't visit was the huge multinational Sony. John Watson – soon to be a key player in Silverchair's rise, and working at that time in Sony's A&R department, the first port of call for anyone pitching a new band – insists that being 'a huge Oils and INXS fan' he would have agreed to meet with Launay who, by then, had produced three Midnight Oil albums (including Daniel Johns's beloved *10, 9, 8, 7, 6, 5, 4, 3, 2, 1*) and INXS's *The Swing*.

On the eve of recording 'Tomorrow', however, Launay fell sick and the production job went to Triple J's in-house producer, Phil McKellar, a veteran of the station's *Live at the Wireless* and *Australian Music Show* programs. (A year later, returning from some production work in America, Launay heard 'Tomorrow' on an in-flight music channel. By then it was a multi-platinum hit. Launay thought the song sounded familiar but couldn't quite place it, or this band named Silverchair. It turned out that the rough edit of 'Tomorrow' was still sitting on his machine at home.)

McKellar recorded the song in one day at ABC's Sydney studio; but because the usual recording studio wasn't available, the band and McKellar were forced to use the drama studio. As McKellar recalled when we spoke in 2006, 'It wasn't a studio used for music, and it had a really old school desk. There wasn't a lot of flashing, blinking lights for the band to look at.' They spent roughly eight hours together in the studio; the Silverparents, who had come down for the session, left their sons in the studio, spending their time either shopping or watching a football game in a nearby pub. Hambling – now incredibly passionate about the band, and professionally involved because of the *nomad* competition – 'baby sat' the session. The only real hold-up was that Chris Joannou had to find a serviceable bass to replace his Dad's 'shitty' four-string. ('It was such a piece of crap,' McKellar laughed, 'every couple of notes would be out of tune.') Fortunately, as McKellar recalled, Sydney band Crow were also in the ABC at the time, so Joannou borrowed a four-string from their bassist, Jim Woff.

While Platinum Studio may have been a shoebox with microphones, the band's recording experience helped them make a smooth transition to the marginally more sophisticated ABC facility. The way Gillies saw it, 'This was just on a more grand scale.' McKellar was thrilled by the band's energy in the studio, and knew that the best way to record them was essentially live. And when Johns opened his mouth to sing, he was floored. 'I remember saying to myself, "How good is this?"'

Once the recording was ready, Hambling and Hutchison travelled north to join up with the band at home. 'It was just me, Chris, Ben, Daniel, their three mums and the cameraman from SBS,' Hambling recalled, neglecting to mention that Hutchison also made the trip. Hambling directed the moody video for 'Tomorrow', which encompassed footage of the streets of Merewether, hardly the rock and roll capital of the universe, and a jail cell in the old Newcastle police station. The video set *nomad* back a whopping $2000. (A typical US video budget at the time was US$200,000.) 'The only special effect was that we screwed a light bulb into a cord and pushed – it was all very George Lucas and R2D2,' Hambling recalls. After the shoot, Hutchison interviewed the band in front of Newcastle landmark, Fort Scratchley.

A little after 8 pm on Thursday 16 June 1994, during what turned out to be its final episode, *nomad* announced that the Innocent Criminals had won the 'Pick Me' competition. They screened the video and aired the interview with the band. No one knew it at the time, but Australian music history was being created.

It was almost three years since Nirvana's 'Smells Like Teen Spirit' had broken out all over, and local music business tastemakers were still searching for an Australian answer to the grunge phenomenon. Sydney act Ratcat had had some chart success with their guitar- and hook-heavy sound, but frontman Simon Day didn't wield Kurt Cobain's couldn't-give-a-fuck charisma or his dysfunctional, heroin-addled menace. Instead, he wore striped tops and was just way too cute. Ratcat's 1991 album, *Blind Love,* raced to Number One in the local charts, but then their 1992 LP, *Insideout,* sank like a stone, proving just how fickle the music world can be. But Johns was a way more interesting character than Day – he not only had an unreasonably sonorous voice that echoed the sound of Seattle, but he was also enigmatic, sullen and serious. There was clearly something going on here.

After the *nomad* announcement, Triple J staffers had circulated the 'Tomorrow' video to record company contacts who they thought would 'get' the band. Enough interest was building in the Innocent Criminals to entice Sydney-based record company talent-spotters (including many of the tastemakers who had rejected the song played to them by Hambling and Launay a few weeks earlier) to check them out. The Innocent Criminals were the complete package; this new band from Newcastle not only rocked like heathens, they also had a growling lead singer whose dirty blond hair and razorblade riffs had scenesters whispering about 'the new Kurt Cobain'. And young girls swooned when he sang, a sound that would have dollar signs swimming in the heads of most music biz players.

Meanwhile, Johns's mother, Julie, was booking the band's shows and dealing with these money men with the caution you'd expect from the parent of a talented fifteen-year-old. The three sets of parents were keeping close tabs on their sons as the opportunists started to circle.

Ex rock and roll journalist John O'Donnell and Sony's John Watson had a copy of the video, even though neither had seen the *nomad* broadcast. The pair were sharing an office at Sony's Sydney base. O'Donnell was only a week into his job with Murmur Records, a boutique 'development' label established in June. A former plumber raised in Sydney's western suburbs, O'Donnell had left his post as founding editor of *Juice* magazine (and an editorial post at *Rolling Stone* before that) after Watson recommended him for the Murmur job. Watson, a former musician (he was in a band called the Spliffs), record shop worker, journalist and manager of Sydney indie band the Whippersnappers, was then Sony's Director of A&R and International Marketing, a global role which would soon help Silver-chair's overseas progress no end. Their backgrounds were ideal for developing a band such as this: they understood how the media machine operated and were aware of how it could chew up an overexposed act.

Both also knew that the lifespan of record company staff could be dangerously short. Murmur had been set up by Sony after much procrastination as a base to release the new, cutting-edge music that the major-label suits had noticed making a mark on the charts. The label had been named by O'Donnell in a nod to his favourite REM record. 'The perception of Sony from the outside wasn't great – it was Margaret Urlich and Rick Price,' recalls O'Donnell, naming two very bland mainstream pop acts. 'That image scared young rock bands off.' O'Donnell and Watson, by contrast, were deeply into the loud flannel-clad bands coming out of America.

Says O'Donnell:

We were listening to all the things they [the Innocent Criminals] were listening to, from Pearl Jam to Nirvana to Screaming Trees and Soundgarden, as well as Sabbath and all that stuff they'd grown up around. We were genuine fans of that music.

However, Sony's generosity only stretched so far: O'Donnell needed a hit to make his new job safe. And Watson was a determined man; previously, in his A&R role, he had tried to sign hot new bands You Am I and Powderfinger, but because of the corporate rigidity of Sony he couldn't offer these bands the flexible deals they needed. Both duly signed with other labels and went on to become two of the country's biggest alternative rock acts; Powderfinger would eventually cross over into the mainstream and sell records and concert tickets by the warehouse-load. Both Watson and O'Donnell were impressed by the Innocent Criminals. They were exactly what Murmur needed to get started: a cool rock act – and a homegrown one at that. And Sony boss Denis Handlin had granted O'Donnell, as head of Murmur, the flexibility to break the company rules; he could offer bands record deals that didn't stitch them up for life (or until the time of their commercial death, whichever came first) – unlike most Sony deals.

As Watson recalled in an interview in 1997:

As A&R manager, I had certain criteria in my head. Silverchair [or the Innocent Criminals, as they were at the time] had it all: with them, all the pieces of the puzzle fit: they played great, had catchy songs, good attitudes and they were fresh, charismatic – and they looked good. They reminded me of why I got into the music business in the first place. When you're that age you don't make music to get laid or to make money or to see your photo on the cover of a magazine. You make music because you like the noise you make when you bang on your guitar. All great music is born from that.

And as Watson pointed out to me in 2003, his and O'Donnell's interest in Silverchair was very much a collaboration: 'The process of signing them truly was a joint effort – neither of us made a move without consulting the other.' O'Donnell called their working relationship a 'tag team'.

Keen to seize the moment, O'Donnell now had a key move to make – he called Julie Johns to find out when the band was next playing. She told them there was a gig on the following Tuesday, but a contingent from Michael Gudinski's Mushroom label, home to such successful homegrown acts as Paul Kelly and Kylie Minogue, had already made enquiries, as had EMI. (Gudinski had seen the Innocent Criminals play at Youthrock in 1993.) Curiously enough, it was the older songs on the Platinum Studio demo tape that interested Mushroom, rather than 'Tomorrow' – they thought the now-discarded 'Won't You Be Mine' was the perfect first single. O'Donnell and Watson were stuck, because a big wheel from Sony's international division was in Sydney on that same night, and they had to toe the corporate line, thereby missing the Criminals show.

Mushroom, however, did make the gig and met with the band and their parents. It looked as though O'Donnell and Watson had missed their chance. But O'Donnell called Johns's mother again and urged them not to sign with anyone. Not yet, anyway.

On 24 June 1994, the Innocent Criminals played Newcastle's Jewell's Tavern. Because the band were under the legal drinking age, they had to set up and play in the bistro and stay in the band room between sets. O'Donnell and Watson – and some bored bikers who kept yelling for the band to play 'Born to Be Wild' – checked out the show, which included early takes on originals 'Acid Rain', 'Stoned' and 'Pure Massacre', as well as Pearl Jam, Hendrix, Kiss and Black Sabbath covers. There may have been only a dozen people in the room – and a few of those seemed keener on the rugby league game airing on the pub TV – but the two record company execs were so impressed that O'Donnell remembers being 'totally speechless. It was like seeing the Beatles at the Cavern before they became stars.'

As Watson remembers:

> It was literally the only time I've been to a show where you go, 'This can't be happening.' I vividly recall driving home and saying to John, 'If I ever leave to manage a band, this is the one.'

On the drive back to Sydney they started formulating a career plan for the band, one that would be sensitive to their ages rather than use their youth as a marketing device. As O'Donnell told me, it was a strategy that would ensure 'they would still be going strong when they were twenty and beyond.' This would prove decisive when the trio's parents sat down to figure out which label would be right for their sons.

Both Mushroom and Murmur made offers to the Innocent Criminals. Mushroom were keen to capitalise on the 'teen rockers' appeal of the band. They loved the band name – which Johns, Joannou and Gillies were tiring of – and planned for them to play concerts in front of a banner that screamed out 'Innocent Criminals'. Mushroom also offered just a little more money up-front, but Murmur's long-term plan appealed to the band, as did the coolness of O'Donnell and Watson, who won the trio over by slipping them rare Pearl Jam live CDs. And, coming from good working-class stock, O'Donnell talked rugby league with Johns's father, which helped sweeten the deal.

The band didn't feel the need to over-think their decision. 'I remember riding our bikes to school one day,' says Joannou, 'and I said to the other two guys, "I like the two John guys the best," and we all agreed.'

According to Gillies:

> They just did it so much more smartly. Mushroom's whole sell wasn't very good. They wanted to put out 'Won't You Be Mine', but the other guys said, 'No, "Tomorrow" is the one.' They were just much cooler. I think if we'd signed with Mushroom it would have been all over after 'Won't You Be Mine'.

The band signed to Murmur, originally for just one album (although by December 1994 the deal had been extended to three albums). They became their second signing, joining up just a week after Perth alt-rockers Ammonia who, despite some chart success locally and some whiffs of interest in America – including support slots on an early Silverchair tour, folded after two albums. The advance paid to the Innocent Criminals – which they would have to recoup through record sales – was modest: less than AUD$ 100,000, which included the recording budget of their first album. They could afford some new gear and not much more.

Murmur might have offered the band less money than other majors but they also allowed them more creative elbow room. As Johns explained at the time, 'We knew if we just signed straight to a big label [Mushroom] they'd really want to promote us. There'd be all this advertising and shit.' How to deal with all this 'advertising and shit' was a key part of the Murmur deal. O'Donnell and Watson didn't want to over-hype the band or position them incorrectly. They knew the band were still too green for such serious music press as *Rolling Stone* and *Juice*, but neither did they want the three to be seen as some kind of teen pin-ups, grinning from the pages of *Girlfriend* magazine. So their first step was to score the band some coverage in the free music press, where they could build credibility and gain the right kind of buzz.

O'Donnell and Watson had drilled what they called an 'anti-marketing strategy' into the heads of their young charges. They stressed that all publicity should focus on the band's music; Watson was aware the media could turn them into 'a teenybopper band, which would have given them a short shelf-life'.

O'Donnell comments:

> Our thing with them was:'You are a real band and from a marketing sense it's almost negative that you are so young.' We wanted to work around that and make sure that didn't hurt their career.

Watson was also concerned about the so-called 'Ratcat syndrome' in which a band explodes and implodes within the course of a couple of years.

This 'cool at all costs' mantra clearly made sense to Johns; he repeated it frequently during interviews:

If we did teen press and things like that, we would be getting the wrong kind of audience. We're not going for the same people that listen to Bon Jovi. We just wanted to reach the alternative press, street press, fanzines, guitar mags and stuff like that. We really didn't do anything like *Rolling Stone* until after people already had an idea of who we were or what we are like.

The band toasted their signing with a now legendary gig on 22 October at Sydney's Vulcan Hotel, a venue Joannou remembers being 'about as big as my kitchen' (and which is now a backpacker's hostel). They were supporting alt-rock acts Nancy Vandal and the Popgun Assassins, but the house was full for the support act. It was so full, in fact, that the stage collapsed due to the crush. 'People were crowd-surfing, hanging onto the roof,' says Joannou. 'It was just madness.' The cover shot for their 'Pure Massacre' single was taken from that gig, which proved that Joannou was right on the money. Similar carnage occurred at a show at Sydney's Phoenician Club, which was captured by director Robert Hambling for the first 'Pure Massacre' video. (A second, shot by Peter Christopherson at a building site on Sydney's north shore, was screened in the US.)

By August 1994, calls started coming in to Request Fest, a listener-driven Triple J program, asking for 'Tomorrow', which had initially been played on Richard Kingsmill's Oz Music Show. This heavy, lyrically naive anthem was striking all the right kind of chords, even if Triple J's then music director, Arnold Frolows, wasn't so sure about the song. 'When it came in,' he told Sydney's *Daily Telegraph* in 1995, 'we didn't think that much of it. It wasn't like we thought, "Oh God, this is a hit."'

As the airplay increased, a concerned John O'Donnell put in a call to producer Phil McKellar. 'Are there two mixes [of "Tomorrow"]?' he asked the producer. After a little sleuthing work, it turned out that Request Fest host Michael Tunn had done his own edit on the song, trimming a part of the instrumental 'breakdown', thereby making it a slightly easier fit for radio. McKellar, every inch the gentleman, quietly suggested that it would be best to stick with his version, and Tunn's was swiftly shelved. 'It was a bit cheeky,' McKellar laughed, looking back.

Johns, Gillies and Joannou, meanwhile, were having some doubts about the name Innocent Criminals, as were Watson and O'Donnell. As Johns said in September 1994, the band had 'started to get sick of it and we found it a bit of a kids' name. We wanted something a bit more mature so people didn't think of us as kids.' 'We thought it was a really bad name,' says O'Donnell. 'It threw too much light on the fact that they were a teenage band.' The band's parents, however, liked the tag and thought, quite justifiably, that a lot of goodwill and recognition had built around it after the Youthrock and *nomad* wins. Around the time of their Youthrock victory, in the salubrious surrounds of a Strathfield pizza joint, the idea for a name change was put forward. Despite the resistance of their parents, the band's casting vote meant they were now operating as Silverchair.

The story of the Innocent Criminals' evolution into Silverchair is deeply entrenched in local rock and roll folklore (and until 2002 that was a lower case 's', because, as Johns explained to Triple J announcer Richard Kingsmill, an upper case 'S' 'just looked spastic'). The band's standard line at the time was that the new name came to them one night when the three had gathered at Gillies's parents' home to make calls to Triple J's Request Fest. Johns wanted to hear You Am I's 'Berlin Chair', while Gillies opted for Nirvana's 'Sliver' – it was suggested they simply ask for 'Sliverchair'. Joannou transcribed this incorrectly, and the name Silverchair – or 'silverchair' – was born. It sounded a whole lot better than some of the other names on their shortlist, which included Grunt Truck and Warm Fish Milkshake, so the name stuck. (Producer Phil McKellar recalls seeing 'Silverchair' amongst a list of names written on a whiteboard during his subsequent ABC recording session with the band.)

John Watson, looking back in 2002, had a different recollection from that of his band: 'It was from the C. S. Lewis Narnia books.' *The Silver Chair* was written by Lewis in 1953, one of seven books in the Narnia series.

Watson continued:

> We had literally hundreds of names on a list. 'Silverchair' came from a catalogue in the Johns household. At that stage, nothing was dismissed

as a potential band name, and through a process of attrition, that's the one that stayed.

And the book title's similarity to the two songs the band loved didn't hurt the choice of name, either.

So the band now had a name and a following, but no new music to share with their hungry audience. 'Tomorrow' was slated for an official release on 16 September. The band played at a Sony music conference in Sydney on 19 August, then returned to the Triple J studios, again with producer McKellar, to cut the tracks 'Stoned', 'Blind' and 'Acid Rain'. McKellar was just as impressed with the band as he'd been at their session a month earlier. 'Like so many young bands, they were very exciting; it was great to get them before they [had time to] become jaded. They just really wanted to play.'

Along with 'Tomorrow', these songs made up the band's debut release, a four-track EP priced at $9.95: three bucks more than a regular single. But this was part of the marketing plan of O'Donnell and Watson – keep it low-key, make the songs the focus, don't oversell the band. As O'Donnell read it, 'We thought if we stopped some young girl buying the record and making it a teen-based thing, great. As it turned out, it didn't hurt sales at all.'

Or as Watson commented in 1996:

> I always liked the way Midnight Oil handled their career. And one of the things they did well was that, in between albums, they kept it low-key – very low-key – so that when they came back, people were hungry to hear more about them again.

Another shrewd move on the part of the two Johns was to hold back on two tracks – 'Pure Massacre' and 'Israel's Son' – for their band's upcoming album, rather than add them to the EP. O'Donnell had told McKellar that the songs, especially the former, were 'killers', which was right on the money.

When Silvermania exploded soon after, O'Donnell stayed true to their low-key philosophy – he even bought up all photos of the band in circulation, buried them in his bottom drawer and shut down all publicity until the eve of their debut LP release. He may have pissed off his former peers in the music media, but O'Donnell was astutely trying to shield the band from overexposure, a sure-fire killer in an environment where credibility is as significant as catchy hooks. At times, Murmur even banned photographers from live shows.

As noted in Watson and O'Donnell's (handwritten) marketing plan, the original goal was to sell 6000 copies of 'Tomorrow'; that way both band and label would be on track to recoup Murmur's (that is, Sony's) minimal investment. Yet an almost indefinable quality about 'Tomorrow' connected with a lot more than 6000 punters. Despite some clumsy high school poetry from Johns – 'There is no bathroom and there is no sink / the water out of the tap is very hard to drink' – the song's stop-start rhythms and Johns's growling vocal, which packed an unclear but quite palpable discontent, hit paydirt. And in keeping with the early 1990s ethos, Johns's guitar howled like a wounded beast. It was a song born of the grunge sound, bound to send moshpits into convulsions.

So what was Johns so angry about? It was nothing personal. The song was inspired, like many of his early songs, by what he witnessed on the evening news; it wasn't some deeply-felt statement.

As he recalled:

I saw something on telly. There was this poor guy taking a rich guy through a hotel to experience the losses of those less fortunate than him. The rich guy is complaining because he just wants to get out and the poor guy is saying, 'You have to wait until tomorrow to get out'. That's one of our least serious songs but it still has meaning to it.

After all, what life experiences did a relatively well-adjusted fifteen-year-old kid have to draw from, anyway?

Meanwhile, the calls kept coming in to Triple J and the Silverchair buzz was gathering momentum. But the band were about to understand that popularity comes with as many lows as highs. In October 1994 a mysterious letter appeared in Melbourne's free 'street press' magazine, *Beat*. A female writer bragged how, along with her girlfriends, she'd snuck Silverchair back to her house and 'took something away from these innocent boys that they'll never be able to give any other girl'. Gillies replied by stating: 'That's the biggest load of crap'. They weren't old enough to drive or drink, they didn't even shave, for God's sake, but already Silverchair were the object of female fantasies. In the wake of this, Watson and O'Donnell became even more wary about the band's dealings with the media.

In November 1994, Silvermania became official, when 'Tomorrow' reached Number One on the Top 40 singles chart, going gold the next week and staying on top for six weeks. In the process, the Merewether three had breezed past Kylie Minogue's 'Confide In Me' on their way to the top spot, and left Boyz II Men (whose current single was called 'I'll Make Love To You') eating their dust. Gillies was getting ready for school when his mother got off the telephone. 'She said, "'Tomorrow' has been number one for six weeks." My first thought was, Fuck, what's going on here? That was really fucking weird.'

By December, 'Tomorrow' had sold 180,000 copies, thirty times more than the Murmur marketing plan goal. This obviously excited the suits, but O'Donnell and Watson were concerned whether the public would give the band the chance to prove themselves more than some faddish, one-hit grunge wonder. They thoroughly understood the fickle nature of rock and roll.

Daniel Johns's expectations had been even lower, as he explained at the time in a neat example of teen hubris.

> We expected it to sell about 2000. And then when it started going up a bit, we're going, 'Oh my God, ha ha ha!' Then when it got to 1 5,000, we're going, 'Hope it doesn't sell any more, we don't want it to sell any more.' When it went to Number One, we were kind of spewing. They're going, 'Congratulations', and we're going, 'Everyone's going to expect every record to go to Number One'.

Gillies, Johns and Joannou were already well aware of the 'tall poppy'syndrome, and their tight group of schoolmates took objection to any sign of rampaging ego. 'As soon as you said something acknowledging yourself, someone would come out and cut you down,' Joannou said. 'So we cut ourselves down. We were always thinking twice.'

In keeping with the anti-everything attitude of grunge, the band didn't want to be stars, at least not publicly. Eddie Vedder of Pearl Jam had declared that uncool, and many bands – Silverchair included – treated his every agitated mumble as gospel. 'We don't want to be very big at all,' Johns said. 'We don't want to be known as the band who think they're rock stars.' At a time when multinationals were offering the band crazy amounts of money to play corporate shows (up to AUD$250,000, according to one report), the band instead opted to do a show at Avalon in Sydney for the Surfrider Foundation. They each received a new surfboard and wetsuit as payment. But nothing could stop the band's momentum. By the end of 1994, 'Tomorrow' was the ninth-highest-selling single of the year and hit Number Five on the tastemaking Triple J Hottest 100 chart. The band then signed on for their first Big Day Out. The madness had begun.

Chapter Two
FROGSTOMPING ALL OVER THE WORLD

> We just loved to play and didn't care about anything else. It was very surreal, wandering around, being part of this big circus.
> Chris Joannou on Silverchair's first Big Day Out, 1995

Australia needed the Big Day Out. For twenty years promoters had tried to establish a workable festival showcasing local and overseas bands, but nothing stuck. One of the earliest and best known attempts was the anything-goes Sunbury Festival, held on Melbourne's outskirts in the early 1970s. It was an acid-, dope-and beer-drenched sweatfest headlined in 1972 by 1960s pop idol Billy Thorpe, who had reinvented himself as a wild-maned hippie with an electric guitar.

A festival veteran, Thorpe had also appeared at the Odyssey Festival, held at Wallacia, on Sydney's outskirts, in 1971. It was another well-intentioned debacle, as he recalled in his ripping yarn of a 1998 memoir, *Most People I Know*. Fried on LSD, Thorpe recalls drifting into a slow blues 'ripped to my toe tips. My guitar felt like it was made of rubber with my fingers growing out of it.' Festivals like these – and their 1980s variants, such as Narara, which managed to entice the Pretenders, Simple Minds and the Talking Heads to a muddy bog two hours north of Sydney, next to the former site of Old Sydney Town – were fuelled by idealism, dope and distant dreams of Woodstock. In keeping with a local music industry still in development, rock festivals were amateurish at best, anarchic at worst.

Ken Lees and Vivian West were Sydney-based promoters heavily into alternative music. They were well connected, with good taste and ambition, in a cool-school, indie-cred kind of way. Since the late 1980s, they had enticed such highly regarded international acts as Billy Bragg, They Might Be Giants and the Violent Femmes to tour Australia. On 25 January 1992, the Australia Day long weekend, they staged the first Big Day Out. The event was closely based on Lollapalooza, the US alternative-rock roadshow established by promoters Marc Geiger and Don Muller. Lollapalooza crisscrossed America between 1991 and 1997 – and was resurrected in 2003 – mixing such cutting-edge acts as Beck, Smashing Pumpkins, Soundgarden and Jane's Addiction with political activism and exotic food not found in your typical strip mall. All this stimulation was held outdoors, spread over several stages. For punters, Lollapalooza offered the chance to get seriously rocked and join Greenpeace, all on the one day. For bands that made the bill, the exposure guaranteed strong record sales, well-paid shows and some wild backstage action.

'As a promoter I've always tried to do things that were interesting,' West said on the day of the inaugural Big Day Out (which, over the years, has been tagged the Big Day Off, because of its easy schedule and generous pay). 'I get bored with just putting together the same old bills.' To drive home his aversion to the 'same old bills', the debut Big Day Out was a musical smorgasbord. Sandwiched between indigenous rockers Yothu Yindi and student favourites the Violent Femmes, was Nirvana, whose second album, *Nevermind*, was about to explode in the US and then all over the world.

Playing before 9000 mad-for-it punters in Sydney's Hordern Pavilion, their set, as described by *Rolling Stone* magazine, was:

> blistering, intense and wildly received, with the moshpit drenched in water and a frenzy of stage divers. They brooded and threatened rather than rocked, and culminated with the animalistic trashing of their equipment to the delight of the devoted audience.

The verdict was unanimous: Nirvana was the shit and the Big Day Out was a hit.

There were attempts to bring Lollapalooza to Australia, but that notion was discarded as the Big Day Out just kept getting bigger. In 1993 the event went national. In 1994, the top five acts on the bill – Soundgarden, the Cruel Sea, Björk, Smashing Pumpkins and Urge Overkill – saw their albums in the Top 10 within two weeks of the event. Major labels found this commercial knock-on effect very attractive, and lobbied Lees and West to get their bands on the bill. And for local acts with just a whiff of ambition, a spot on any of the four main outdoor stages guaranteed some decent record sales, a leg-up for their career – and the chance to hang out with their heroes. It was also confirmation that they'd been accepted by the alterna-rock movement, which had started to break down barriers between mainstream and independent music in the early 1990s. 'It's the spirit of the event that counts,' promoter West said in 1994, 'so audiences are open to seeing all bands on the bill.'

Well, yes, but there was really only one band that had 'must see' written all over them at the Big Day Out 1995: Silverchair. They'd ended 1994 with a platinum-selling Number One single (the follow-up, the grinding 'Pure Massacre', debuted at Number Two three days after their first Big Day Out show). The buzz surrounding the band's appearance almost matched Nirvana's three years earlier.

The band had been signed up at a bargain price – shades of the Beatles' 1964 Australian tour, when the deal was done with a local promoter days before Beatlemania broke out in the USA – when O'Donnell approached West in late 1994. He had met with the promoter for an hour, slipping him a pre-release copy of the 'Tomorrow' EP and talking up the band. On the urging of their booking agent, Owen Orford, West checked out the chaos at the band's Vulcan show and was sold. Orford delivered the good news to the band while they were in the studio. 'He [West] got it straight away,' says O'Donnell. 'They got the band for next to nothing and it created all this excitement. We needed the band to play the right kind of shows – and with other credible bands.' (Silverchair management are still reluctant to name the exact figure, more than a decade later. 'We'd rather leave the BDO fee as the quoted "bargain of the century",' replied Melissa Chenery.)

In keeping with Watson and O'Donnell's softly-softly strategy for the band, at the Sydney Big Day Out, Silverchair were booked for a mid-afternoon spot on the outdoor Skate Stage, 100 metres away from the main stage inside the Hordern Pavilion. At a stretch, 5000 punters could see the band. Instead, 15,000 sun- and beer-drenched fans tried to squeeze together, sardine style, to check out this new band of baggy-shorted, T-shirted teen hotshots. This first Big Day Out appearance not only made clear just how popular the band were, it also proved to the hard-to-please alt-rock audience that the band could really play.

David Fricke, a senior editor from American *Rolling Stone,* was in Australia to attend the Big Day Out and see how it stacked up against America's Lollapalooza. Every band Fricke encountered who had played the Big Day Out had praised it, so he was keen to get a taste for himself. Still, he couldn't quite believe what he witnessed when Silverchair hit the stage, as he wrote in his report of the carnage.

> Tsunami-force waves of crowd surfers repeatedly roll towards the stage, damn near crushing the packs of defiant, cheering teenage girls pressed against the security barrier. Several enterprising fans, determined to get a better view, scramble up a drainpipe to the roof of an adjacent building, breaking the pipe and yanking part of it off the wall in the process.
>
> Then a shirtless loon bored with rooftop slamdancing shimmies up a light pole overlooking the heaving moshpit. He dangles from his perch with one hand and a huge doofus grin on his face, poised to execute what looks like the ultimate stage dive – four storeys down. Fortunately, security gets to him first as Silverchair, to their wry amusement, are rushed off the stage.

(In Melbourne, punters actually jumped off nearby rooftops into the huge moshpit and trampolined on the tarpaulin hanging over the band.)

It was 3 pm when Silverchair exited the Sydney stage. Still to play at Big Day Out was Hole, fronted by Courtney Love, the widow of Nirvana's Kurt Cobain, and Offspring, the Californian punk band that had recently run roughshod over the charts with their hit album *Smash.* But it was Silverchair that everyone was talking about.

Fricke again:

> Johns sings with a full-blooded voice that belies his age. The madhouse atmosphere is not a Pavlovian reaction to overnight success; the Seattle-fried crunch of 'Stoned' and 'Pure Massacre' is truly potent stuff.

The mouthy Love was in the midst of a drug-fuelled mourning period for her husband, who'd shot himself in their Seattle garage the year before. Yet she was sufficiently aware to notice the attention directed towards the Novo-castrian trio. In typical Love fashion, she decided to bring Silverchair down a notch or two. 'So this young guy from Silverchair looks like my dead husband, Kurt, and sings like Eddie Vedder,' she drawled during her set. 'How lame.' She repeated this observation a few nights later at her band's show at Sydney nightspot, Selinas. Whatever her intention, Love's comments showed that, almost against their wills, Daniel Johns and Silverchair were leaving their mark on the rock world beyond Australia. An insult from Love meant that they were definitely on the cool radar. (Four years later, in St Louis, Love and Silverchair again crossed paths. Only this time, she was topless. As Joannou tells it, 'She passed Daniel in the hallway, stopped, and said, "Are you doing heroin?" He said, "No." She said, "Good, because that's so 1995."')

Other international acts at the 1995 Big Day Out paid Silverchair more respect than Courtney Love. Brit rockers the Cult called them up onstage in Perth during the final date of the festival and declared them 'Australia's finest'. Backstage, the Cult had given them penknives as gifts. Silverchair responded by donning wigs and dancing onstage, badly, as the Cult riffed on.

But it was all becoming a bit much for the fifteen-year-olds of Silverchair. Johns had summed up the mixed emotions they felt about their success when he introduced the mosh-inducing 'Tomorrow' at the Sydney Big Day Out: 'This one is called "Cat's Scrotum",' he mumbled. Gillies and Joannou didn't say a word.

Another American in the Big Day Out melee was David Massey, the Vice President of A&R with Epic Records, a subsidiary of Sony Music. Given that Murmur was part of the giant Sony group, Massey had an option to release Silverchair's music in North America. He was smitten by the band, and especially by Johns, and promptly agreed to release *Frogstomp*.

Massey surmised:

He's fifteen years old, he's got blond hair but he's nothing like Kurt [Cobain], He's a bright, young surfer kid. They have their own identity. What impressed me most about them live was how well they actually played, how much presence they had on stage, and how developed their sound is for their age. The audience response was pretty rapturous and it made me realise there wasn't the tiniest issue of novelty.

Well, maybe not, but any A&R guy worth his corporate credit card could spot the obvious appeal of the band – they were young, a little wild, had some great songs, and their ages gave journalists an angle. Silverchair had something for everyone.

'We were learning a lot of things then,' Joannou figures, recalling their Big Day Out experiences. 'We just loved to play and didn't care about anything else. It was very surreal, wandering around, being part of this big circus.'

It was clearly a crazy time for the trio. They were caught up in a whirlwind of manic shows, and they were also about to travel overseas for the first time, where Silver-mania would be crazier still. Even going to Sydney had been a big event for these three small-town teenagers: now they were venturing into the largest rock and roll marketplace in the world.

While Big Day Out madness was happening all around them, the band were keen to prove they weren't two-hit wonders – and Watson and O'Donnell needed to prove their new stars didn't have a short shelf life. During December 1994 and January 1995, the band spent nine days with South African-born, Australian-based producer Kevin 'Caveman' Shirley in Sydney, recording what would become *Frogstoinp*, their debut album.

Originally based in Newcastle, Shirley had worked the desk for some well-regarded but small-selling Australian bands, including power-riffers the Dubrovniks, and had engineered the Baby Animals's 1991 debut album, which reached Number One in Australia and sold 300,000 copies. But he was an unknown quantity as a producer. Watson, however, was keen to have Shirley work on the album, in part on the strength of some demos he'd produced for the Poor, a low-rent AC/DC that Sony had signed in 1994. ('They were fucking great, sonically,' according to Watson, although Shirley couldn't actually recall making the demos when we spoke in 2006.) And O'Donnell liked Shirley's work with the Dubrovniks. Although many at Sony thought this a risky choice, it turned out to be another smart move by the two Johns. And even though Phil McKellar, who was on the shortlist, would have loved to have a shot at producing the album, he respected the choice of Shirley. 'Was he the right guy?' he asked when we spoke. 'I'd have to say yeah. That album really represented what the band was like live.'

But Shirley, an unapologetically commercially minded producer, whose attitude had always been 'Why make an album that doesn't sell?', wasn't sure he was the man for the job. 'I wasn't really that interested in working with them,' he said. 'They had such a cool thing going with Phil [McKellar] and Nick [Launay]; I thought they had a winning formula.' Shirley reluctantly agreed to spend a weekend with the band and record two songs – 'Pure Massacre' and 'Leave Me Out' – as 'an experiment'. Pleasantly surprised by the results, he signed on for the album, for a fee of AUD$20,000 and three 'points' in the album, a deal which netted him upwards of half a million dollars and made him one of the many people to benefit enormously from the album's success. Before the band set up base at Festival Studios, Shirley spent a fortnight with them in Newcastle, working through each song that would make the album. 'I think I spent more time in pre-production than the studio,' he recalled.

Shirley was known widely as a true 'rock dog'. A gradually emptying bottle of Jack Daniel's sat on the desk throughout every session he worked on. It was a sight that didn't rest well with Silverchair's parents, still the band's surrogate managers, who came into the studio each afternoon to check out their boys' progress, after a day of shopping. The Silverparents said little, but Julie Johns did take Shirley aside after hearing how he'd double-tracked her son's voice during 'Israel's Son'. As Shirley recalled, 'She asked me, "Is it really necessary to have that distortion? He has such a beautiful voice."' Shirley smiled and got back to work. Nor did the two Johns intrude greatly on the album-in-progress. 'They were involved,'

Shirley said, 'but knew we were going in the right direction. I don't recall them ever saying, "This song isn't right."'

But Shirley's reputation wasn't fully deserved. A single parent, he brought his six-year-old son, who was on school holidays, into most sessions, and although Shirley 'did have a drink each day,' as O'Donnell recalls, 'he was totally tied in.' 'I lived and breathed that record,' Shirley told me. 'I had an incredible feeling about it.' Shirley also supplied the guitar – a vintage 1955 Les Paul – that can be heard throughout the LP. He just didn't think that Johns's favourite axe from the time, a Steve Vai signature Ibanez, could provide the necessary grunt. It was a good call on his part.

A fast worker, Shirley did his best to get the teen trio interested in the workings of the studio and the recording process, even if their short attention spans usually got the better of them. When that happened, he'd send them outside to play cricket, or lock them in a room with a porn video featuring Ron 'The Hedgehog' Jeremy, which kept them titillated for hours. As Shirley explained, 'Sometimes in the studio you're a policeman, sometimes you're a babysitter or a friend. This time around, I was a rebel schoolteacher.' Shirley's approach in the studio was smart. Rather than the traditional method of recording rhythm tracks first, then adding guitars and vocals, he worked song by song. By the end of each day, one – sometimes two – songs were ready for playback. He understood that these guys were teenagers and they needed some immediate gratification for their work. While Shirley set up takes, he would let them crash about the studio corridors. Joannou laughs at the memory. 'We were just having fun. He was perfect; he'd call us in and say, "Right, we need you now." We'd go in, do it and then see what other stuff there was to break.'

If Shirley had any hassles with recording *Frogstomp*, it was recreating the 'feel' that Phil McKellar had captured so well on 'Tomorrow', the album's key track. Shirley mentioned this to McKellar in passing, when they ran into each other at Sydney venue Selinas during the period Shirley was working on the album. '[Shirley's version] sounded a bit more polished, a bit faster,' McKellar said. 'I prefer mine.' 'The guys didn't cut it at the same tempo,' Shirley said. 'It was too slow.' The finished version of the song, which would become the catalyst for Silverchair's supernova rise, is actually the result of painstaking editing on the part of Shirley and his crew; like a sonic jigsaw, the song was seamlessly stitched together and then digitally sped up.

Band and producer spent four days in Festival Studios in Pyrmont recording the basic instrumental tracks, and another five days recording overdubs and Johns's vocal parts. Capturing those world-weary vocals – so unsettling from a teenager, and such a major part of the band's sound – was the most difficult part of the recording. On the first day, thanks to studio inexperience and a lack of proper vocal training, Johns simply ran out of voice. Then he caught a cold, which meant he had to return a fortnight later to finish five tracks. In an effort to get Johns motivated, Gillies and Joannou decorated his vocal booth with *Playboy* and *Penthouse* centrefolds and then rattled around the studio's corridors on equipment trolleys, just like typical fifteen-year-olds . One Festival staffer from the tune recalls the band vividly. 'They made so much fucking noise,' I was told.

'He has the best sounds – drum-wise, everything-wise,' Joannou said of Shirley in 1995. 'He's great to work with and he's got a good brain. He mainly made things a bit longer or shorter.' The views the band was expressing about Shirley changed at the time of their second album's release, with indirect accusations that he was a control freak. But those close to the band believe the boys were blowing smoke in an effort to blame the inevitable Seattle/grunge comparisons on something – or someone – other than their songs.

When asked about *Frogstomp* in 2003, Johns was very proud of the album:

> Kevin did a really good job. We were so young and inexperienced at the time that we probably needed somebody who could take control of the recording side of things and that's exactly what he did. A year or two after we made *Frogstomp* I really didn't like it, because it pigeonholed us and felt restricting. But that wasn't Kevin's fault – it had more to do with the songs and some of the stuff that happened around the album. These days some of the songs on *Frogstomp* make me wince, but overall I think it's a fun record.

Frogstomp was wrapped for the bargain price of around AUD$40,000. What wasn't absorbed by studio rental costs was mostly spent on Shirley's fee, travel expenses and accommodation. It was a relatively low-budget effort that would recoup its investment many times over, and then some. Joannou commented:

> We did the album pretty quick because we didn't have a lot of time. You know how people say it takes, like, three months to do an album? That's a load of crap. You can do it in ten days – piece of cake.

(However, by the time of *Diorama,* their fourth album, they too would be spending months in the studio.)

Shirley said in 1996:

> The alarming thing is that the guys sound as mature as they do. You can definitely hear the influences. But they weren't embarrassed about showing those influences. I think the age card is a funny one. George Harrison was sixteen when he joined the Beatles. Michael Jackson was going a long time before that age. It's nothing unusual in the history of rock and roll.

Frogs to nip – named after a Floyd Newman song Johns spotted on a Stax-Volt singles compilation among Watson's record collection – was released in Australia on 27 March 1995, debuting at Number One in the album charts and staying in the top spot for three weeks. (Producer Kevin Shirley was shocked when he saw the album cover; although he hadn't mentioned it to the band, his one phobia was frogs – and there they were, glaring at him from the cover. 'I though they were going to call it *Llama-something*!' he exclaimed.) It was the first debut album by an Australian act to chart at Number One in its first week. By 10 April, it had been certified platinum (70,000 copies sold). By May it had sold more than 100,000 copies, principally on the strength of Triple J airplay and live shows. The two Johns did their best to uphold their low-key, street-cred strategy; in fact, it was only at the end of the year, under pressure from Sony executives, that Watson and O'Donnell agreed to a week's worth of TV advertising – and only if they could produce what amounted to an 'anti ad'. According to O'Donnell, 'We just didn't want to be greedy.'

For a trio of fifteen-year-olds still finding their own rock and roll voice, *Frogstomp* was a remarkably solid, if hugely derivative album. More than anything else, it was an album of its time, propelled by what would be recognised as the signature sound of Silverchair: Johns's full-throated roar and serrated riffs (check out 'Pure Massacre'), Joannou's fat, fuzzy basslines (best heard in 'Israel's Son') and Gillies's muscular tub-thumping (heard everywhere). They worked from the definitive grunge template as perfected by Soundgarden, Nirvana and Pearl Jam: quiet verses followed by loud choruses and a sound as thick as sludge. However, Johns's old-beyond-his-years growl and the melodies that broke through the sonic murk were distinctive. Though they weren't quite the innovators they would become with later albums, *Frogstomp* proved that Silverchair were far more than slavish imitators.

Johns, who still insisted that he drew most of his lyrical ideas from watching television, whipped up a batch of songs dominated by death, violence and powerhouse rock riffs. 'Faultline', for starters, was written about the New-castle earthquake of December 1989, which killed thirteen people. 'I just saw on the news that a guy's brother was killed, so I wrote lyrics about it three years later when I remembered it in a dream,' Johns explained.

Of the rest of *Frogstomp*, 'Shade' was a howling power ballad that hinted at such future hits as 'Ana's Song', 'Leave Me Out' wielded a simple 'back off' message and 'Cicada' was pure teen angst (with guitars). The sombre, surprisingly restrained 'Suicidal Dream' was the album's most disturbing track. Johns calmly sang the lyric: 'I fantasise about my death / I'll kill myself by holding my breath' as if it were just another pop song. 'It's not about me,' Johns insisted. 'It's about teenage suicide and the ideas people have. I don't try and write lyrics about me.'

Regardless of Johns's lyrical influences, *Frogstomp* connected with more record-buying teenagers than the band or their label could ever have imagined. And although it attracted such condescending tags as 'Nirvana in Pyjanaas', 'silverhighchair' and 'Not Soundgarden, Kindergarten', most critics treated the album with respect. Writing in the *Sydney Morning Herald*, buzzkilhng journalist Shane Danielsen called it 'an impressive debut', noting their 'ability to pile layers of punishing noise atop a tune worth humming'. Australian *Rolling Stone* gushed that 'Silverchair make a noise like they're here to stay,' concluding, with only the faintest hint of condescension, that 'this is eminently moshable stuff, guaranteed to cause carnage in lounge rooms across the country.'

While they mightn't have a sound to call their own, Silverchair had grabbed hold of the grunge Zeitgeist with all six hands, even down to the fine detail of wearing the right T-shirts – featuring the names of local heroes You Am I and Ammonia, and US bands Ministry, Helmet and the Offspring – in band photos. Some wear their influences on their sleeve; Silverchair wore them on their skinny, hairless chests.

The band were big winners in the annual Australian *Rolling Stone* Reader's Poll awards, published in April 1995, winning Artist of the Year, Best New Band, Best Hard Rock Band and Brightest Hope. 'Tomorrow' picked up Best Single, while the obligatory naysayers also gave them the tag Hype of the Year. But Silverchair were getting used to their critics.

The band readily admitted the influence of Pearl Jam on their runaway hit of a single 'Tomorrow', but began to play down the long-term impact of the multi-platinum grungers. 'When you hear the album, it doesn't sound anything like that,' Joannou assured writer Mel Toltz.

'That was early,' Johns threw in.

> That was on the first EP. At that time we were very strongly influenced by Pearl Jam. That's all we ever listened to. And then we started listening to Soundgarden and Helmet and stopped listening to Pearl Jam.

A defensive tone crept into his diatribe: 'Because we were just starting out, we didn't know.'

Even as fifteen-year-olds, the trio were already developing a solid defence to the tall-poppy syndrome that is such an intrinsic part of Australian culture.

'People give us shit,' Johns said.

> It's good in some ways. It stops you from getting a big head if you know like millions and millions of people hate you. And if people hate you, it makes you want to keep going, 'cause you want to prove them wrong.

Ben Lee, the teen hipster from Noise Addict, was a very public critic of Silverchair. His band had emerged at the same time, but whereas the Newcastle three were immediately embraced by the mainstream, Lee's outfit stayed resolutely in the margins, maintaining their indie cred and the coolest possible connections (their second-ever gig was opening for New York art-rockers Sonic Youth). Lee's scorn for Silverchair was clear when he told *Rolling Stone* magazine: 'There's no way they're ever going to live this down. They'll always be "the kids from Silverchair". Those kids, they don't know what they're letting themselves in for.'

On 12 April, 'Israel's Son', the third single from *Frogstomp*, was released. But it was a limited release; the single was only available commercially for three weeks. This was another Watson and O'Donnell move to control the band's exposure, in the face of an alterna-rock-hungry public that couldn't get enough of them. And still the song bruised the Top 10, peaking at Number Eleven. The Sony-employed pair were now acting as caretaker managers for the band, along with the boys' parents, especially Julie Johns. But what Silverchair really needed was someone to take on the management role full time.

Watson had never hidden his interest in managing the band, and in August 1995, the worst kept secret in the local rock biz was revealed: Watson decided he was ready to look after Silverchair, quitting his A&R position with Sony. Watson had been planning his move since March. Despite a few expressions of interest – John Woodruff, who had checked them out when they won Youthrock 1994, was the highest profile manager keen on the band – there was no other logical contender for the job. The deal was sealed over a few lunches with the trio's parents. According to Watson, 'It was just a question of when I was going to jump ship.'

Speaking with rock scribe Stuart Coupe in his Music Industry News & Gossip column in Sydney free press mag *Drum Media,* Watson explained:

> After more than four years at Sony Music this has been a very difficult decision to make. However, things have finally reached the point where Silverchair really do need full-time management rather than part-time career guidance which John O'Donnell and I have been trying to provide since the band signed to Murmur last year. The support

I had from the band, their parents and everyone at the record company has been tremendous and I am excited at now being able to focus 100 per cent on helping Silverchair achieve the international success they deserve.

As for the band themselves, they were happy enough about Watson taking over, but as Gillies put it, 'We so weren't thinking about it; we didn't give a shit.'

Around the time that Watson took over management of the band, murmurs of Silverchair interest emerged in America. And it came from a variety of sources.

'The Big Backyard' was a government-subsidised initiative that produced half-hour radio-ready programs – DJ voiceover and all – of new Australian music. It was burnt onto CD, and distributed via embassies and diplomatic posts to more than 750 radio stations in 100-odd countries. In an effort to get the band's US label, Epic, excited about the act, Watson bought the Big Backyard mailing list and fired off a Murmur mailout. It included a letter from the program suggesting stations check out this new Australian music.

Back in March 1995, a Perth-based fan had mailed a copy of 'Tomorrow' to a relative who worked at Detroit radio station 89X, which, on 27 March became the first US radio station to playlist the song. Brian Philips, the chief programmer for Atlanta's 99X station, was in Australia on a junket to check out the Cruel Sea just as 'Tomorrow' fever started to spread. He grabbed a copy of the song everyone was talking about and playlisted it on his return to Atlanta. Within a week, it was one of the top five songs requested by listeners. Chicago's Q101 also added 'Tomorrow' to their playlist; soon Seattle's KNDD did the same, as did Milwaukee's WLUM.

The band had already played three fly-by European dates, in Frankfurt, London and Amsterdam, between 29 March and 3 April, which bassist Joannou casually dismissed as 'just a bit of a thing to spread the word that we were a new Australian band'. The amiable Gillies decided London would have been 'legendary if it was warmer and had a beach'. But America was where serious interest was developing in the band, and as Watson and O'Donnell knew, it was also where the serious money was to be made.

Epic had planned to run with 'Israel's Son' as Silverchair's first US single and have the band tour to coincide with *Frogstomp*'s release late in the year. Now they had to change their plans and lead with 'Tomorrow' – and get the band over for at least a few dates. By 6 June, when the single was officially released to radio, David Massey knew he had a phenomenon on his hands. As he told *Rolling Stone* magazine, this wasn't record company spin at work. 'Tomorrow' had been 'getting an amazing response from the public,' he said.' It comes from the public as opposed to industry hype.'

On 21 June, the band played their first American date, in Atlanta (even though a visa hassle in Sydney meant they almost didn't make the trip at all). Although they made a press stopover in Los Angeles, they didn't play shows there. Instead, they opted to do gigs in the cities where radio response to 'Tomorrow' was strongest: Atlanta, Chicago (on 23 June) and Detroit (24 June), at the 'birthday bash' for station 89X. It was a smart move by the band's management: make a few splashes and let the ripples spread from there. And by playing radio-sponsored shows, the band were establishing some goodwill. It is one of modern rock and roll's unspoken rules that by playing a free radio show a band becomes entitled to good treatment by that station's playlist programmers.

Despite the impressive local radio interest, no one could have expected the response at the Atlanta show. The venue, the Roxy, housed 1500 punters at a squeeze. Mid-afternoon, a shocked Watson put in a call to O'Donnell back in Sydney: 'You're not going to believe this,' he reported, 'but we're at soundcheck and there's a queue of 150 people going around the corner.' By six o'clock, two hours before the doors were due to open, a line of 3000 hopefuls snaked a kilometre down the street. On a home video made at the show, Watson can be heard muttering about the out-of-control crowd response.

The mayhem continued throughout the short tour. At their Chicago gig two days later, while the crowd moshed themselves senseless, a female voice shrieked from the balcony, 'Oh my God, they're so cute I can't believe it.'

The *Chicago Tribune's* Greg Kot reviewed the show, describing how the band overcame a wobbly start to:

> put some wallop behind the insidious melodies of 'Tomorrow', 'Real [sic] Massacre' and 'Israel's Son'. There was no denying the savvy sense of dynamics, muscular melodies and tight ensemble playing.

All of which suggested that Silverchair has the potential to match the impact of some of its influences, if not make Mom and Dad sell off their old Zeppelin albums.

The band was brought back down to earth, however, when Johns broke a microphone stand during their set, and the venue insisted they pay for the damage.

Watson and O'Donnell had suspected the band would draw a strong response, but this was the stuff of which managers dream. By the time of the Chicago show, *Frogstomp*, which had been released less than a week before, had sold 5000 copies – 2000 in Atlanta alone, where it debuted at Number Eleven even before it was fully stocked in stores. The following week, sales doubled. As 99X programmer Philips stated: 'It is not in my experience for a band to launch itself into the stratosphere this quickly. This is a very special thing.'

Watson and O'Donnell insisted, just as they did in Australia, that the band would only accommodate the 'right' type of media, even to the extent of turning down *Time* magazine's request for an interview. Their first US radio interview, with Sean Demory from WNNX, Atlanta, was a useful reminder that, after all, these rock-stars-in-the-making were still teenagers. Whereas most bands would have been talking up whatever product they had to sell, Silverchair were more interested in discussing the merits of rollercoasters, especially those at Magic Mountain, an amusement park in LA. 'That is the best place in the whole world!' Johns gushed. Their exchange touched on everything from seeing hardcore favourites Helmet at Brisbane's Livid Festival (Gillies: 'And that was very legendary') to in-flight meals, arcade games and the lack of American beaches. It was all good-natured chaos, with the band maintaining their credibility by requesting a Helmet song rather than the track off *Frogstomp* that the DJ had already cued up. 'You don't have to play something off that CD,' Gillies and Johns shouted in unison.

After the Detroit show, the band returned to Europe, playing the Roskilde festival, Denmark's answer to Lolla-palooza and the Big Day Out, on 30 June. There were more European festival dates in France (where they were almost wiped out by a speeding truck in the middle of the night),

Switzerland and England, before they returned home in mid July. Back in Australia, they toasted *Frogstomp*'s success with a hometown show on 12 August at the Newcastle Workers Club, at the curiously named Llama Ball. The llama was a favourite animal of the teen wonders for a short time, and they would name their fan club the Llama Appreciation Society – Johns even titled his publishing company Big Fat Llama Music. *Frogstomp*'s liner notes declared 'no llamas were harmed in the making of this album' and encouraged fans to 'support the liberation of the llama nation'. As Watson explained, 'They were fifteen-year old guys; llamas were funny.'

These llama-lovers were also homecoming heroes.

Meanwhile, Epic wanted a bigger-budget video for 'Tomorrow', rather than Robert Hambling's cheap-as-chips clip, so they hired director Mark Pellington, later to become the director of such Hollywood flicks as *The Mothman Prophecies*. MTV soon had the clip in their 'Buzz Bin', on high rotation.

Silverchair's timing couldn't have been better. Nirvana were all over when Cobain killed himself in 1994; grunge giants Pearl Jam were off the road, immersed in a legal battle with Ticketmaster over concert prices, while both the Smashing Pumpkins and Soundgarden had retreated to the studio. American rock lovers wanted something loud and energetic and youthful, and they wanted it now. Silverchair was just the band – and Epic fully understood this. '"Tomorrow" is a stone-cold smash,' Massey said at the time.' It's a really American sound. It fits in perfectly.' It also didn't hurt that their lead singer was desired by girls and envied by their boyfriends.

Even parents loved Silverchair, as New York writer Geoff Stead observed:

> Silverchair's image has received the stamp of approval from the mums and dads of America. They believe the young Australian band is not tainted by the drugs and sex scandals which surround many groups.

'I'm not a fan of their music,' said Glen Bernard, a parent of four Silverchair fans, 'but my kids love them and it's good, clean fun.'

Timing, business-wise, also helped their American invasion. At this time Epic had no in-house A&R head (they were waiting on a new recruit to shift over from Virgin), so they weren't signing many new US acts. This gave priority to such non-American Sony signmgs as Oasis, Deep Forest, Des'ree and Silverchair – all big sellers in 1995. Usually, American signings are favoured, because a homegrown hit meant that Epic wouldn't have to pay a 'matrix royalty' to the country where the act is signed, thereby earning larger profits. But in 1995, Sony had no option. On 10 July, *Frogstomp* debuted in the *Billboard* Top 200 at Number 106. By 7 August, it was certified gold, having sold half a million copies. And it just kept selling. In the format-crazy world of US radio, it was a far-reaching success, ranking highly in everything from the New Artist and the Mainstream Rock lists to the Top Heatseekers chart, as well as the all-important *Billboard* Top 200, where it peaked at an impressive Number Nine.

Proving what a listener- and public-driven success this was, *Frogstomp* was certified platinum on 11 September 1995, well before most reviews of the album appeared. American *Rolling Stone* wrote that the band 'exude a rugged confidence and an otherworldly grasp of noise rock that belies their tender ages.' Fort Lauderdale's *Sun-Sentinel* newspaper declared that 'Silverchair's music is in a realm of its own.'

The *New York Times*'s Dmitri Ehrlich wasn't completely sold, but could spot the band's strengths:

> Obviously derivative of Stone Temple Pilots, Nirvana, Pearl Jam and Soundgarden, the group proffers dark musical theatrics with a tossed-off air and a visceral, corrosive texture. Aggressive to a fault, Chris Joannou makes use of intentionally distorted bass line[s] juxtaposed against Mr Johns's shimmery man-child vocals.

Request magazine's Jim Testa noted that:

> [*Frogstomp*] may not be the most original album of the year, but it's certainly one of the most accomplished, displaying a vaunting command of dynamics and tempo changes, and an impeccable grasp of the nihilism and frustrations shared by most young Americans.

Not a bad rap for three Aussie brats still in high school.

Silverchair's first full-scale North American tour started with a sold-out show at Toronto's Opera House on 31 August, followed by another full house at Chicago's 1100-capacity Metro on 2 September, and subsequent sold-out dates in Boston, Washington DC, Atlanta, Los Angeles (at the legendary Whisky A Go-Go), San Francisco and Seattle, before ending with a free show on Santa Monica pier on 17 September. By that time, *Frogstomp* had sold more than two million copies in the US alone and was Number Nine on the *Billboard* chart – outselling even Michael Jackson's *HIStory*. 'Tomorrow', meanwhile, was in the middle of a twenty-six-week residency in *Billboard*'s influential Modern Rock chart. No Australian band since INXS had steamrolled the American charts in that way – and it took INXS several years on the road, sleeping in the tour van and eating at diners, to make the slightest impact. Silverchair, however, broke overnight. Despite their 'don't give a shit' attitude, the band were fully aware of their good fortune. As Joannou told me in 2003, 'Watto [Watson] made it very clear how lucky we were that we weren't stuck in a van, trudging around, playing gigs to three people.'

But still the band behaved as you'd expect fifteen-year-olds to behave. Life on the road with Silverchair was something like a three-way version of *Bill&Ted's Excellent Adventure*. 'They seem oblivious to the Silvermania that is sweeping the US,' wrote *Rolling Stones* Mel Toltz, who caught up with the band during their American tour. 'Odd remarks and crude comments appear from nowhere and are volleyed back and forth across the room over an imaginary net.'

Curiously enough, this happened even though the band's entourage included their parents. The Silvermums and Silverdads would take turns travelling with their sons; Joannou's father, for one, enjoyed the life so much he even grew his hair halfway down his back, just to keep up with his bass-playing offspring. Gillies believes that his mother was the strictest of all when it came to band curfews. 'It was just a pain,' he said. 'She managed, for a little while, until I was about sixteen, to keep the reins on me. She'd make sure I was back by 1.30.' (The mothers did warm to touring, nonetheless. Today the band joke that their parents still ask when they're next touring, so they can join them and shop till they drop.)

In the midst of the madness, on 7 September, the band took part in the MTV Music Awards in New York, the night before another full house, this time at the Academy, a 1250-capacity Manhattan venue. They performed 'Pure Massacre' and 'Tomorrow' while perched on a stage atop Radio City Music Hall's entrance marquee; between songs they had to crawl back inside through a large window. The three tore through their performance, more bemused than excited by the company of America's A-list of rock stars (including Courtney Love) and such movers and shakers as Sony chief Tommy Mottola – also known as Mr Mariah Carey, at the time – who introduced himself to the band in their dressing room. The only time the trio truly loosened up was when human livewire Taylor Hawkins, then drumming for Alanis Morissette but soon to become a Foo Fighter, introduced himself and wished them luck. And rather than walk the red carpet with the other stars, the band walked around it – it was their way of staying one step removed from the glitterati. Chris Joannou joked, 'We thought we would've got in trouble if we walked on it.'

Craig Mathieson captured the frenzied atmosphere in *Hi Fi Days*:

> As 'Pure Massacre' ends, Johns coaxes spasms of feedback from his guitar, Gillies (literally) attacks his drums with fervour and Joannou unceremoniously drops his bass. Noise rings from the stage as Silverchair walk off. For a few seconds the camera lingers on the abandoned instruments as the white noise fades. The camera cuts to co-host Tabitha Soren, who looks taken aback by Silverchair's firestorm and grins nervously before putting everything into perspective with a clarifying comment: 'Whew'.

On 10 September, the band supported the Ramones in front of a 20,000-strong crowd in Atlanta, at a show, not coincidentally, entitled The Big Day Out. (Station programmer Philips had obviously returned from Australia with more than a Silverchair CD.) Few rock stars outwardly impressed Silverchair, but this was a show that stuck with them for some time. 'They were legends; they were hell men,' Johns declared of the original New York punks, who'd split soon after.

Silverchair were at the centre of a major buzz, and the album kept selling; *Frogstomp* eventually spent a remarkable forty-eight weeks in the *Billboard* album chart. And the big names kept gravitating towards the band, including Nirvana bassist Kris Novoselic, who fronted at their 15 September show at Seattle. 'He was sitting on the side of the stage with his girlfriend [wife, actually],' Johns remembered of his encounter with the lanky man from Nirvana. 'He kept telling us about his toothache. It was so funny.'

Their American tour, however, ended on a bloody note. During their free final show on the Santa Monica Pier, the band experienced technical problems, which slowed down their set and upset the crowd. Someone in the surly mob hurled a bottle onstage, which hit Johns on the left side of his head, opening a gaping wound. He kept playing, finishing the show with blood streaming down his face, looking more like one of the Newcastle rugby league Johnses than the softly spoken frontman of Silverchair. As soon as the gig ended he was carted off to hospital.

It was Johns's first real taste of the downside of fame, even though he laughed about it later on.

> I got stitches and everything and came back and our sound guy was complaining about the PA and shit. It was so funny. It was heaps good fun. Everything went wrong.

Joannou remembers that crowd as one of the roughest they'd ever fronted.

> It was really hardcore. It had one of the craziest mosh circle things I'd ever seen. [In the US, moshpits have a tendency to develop into strange, dangerous 'circles' of slam-dancers, who look as though they're performing some bizarre ritual dance.] Big dudes were running around slamming their mates; these guys were crazy. They'd whack some guy really hard and then pat him on the back.

If Santa Monica was a bust, Silverchair's return to Australia was a dazzling high – even better than the Magic Mountain rollercoaster. The annual ARIAs were held on Monday 2 October at Sydney's Darling Harbour. The word doing the rounds was that the 'old guard' of Farnsey, Barnesy and co.

were about to be dethroned by three punks from Newcastle. There were other bands at the front of the alt-rock revolution, too, such as Sydney trio You Am I, who'd just released their second and best album, *Hi Fi Way*. Even though Janet Jackson was the guest of honour and mainstream pop star Tina Arena won four gongs, including Best Australian Album for *Don't Ask,* it was Silverchair's night of nights.

The band cleaned up, winning awards for Best New Talent, Best Debut Single, Best Australian Single and Highest Selling Single ('Tomorrow'), as well as Best Debut Album for *Frogstomp*. Typically, rather than come off like a bunch of poseurs and accept the awards themselves, the band sent along Josh Shirley, the son of *Frogstomp*'s producer, to collect each of their pointy statuettes. (Or at least he collected the first two ARIAs; jet-lagged after an overnight flight from New York, and an interminable performance from Merril 'Mouth' Bainbridge, he fell asleep at the winner's table and left his father to collect the subsequent trophies.) No one, apart from 'Chair insiders, had any idea who this kid was who was collecting the silverware.

But the band weren't just being whimsical. Josh Shirley was the only person, apart from Johns, Gillies and Joannou, to actually play on *Frogstomp*. You can hear him flailing about on the drums just before the start of the album's final track, 'Findaway'. 'It was just funny,' explained producer Shirley. 'That was part of the spirit of the recording sessions; it was fun in the studio, even though they came perilously close to taking themselves – or being taken – too seriously.' The link was meant to be explained by presenter Meatloaf, but the big guy didn't quite make it to that part of his cue card. The press, who the next day tore a few layers off the band for being smug, were actually missing out on a great story. 'It got a bit lost in translation,' Shirley accepted.

It didn't matter to Silverchair, though. They hooked up with You Am I's Tim Rogers to close the night with a tearaway cover of Radio Birdman's 'New Race', and had the rockingest time of their life. Rogers was as big a hero to the Silver-trio as Eddie Vedder; Johns had even sported a You Am I T-shirt on an American TV broadcast. 'We only practised for about an hour and thought, "Yeah, that's all right",' Johns said afterwards. 'Shit, it was funny.' The new guard had entered the building, even if they didn't bother stepping onstage to collect their trophies. The lines between mainstream and so-called 'alternative' acts were blurring, with Silverchair leading the way. Such multi-syllabled acts as Regurgitator, Powderfmger and Spiderbait would soon be riding Silverchair's coat-tails right to the top of the pop charts.

Just as satisfying was the band's success at the 1995 Australian Performing Rights Association (APRA) Songwriter Awards, held on 12 December, when Johns and Gillies shared the 'Songwriter of the Year' award. These awards are greatly valued by musicians because they're judged by music-making peers, not the industry players who make the decisions at the ARIAs. So Silverchair didn't just have industry approval; their fellow musos thought they were pretty cool, too.

The rest of Silverchair's 1995 was spent in motion. And there were more injuries. During a 27 October gig at the Palace in St Kilda, Johns stage-dived into the crowd. Joannou and Gillies kept playing, while keeping a wary eye on their frontman. When Johns hadn't surfaced after a minute, they started to panic. Local rock and roll legend maintains that when Johns dived, the crowd parted and he hit the deck. The truth, of course, is slightly different. As Joannou told me, 'Daniel stage-dived and then people started to grab his shirt and stuff and he went, "Whoom!", straight to the bottom.' Plucked out of the sweaty mass by security guards, Johns made it back to the stage with his clothes ripped. When his eyes started rolling back in his head, the show was over. (Joannou: 'We went, "Fuck, he's dead!"') Thankfully, there was an off-duty police car parked outside; Johns was raced to hospital, where he was held for observation. But still the show went on – within two days, Silverchair were playing another (this time incident-free) gig at the same venue.

Their next North American jaunt – hastily arranged after an injury to Chili Pepper Chad Smith forced the cancellation of a shared tour – started on 25 November, with another full house, this time in San Diego. Dates followed in Vancouver, and continued on to 18 December, where they shared the bill at LA's Universal Amphitheater with Radiohead, Oasis and British Nirvana clones Bush. They put in a *Saturday Night Live* appearance on 9 December, and four days later played New Jersey's legendary Stone Pony, the club whose place in rock and roll folklore was secured because it was the starting point for Bruce Springsteen and his E-Street Band.

Rock writer Stuart Coupe found himself in the eye of the Silverchair storm when he caught an all-ages show in Philadelphia. Backstage, Coupe noted 'how remarkably down-to-earth and relaxed' the band seemed, despite the pressure of photo shoots, interviews and pressing the flesh, which are required to break new albums, especially in America. Nonetheless, the controlling hand of manager Watson was ever-present. 'An interview?' Coupe wrote in Sydney's *Drum Media*. 'Watson says he'll think about it but reckons he doesn't want to do any Australian press for the moment.' Coupe knew that American *Rolling Stone* writer David Fricke had just spent a few days with the band, and he was justifiably pissed off. Coupe observed, 'It was hard not to think about the situation with INXS when they were just *toooo* big for the Australian media.' (In his defence, Watson insists that he was merely trying to maintain a 'level playing field' with all Australian media at the time.)

Coupe met up with Fricke a few nights later, at the band's show in New York's Roseland Ballroom, on 10 December. He asked the respected US scribe how Silverchair stacked up next to Nirvana. 'He tells me that Kurt had a bit more angst and menace,' Coupe wrote, 'but aside from that, Silverchair are putting on a show to rival that band.' Right then in the United States, that was more than enough to satisfy an alt-rock crowd short on heroes.

Silverchair closed 1995 with an outdoor New Year's Eve show in Perth. By then, *Frogstomp* was rapidly heading toward global sales of 2,898,000. The band had cleaned up at the ARIAs. Their estimated gross earnings for the year were AUD$6.4 million. They'd rocked Europe, Australia and America, coast to coast. You want an excellent adventure? It had been the biggest year of these kids' lives. Bill and Ted would have been proud.

All of three days separated the band's New Year's Eve show and their opening date of 1996, where they put in a rapturously received set at the inaugural Homebake (renamed 'Mudbake' for the day) – an Australian-only rock festival held in Byron Bay on the NSW north coast. The crowd's response to Silverchair was manic, despite the teeming rain and horrendous conditions that necessitated a shortened set for fear of the band being electrocuted. Producer Phil McKellar was in the crowd, taking in the muddy chaos. 'People were just so excited to see them,' he said. 'It was huge.'

But in January, the band learned – just as Johns had in Santa Monica – that fame's yang can often outweigh its yin. Success really had a funny way of biting them on the arse and bringing them down, just when their outlook was ridiculously bright.

It all started with a *Daily Telegraph* headline, which shouted: 'Silverchair shocked. Violence appals us, band says.' Another headline yelled: 'A script for murder.'

On 11 August 1995, in Washington State, sixteen-year-old Brian Bassett and his friend Nicholaus McDonald had shot Bassett's parents and drowned his five-year-old brother. When caught, they told police they were playing 'Israel's Son' at the time. Their trial opened on 18 January, and both were being tried as adults, which guaranteed far more media coverage than yet another tragic case of American patricide. McDonald's lawyer, Tom Copland, claimed that both his client and Bassett had been driven to kill by the Silverchair song; he insisted that the track should be admissible evidence. He stated that the song was 'almost a script' for the murders. There was even talk of subpoenaing Daniel Johns, who wrote the song.

Naturally, Watson sprang to the band's defence, making an official statement that read:

> Silverchair do not, have not, and never would condone violence of any sort. The band is appalled by this horrific crime and they hope that justice will prevail in prosecuting whoever is responsible for it. Silverchair absolutely rejects any allegation that their song is in any way responsible for the action of the alleged murderers. It is a matter of public record that the song in question is inspired by a television documentary about wartime atrocities. The song seeks to criticise violence and war by portraying them in all their horror.

While the song's author remained silent, *Frogstomp* producer Kevin Shirley was shaken to his core, crying 'for hours'. 'It freaked me out completely,' he said, when told of the murders. He immediately sought the reassurance of some close friends, but still 'felt very much responsible' for what had happened.

Responding to Copland's argument, deputy prosecutor Jerry Fuller asked:

> What does it prove? Does it prove that Bassett hated his parents? Does it prove he had the motive to kill his parents? No. All it proves is that it was a song that he played.

The next day, Judge Mark McCauley ruled that 'Israel's Son' could not be played during opening statements and reserved judgement on whether the song could be played at all during the trial.

But the damage was done: suddenly a very green bunch of sixteen-year-olds from Newcastle were receiving a similar treatment to British metal outfit Judas Priest, who were being sued in an American court by two families who blamed their 1978 album *Stained Class* for the suicides of their sons. That case was also dismissed, but the stigma was pervasive. O'Donnell, Watson and Silverchair's parents had every reason to close ranks just a little tighter around their charges.

Speaking eight years down the line, Watson considers this a pivotal moment for Johns; one that triggered his increased wariness of the limelight and which would soon turn him into a virtual recluse. A *Daily Telegraph Mirror* article from October 1995, headlined 'How a $6m boy gets to school' that showed Johns, in school uniform, riding his push-bike, only exacerbated the problem. 'I'm not saying the media caused the problems which happened later,' says Watson, 'but there is not a doubt in my mind that they were one of several contributing factors.' O'Donnell agrees: 'I think the "Israel's Son" thing hit him really hard.' (Johns would have the last laugh when it came time to vent his anger and write the bitter lyrics for future albums *Freak Show* and *Neon Ballroom*.)

But it wasn't as if the band went into hiding. Next move for Silverchair was their biggest yet: a US stadium tour with the Red Hot Chili Peppers, rescheduled from the previous November because Chili Peppers drummer Chad Smith had been injured in a sporting mishap. The two bands connected well; Silverchair got on famously with Smith, the most sociable Chili Pepper, who Joannou described as 'quite a dude'. The shows were huge, including a 9 February stop at New York's Madison Square Garden, the biggest indoor gig in the city that never sleeps. Twenty thousand people turned up. It was almost a year to the day since the band had played Melbourne's inner city Prince of Wales Hotel. Things had changed.

Said Johns:

> Playing the Garden was a dream come true for us. We used to watch Led Zeppelin's video *The Song Remains the Same* [which was filmed

at Madison Square Garden] two times a day, and to play there was mind-blowing.

Gillies was an even more hardcore fan; he'd watch John Bonham's drum blitz, 'Moby Dick', in slow-mo, then he'd flail away on his bedroom kit, copying Bonham's moves. To this day, it's still his favourite rock movie. 'It was this buzz,' he said just prior to the Madison Square Garden show. 'I'm going to play where one of my biggest idols had played.'

One thing in particular that had changed for the band was the kind of attention they were receiving from women. They'd moved on from simply being 'cute'; now they were subjects of genuine female desire. During a warm-up show in Los Angeles on 4 February, a tiny scarlet-coloured bikini bottom fluttered through the air, landing at the feet of a bewildered Daniel Johns. And on the final night of the tour, 16 February, at Long Island's Nassau Coliseum, the band were in for a shock when the Chili Peppers hired two strippers to parade around the stage, topless, while the band played on, desperately hiding their red faces from the crowd – and the chuckling Peppers. The trio's parents – stone-faced – observed from side stage.

After the tour, Joannou told the *Sydney Morning Herald*:

The Red Hot Chili Peppers thought we'd be little arse-holes. When a band starts out sleeping in the backs of cars and in $50 hotels, then works their way up to 15,000 [seat] arenas, then they're, like, really good guys. But the guys that get successful really quick are [supposedly] total wankers. The Chili Peppers thought that because our album went pretty good in America quickly, we'd be real little shits. After they got to know us, it was cool.

The fun ended pretty swiftly, because the band was having more trouble with 'Israel's Son'. Their US label had asked them to reshoot the video. Johns claimed that the label thought it too violent. 'I thought, "That is a good clip for us,"' Johns told MTV in February 1996. 'Then someone had to go and have a whinge about it [and] now we've got to change it all because of [a] stupid thing.' According to Chris Joannou, the one image that bothered Sony 'just had a noose hanging off a beam of wood.' 'And a dog in a cage,' Johns added. 'They said it was too violent. It's bad.'

Curiously, in the reworked video, the use of lighting and colours is very reminiscent of Nirvana's 'Smells Like Teen Spirit', while Johns wears what one fan described as a 'grandpa sweater' – exactly the type Kurt Cobain used to fancy. In an even more perverse twist, Johns wears a shirt with the number 27 on it – the age Cobain (and Janis Joplin and Jim Morrison, amongst other famous rock deaths) was when he died. It was becoming clear how Epic was positioning the group for American youth: Nirvana reborn. The band were learning a big lesson about the role mythology and hype played in selling rock and roll records. The label's move, however, was unwise: 'Israel's Son' didn't chart with any of the impact of *Frogstomp*'s other two singles, 'Tomorrow' – which clung to the *Billboard* charts for seven months – and 'Pure Massacre', which hung around the chart for three months.

By the time the band reached Europe on 20 February for a run of shows in England, France, Germany and Holland, they were already looking ahead to their second album, while vocally defending themselves against assertions they were purely a grunge band.

'The same fucking people are always comparing us to Pearl Jam and Nirvana,' Gillies told Holland's *Oor* magazine. 'The album [*Frogstomp*] doesn't have a Seattle grunge sound at all.'

To which Johns added:

> In a couple of months, after the European tour, we'll start with recordings for a new album. You'll hear jazz, funk and rap. We already have a lot of new songs.

Gillies threw in:

> The next album will be hard and dark. The sound has to be even more fuller and fatter. We can do that now because we have a much bigger budget. Maybe we'll put a more cheerful song on the middle of the album to cheer the listener up. But the rest of the songs are meant to go cry with.

Silverchair played – and filled – bigger venues when they returned to the USA in February, including the 4500-capacity Odeum Sports & Expo Center in Villa Park, Illinois, the 3500-seat International Ballroom in Atlanta and the Electric Factory in Philadelphia, which held 3000 punters.

Naturally, their concert grosses increased – the Illinois show turned over US$74,500; more than US$44,000 was generated at their Philadelphia gig. Commercially speaking, it was the best of times for a band who'd never had to endure the hardships of the sticky carpet circuit.

The trio returned to Australia after a 6 March show in Cologne, breaking for shows in Japan on 2 and 3 April. Again, they cleaned up in the Australian *Rolling Stone* Readers' Poll, winning Best Band, Best Single (for 'Tomorrow' – a repeat of 1995), Best Male Singer, Best Hard Rock Band, Best Album Cover and Brightest Hope for 1996. And Johns was voted Best New Talent in *Guitar World*'s Readers' Poll, rolling Foo Fighter Dave Grohl and Korn. Johns's solo on 'Tomorrow' ruled over such wannabes as Eddie Van Halen, Dave Navarro and one Larry Lalonde, whose six-stringed blitz during the tasteful track 'Wynona's Big Brown Beaver' was hard to miss. As the magazine stated in their editorial, 'We suspected the teenaged phenoms of Silverchair were popular, but we didn't know they were immensely popular.' Johns, typically, played down the award. 'I don't really rate that as a solo. Basically, we really don't think that solos are worth doing for our music.' He was right on the money; it was more an explosion of noise than the type of solo that would give life to a million air guitarists.

The band had one more show to close the globetrotting *Frogstomp* tour: a 9 April set on the final day of the Royal Easter Show in Sydney. It was kids' day at the show; it made perfect sense that the prime entertainment for the day was a band of guys who could just as easily have been part of the crowd, shopping for showbags and riding the ghost train.

Twenty thousand fans fronted for the show. Backstage, among the music business insiders, the whisper was that the band was about to collect AUD$5 million for the publishing rights to *Frogstomp* and their next album. Onstage, the band ripped through a 75-minute set, with Gillies performing the ritualistic trashing of his drum kit at the close of 'Israel's Son'. As fireworks lit up the sky, a hundred teens in the moshpit were led away and treated for cuts, scratches and bruises.

Just under ninety gigs and several million sales of *Frogstomp* down the line, Silverchair were the kings of the world. So what next? Just as importantly, could it last?

* * *

A NEW TOMORROW

Madness in the Moshpit: An interview with David Fricke

Renowned American music writer David Fricke joined *Rolling Stone* in 1985 as Music Editor; he's now a Senior Editor. He was the first influential American writer to see Silverchair in action when he caught their legendary set at the 1995 Sydney Big Day Out. He then hit the road with the band when they toured America in the northern winter of 1995, as the band went platinum with 'Tomorrow' and its parent album, *Frogstomp*. Very much a Silverchair advocate, and an Australian music buff, he has tracked the band's career ever since.

What brought you to Australia in 1995?
I went because REM were opening their world tour there. I got there in time for two of their Sydney shows and the Big Day Out was within that ten-day period. Being Music Editor at the time, I was able to give myself special dispensation to stick around for the Big Day Out. I'd never seen one and figuring that we'd given so much coverage to Lollapalooza, and all the festivals that had sprung up in its wake, I thought it was worth seeing.

Had you heard much about the Big Day Out through bands you'd interviewed? Did the festival have a buzz overseas?
It had started to get a reputation because of the year Nirvana played there [1992]. And there was a buzz from Australian musicians and writers I knew. I also thought it was worthwhile covering because Hole was playing there, Ministry was playing there, plus all the Australian stuff, which I'd always been interested in. We ended up running a lot of photos and my blow-by-blow account.

What was your awareness of Silverchair at that time?
By that point, John O'Donnell, who I knew through his time at *Rolling Stone* – and who'd given me the heads-up when he started at Murmur with [John] Watson – had started sending me stuff. I'm pretty sure that an early copy of the EP had gotten to me. I was familiar with those songs, particularly 'Tomorrow'.

Other than that, all I knew was that they were real young and that John [O'Donnell] was very excited about them. I'd seen John while I was in Sydney and he was talking them up. By the time I saw him at the Sydney show, everyone was raving about the Melbourne show a few days before, where people were jumping up and down on the roof and all this sort of stuff. Obviously there was a buzz going on. Fortunately, they were [playing] on the day I made the festival.

What are your recollections of the gig?
When the afternoon started, the crowd started lining up to see them – and it was out of control. They were obviously playing in a space too small. I'm sure the fire department would have had objections. People were up on the roof, they were standing at the back – and as for people up in the front, well, you could just imagine the rib cages cracking. It was really packed. It was an amazing buzz. It's really hard these days to get that sense of anticipation at a rock show because we all know how they are; they've evolved into ritual. But this was a band that was way too young to be part of the ritual – and a lot of the crowd were way too young to be jaded.

Did you get a sense of ownership from the crowd?
I definitely got a sense of pride. It was excitement, it was pride, it was anticipation. It was something you definitely didn't get when Hole was on stage, or Ministry. You got it as well when You Am I played the bigger stage later on, although it wasn't as packed. It was something that was shared throughout the entire day; that this was the first major surfacing, nationally, for a lot of those bands, rather than a regional situation. But Silverchair were the one: they'd gone Number One, they were so young – and the combination of the novelty and the achievement made them unbeatable.

How did they stack up against other acts on the bill?
They killed me; they absolutely killed me. It wasn't anything special that they did, but they were so good, unselfconscious, and they didn't seem cowed by the fact that they were the hottest thing since the invention of the wheel. John [O'Donnell] took me backstage briefly before the gig and introduced me to John Watson for the first time, and the three guys were

just sitting against a wall, on the floor. They were so, you know, 'whatever'. They were so nonchalant. Meeting me was no big deal – John was going, 'David Fricke, *Rolling Stone*, America, dah, dah, dah,' and they just went, 'Cool.' I wasn't offended; I just figured that these guys have it under control; they didn't give a shit in the best kind of way. They were ready to go out and play.

To them, the playing, the songs, the music, and all the excitement that came back from the crowd was the thing. It wasn't about the fact that some guy from a magazine was there, or the zillion record company people – it wasn't like they were surrounded by friends. They were surrounded by adults. It wasn't worth getting excited about. The real excitement was to get out and play. That's how I read it.

And what about their set: it was quite brief, right?
It was fairly short; it was essentially the first album. I'm not sure how much was finished by that stage. 'Israel's Son' just blew me away – if I remember correctly, that was the last number. In a sense, 'Tomorrow' almost sounded old compared to that and songs like 'Pure Massacre'. It's got that soft/loud dynamic, but it was almost like a ballad compared to 'Massacre' or 'Israel's Son'. Not only was 'Tomorrow' good, and these guys were good and loud and looked great, but they had some serious songs that were worth banging your head to.

Where were you while all the action was happening?
I was standing right to the side of the stage, in the pit, near the corner where Daniel was standing. It was loud; I was right there. If I was any closer I would have been on stage. I was blown away. It was a day of really great stuff– You Am I were great, Spiderbait were great, it was a real blast to see Deniz Tek after being a Radio Birdman fan for twenty years – but Silverchair was the great shock. I came back to New York and didn't stop talking about them.

Did Courtney Love give Johns the once over?
Certainly at the Sydney Big Day Out, Courtney was rocking and reeling all over the place, so why shouldn't Daniel get a taste? The whole atmosphere

backstage was so freewheeling but, at least in Sydney, they didn't seem to take too much part in it.

What happened next?
Frogstomp came out here in the fall and did its inexorable climb. I went out on the road with them in December 1995 – I remember, because it was fucking cold. The record was breaking in a way that deserved a feature story, so I got myself assigned to go out on the road with them for a couple of dates in Canada and then went to Detroit with them.

Had they changed much by this stage?
They were a lot more at ease around me. My previous meeting with them was kind of, 'Hi, huh,' in that teenage, don't-give-a-shit way. And I have zero problem with that. But once I got out there with them, and knew John [Watson] a bit better – I think he might have told them that I was an OK guy to hang out with – they loosened up. And they were having some fun at my expense. I mean, they were sixteen years old. They were laughing and cracking wise and making all kinds of bodily function jokes and stuff like that. It was like going back to high school.

Were their chaperones on the road with them?
The dads were there, and I think, with all due respect, they were a bi t looser because the dads were there and not the mums. The dads were enjoying the trip as much as the guys. Although they kept the discipline thing going on, it was more like going on the road with your best friend than being on the road with your mum. It was a different atmosphere. They were actually cool to talk to. The parents did not do interviews, but they all agreed to sit there, all three of them, and do an interview at the hotel in Detroit. They were quite funny. They were all working class guys; their thing was that it was as much fun for them as the guys. In a way they were growing up with their sons all over again. It was like a big camping trip.

Did the dads spend their time warning their sons of the evils of the music industry?

Not as much as you might expect. By that point the mums and dads had been in the thick of it with regards to negotiating a record deal and everything going nuclear in Australia, so they already had some expertise in what was stupid and what wasn't. The one thing I could detect in all three dads was that as goofy as the guys could get, they didn't seem to fear that they [the band] would go running off, picking up hookers and doing drugs. The one thing that was weird for everyone was drinking, because the drinking age here is twenty-one. And in some cases they played clubs that served alcohol. But then again, they'd played pubs in Australia. They'd had a year of that. The only difference here was that it was bigger: there was more of it.

Did the American media focus on the ages of the guys in the band? Was that their key angle?
I think it was less of an issue with people buying the record than those writing about it. In Detroit they were playing to an audience older than them, who were there because they liked the songs and liked the sound. It wasn't Noise Addict or Jimmy Osmond; they didn't look like they were eight years old. These guys could play; Ben was a thundering drummer, Chris really held the bottom end down well and Daniel could project. He wasn't projecting as well as he would two tours down the line, he didn't have the eyeliner or the devil beard, but he knew how to hold his own on stage. You didn't think about age unless someone brought it up. The only time it became an age thing was when they would moon someone from the bus; then you went, 'Oh yeah, they're sixteen.'

Was Johns regularly compared to Kurt Cobain?
You'd read about it, people would talk about it, but personally I didn't give a shit. I'd interviewed Cobain, I'd seen Nirvana and I thought they were two different things. Daniel was young, he was blond and he screamed a lot. It's a grand tradition – look at [the Vines's] Craig Nicholls.

What about their 'Australian-ness' – did media focus on that?
I was interested in them initially because they were Australian and because I've had a long-time love affair with what goes down there musically. But

the radio wouldn't announce 'Tomorrow' as 'that song from the Australian band Silverchair'. By the time it hit they were just Silverchair. It wasn't like they were waving the Australian flag or had wallabies dancing in the videos. They didn't make a big deal about it. Because of their ages they were developing their own personal identities, much less some kind of weirdo nationalism.

One of the truly Australian characteristics about their story was the way they got that record deal. Here, you don't have hip national radio contests that involve young bands with demos. What do we have? *American Idol* [the US version of *Australian Idol*]. The idea that Triple J could be that instrumental in developing one act, average age fifteen, from Newcastle and help propel them to international stardom, is unheard of. Even the Strokes had to go to England – and a lot of their fame rebounded here. The Vines did that as well. [As did Jet soon after.]

So the most Australian characteristic about Silverchair is that you have a country where the population is small enough, and the media, especially Triple J, is hip enough, that they could have that kind of immediate effect and have that blow up overseas. By the same token, if Triple J had done all that stuff in exactly the same way and the record sucked, they wouldn't have gotten much past Tahiti. If the music hadn't been there, it wouldn't have mattered if they were Australian or not. But because of the channels that were available to them and the fact that they had the goods, I think that was a leg up they mightn't have got if they were from Bloomington, Indiana.

Were the band enjoying all the travelling and promotion and playing while you were with them?
It was one great, enormous good time. Sure there was a lot of work, but when you're sixteen and in a big rock band – this is work? Would you rather be in school? I don't think so. It was interesting when you talked to them, too – their references were younger, while the dads would talk about Ritchie Blackmore and Deep Purple. To the guys, Tim Rogers was God.

Yet they often talked up the influence of their parents' record collections on their own music.

A NEW TOMORROW

Kids do that in any case more than they care to admit. The idea is not to admit it. But they did cop to that. I remember asking Daniel something about influences and he said, 'Some dude named Donovan.' That put it all in perspective. But it just goes to show that he was paying attention. He may be coming at it from a different generation, a different decade, but he was listening to a lot of what was around him, be it Kurt Cobain, Tim Rogers or some dude named Donovan.

So who was the Silverchair class clown?
They were equals. Chris was probably a little quieter than the other guys; Ben and Daniel took the lead in these things. But Chris gave as good if not better in the exchanges with the outside world. And the outside world meant anyone on tside those three, including the dads and Watson. Watson took all kinds of grief; they were always cracking wise and were at him. But that's what you do when you're young; you think you've got the world by the balls.

Did they care about anything at all?
You could tell they cared about what they did and that's what was really impressive. They were that young and that focused and that committed. When it was time to go out [on stage], there was no screwing around. On the bus there was a lot of screwing around but once they got onstage it wasn't a game. They really worked hard and clearly enjoyed the work. And that's why the shows were so rocking, whether they were playing outdoors or at this little St Andrew's Hall in Detroit, or later on when I saw them at Roseland in New York [on 10 December 1995]. I saw them at different venues and they measured up to the space no matter what it was or who was in it.

Tell me about the heater . . .
[Laughs] I don't know where they got this bus. It was sub-freezing; it was December. At some point the heater on the bus packed it in. It was really, really cold. I could kind of deal with it, being used to it, but being from Australia I don't think they were quite prepared for how cold it was. We stopped at some anonymous place along the road and the driver, or it could have been one of the dads, came up with the idea of getting a space heater, which made sense. Apparently the only one they could find was

a kerosene heater, which they put in the centre of the main lounge area of the bus. They lit this thing up and it was a little scary. Never mind fire; what about smoke inhalation?

We all laughed about it, but when I came back and told my wife, she said, 'Are you crazy?' It was cold, it was a long drive, and people were bundled up. Daniel was wearing about four coats. Afterwards we realised what a colossally stupid thing to do it was. But it was either that or be found frozen to death by the side of the road. We were like Neanderthals around a fire in the middle of the Ice Age.

Do you have fond memories of the tour?
I loved it. It was only a week, maybe a little less, but it was great. They were fun to be with, the shows were great and that's everything I like about being on the road. And the story hadn't been told to death; they hadn't really been interviewed that extensively and the parents hadn't done anything at all, which was something John Watson really worked at for me.

They didn't want to become part of the story and highlight the adolescence of the band. They wanted to present the guys as individuals with real brains and hearts of their own. It was clear the band hadn't been talked to death; I spoke with them each for an hour plus, which must have felt like an eternity for them. I was able to get things from them I hadn't read, even in Australian stories about the band.

So during winter 1995 and onwards into early 1996 in the USA, was 'Tomorrow' unavoidable?
Not in a way that made you sick of it. Let's face it, 1995 was a good year tor stuff here: there was *Mellon Collie [and the Infinite Sadness]* from the Smashing Pumpkins, the Beastie Boys headlined Lollapalooza. 1 think it was the post-Cobain apex of alternative rock in this country. In fact, Silverchair fit in perfectly. They benefited from timing as well as craft and talent. Tool was coming up, the Pumpkins, Hole, Ministry, Nine Inch Nails – there was a lot blowing up. That was before Top 40 radio in this country restricted itself to hip-hop and dance. You'll get no rock on Top 40 radio now. It's been subdivided to death. That's why it's so hard for Silverchair to get radio play

now, because it's impossible to find a format that has a broad enough appeal. All you have to do is see MTV. It's all about targeting. It's very specific.

You hooked up with the band the next year in New York, right?
That was a real trip. They'd come in to do some post-production or some B-sides [for the 'Freak' single] and Watson called me and said, 'Why don't you come on down?' It was some studio down on 14th Street. I went down, it was early evening, we got to talk for a little bit, and Nick [Launay, the producer] was doing whatever people do in recording studios. Then it was time to do the B-sides and they had decided to do a version of 'New Race' – and Deniz Tek was there. I was thinking, 'Great, Deniz Tek twice in one year.' Radio Birdman had never played here, so to see him working here was great.

Everyone's having a good time. They do the basic track – the track, the vocal, Deniz's guitar solo – it doesn't take more than an hour. At the end, they're going to do the, 'Yeah, hup!' part of the background vocals. Daniel goes out; Ben goes out; Chris goes out; Deniz goes out. Then Nick turns to me and says, 'Get out there!' I went, 'You've got to be kidding.' He reminded me that it was my dream come true – Radio Birdman and Silverchair. So he gave me a set of headphones and we all stood around a mike going, 'Yeah, hup! Yeah, hup!' Fuck me, it was the best. I said, 'Now I have completely lived – I've sung with Deniz Tek and Silverchair on a Radio Birdman song! Thank you, God.' It was Aussie rock history in a bottle.

Did you get treated well in the mix of the song?
I was very conscious that since I was the ringer in the line, I better not screw up. Maybe it's just my imagination or my ego, but I think I can hear myself in the mix. I don't know. We were all around one mic; it wasn't like Queen or anything. When they issued the single they put my name in the credit, which was a really big thrill. It was my first time on a Number One record. That won't happen again.

What was your take on Freak Show, *the so-called 'difficult second album'?*
The thing is that they blew up with that first record, but I think *Freak Show* did better than a lot of people whose first records have blown up as big

and immediately as theirs did. The novelty had worn off, so its success was based on the quality of the songs.

They were headlining bigger venues, too, the second time around. When people say the record's a failure, by what standard? I thought *Freak Show* was really good, I really enjoyed it. They were growing as players and I think Daniel was really growing as a songwriter. He's actually a really good ballad writer.

Do you think the band has gotten a reasonable rap over the course of their career?
A lot of people associate Silverchair with that mid 1990s quasi grunge thing, and a lot of people forget he was fifteen at the time. Not many people are writing songs then. They're playing in covers bands, probably playing Nirvana songs. So he's done his growing up as he's doing the thing. You're seeing the process, both the mistakes and the improvements. A lot of guys don't have to go through that. I think Daniel's underrated because everybody thinks they overrated him as a teenager.

Chapter Three
THE FREAK SHOW

It's really weird for our friends. I've asked them a few times, 'Is it weird for you, us just saying, "We're going to New York for a week"?' And they're like, 'Fuckin' oath it is!'

Ben Gillies's take on success, 1996

The Easter Show might have been a mighty way to wrap up *Frogstomp*, but the band's first priority, by April 1996, was to get back to school. As Ben Gillies told Australian *Rolling Stone*, in the wake of *Frogstomp*'s runaway success, the trio needed to 'chill, and shit – go to school and hang out with our mates'. Swiftly, these three regular Newcastle dudes had become international rock stars, but their mates back home were all too ready to remind them where they came from. There were clear signs that the trio was uncomfortable in the glare of fame's spotlight, a part of their public lives to which they had never fully adjusted. Barely a day went past when the band didn't encounter a voice shouting, 'Silverchair suck! Silverchair are wankers!' from a passing car.

Gillies mused:

It's really weird for our friends. A couple of my really close friends at home, I've asked them a few times, 'Is it weird for you, us just saying, "We're going to New York for a week"?' and they're like, 'Fuckin' oath it is!' Even for them, it's a spin-out that one day we'll be there talking to them, going to parties, and the next day we'll be on the other side of the world.

Johns insisted that:

> Our friends are cool, because we don't change at all, we don't think we're any better than anyone else. Our friends treat us the same. We're just the same people [who] go to our mate's house and hang out and play pool and fall asleep on the lounge.

The truth, however, was slightly different. The singer/guitarist suffered his first bout of depression after the madness of *Frogstomp*; it was a pattern that would repeat itself, more intensely, in mid 1997 and early 1998. Gillies and Joannou, meanwhile, also had their own dark patches. The songs Johns was about to write for their second album would express the discontent he was feeling towards the rock life.

When they came off the road after touring the life out of *Frogstomp*, Johns, Gillies and Joannou had two years of high school to complete, and it was a bit of a struggle to keep up academically. 'We do a lot of catch-up work when we get back,' Joannou commented, 'and we do have tutors.' Ever wary about 'rock star ego syndrome', Gillies noted that 'school is a priority to keep our feet on the ground, basically so we don't turn into rock stars'. 'I want to do music for the rest of my life,' Johns commented, 'and how well I go in Maths isn't going to help at all. Music comes before school for me because you can always go back and finish school.' His words strongly echoed those of Dave Grohl, whose new band, the Foo Fighters, were fast developing a reputation almost as strong as his former group, Nirvana. When asked why he chose to leave school and join a band, Grohl replied: 'I knew in ten years I wouldn't be using much trigonometry.' Gillies, Joannou and Johns felt exactly the same.

Despite the intrusions of Silverchair duties, the trio's ever watchful parents ensured that their education wasn't neglected.

As Peter McNair, former principal of Newcastle High School, recalls:

> The families' wishes were for school to be a separate life from their rock star [life]. Their peers were very cool about it, they didn't treat them any differently. School was a place of normality for these young men who were going through this amazing experience.

The band and their parents struck up a workable arrangement with McNair: the trio received special credits in music, after organising to have a music program (which the band funded) added to the school curriculum. As Gillies said at the time, this made graduation way easier. 'It's really great,' he said, 'because one of the requirements of this course is to give them a recorded piece of music. So we can just give 'em the CD.'

In early May, producer Nick Launay – the man who'd edited the original version of 'Tomorrow' – headed up to Merewether to meet the band and listen to their new songs. But the three teens were keener to have him sit with them in Gillies's car as Gillies screamed around Newcastle at dangerous speeds, with Launay as the legally required adult 'supervisor' to a driver still on his L plates. During rehearsals, Launay found it a struggle to hold the band's interest for more than a few songs at a time. But by 17 May, the band were formally rehearsing new songs for their second album, which they previewed at a Newcastle University show six days later.

Events off-stage made this a significant gig in Silverchair history. Watson – and Sony – were keen for the band to establish a cyber-identity, to capitalise on the unstoppable rise of the Internet. Sony's technical department had created a prototype website for the band, but postings were slow and the look of the site was no different from the sites of such other Sony acts as Celine Dion. Watson sensed that the band needed a more grassroots approach. The morning after the Newcastle University show, he logged onto an unofficial Silverchair site based in New Jersey and was shocked to find not only the show's setlist and a song-by-song review of the gig, but quotes from Joannou's mother about the concert. 'That was the moment,' Watson says, 'that I realised you could never be as reactive to this kind of technology wearing a corporate hat as you could being a fan.'

Watson learned that an Australian fan of the band, Duane Dowse, had filed the review. He talked Sony into providing some funding to help Dowse and several US-based volunteers set up and maintain what became the award-winning www.chairpage.com ('www.Silverchair.com' actually belongs to an American HMO). Watson then actively began to stream information to Dowse for posting on the site, with updates on concerts, new releases and band-related activities. In the subsequent ten years, www.chairpage.com has created as good a virtual community as any band could hope for. It certainly hasn't harmed Silverchair's reputation as a 'band of the people'. Because of its connection with a worldwide network of true believers, the band has maintained a 'cyberlife' of its own, without relying on the traditional record company PR methods. It helped, too, that their followers were young and web-sawy; they embraced the new technology. And by providing special offers to members, www.chairpage.com encouraged loyalty, and also raked in a few handy merchandising bucks for the band.

To chairpage members, the band was cool; they weren't just part of the music industry machine. This underground network was the next logical step of the alternative rock world's doctrine of band/fan connectivity. Within a few years, a fully functional website became an essential part of every band's information machine.

Recording for Silverchair's second album was set to begin on 30 May, after three days of pre-production, at Sydney's Festival Studios, where *Frogstomp* had been recorded. The official line at the time was that Nick Launay, who had very nearly struck gold with 'Tomorrow' in 1994, had been chosen over *Frogstomp* producer Kevin Shirley 'to complement the heavier, darker sound' the band was after. The truth, however, was that Shirley had been offered the Silverchair album but opted to continue recording with American stadium screamers Journey, whose big-budget album had run overtime.

Shirley had wanted to work with Silverchair again, but, according to his recollection, had an 'unhappy meeting' with Watson in LA. 'He was already talking about "restructuring" my deal,' Shirley recalled. 'I think he was drunk with power.' Shirley remains convinced that the Journey situation was simply an excuse to elbow him aside in favour of Launay, although he has 'no idea what was behind that'.

John Watson's version of events is quite different. 'Silverchair really needed to record their second album during a particular two-month window due to school holidays and to allow the possibility of a 1996 release,' he replied via email. 'The band's timing needs had been clearly explained to Kevin, but he decided to work with an '80s band during that time instead, so Silverchair was left with no choice but to find someone else. There was no other agenda at work here whatsoever. Kevin acted like he thought he was the organ grinder and the band were his monkeys. He thought he could do anything he wanted and everybody would change their plans to accommodate him. He was mistaken.' (Shirley, however, would later return to Silverchair, to mix *Neon Ballroom*'s 'Miss You Love' and the single version of 'Anthem for the Year 2000'. He also recorded the band's set at 2001's Rock in Rio, with a view to a future, as yet unreleased, live set.)

At the top of the band's wishlist has been Seattle-based producer Steve Albini, who had worked on Nirvana's final studio album, *In Utero,* and was renowned for capturing a raw, vital sound using little studio trickery – in fact, his method of producing an album consisted of hitting 'Record' and letting the band get on with it. Johns frequently dropped Albini's name during interviews. Always wary of people's opinion, however, Johns figured that hiring Albini to produce *Freak Show* would make them easy targets. 'Everyone would say we did it because Nirvana did,' he told American *Rolling Stone* in February 1997. Manager Watson confirms this. It was as though Silverchair just couldn't shake off the ghosts of the grunge gurus.

Launay's relationship with the band was strong. He stayed at the Johns family home during album pre-production, and even sold Gillies a snare drum he owned that had been used by grunge heroes Soundgarden when recording their hit album *Superunknown.* Launay had lugged the drum with him on the train to Newcastle, fully aware that Gillies would love to own the thing. (Gillies loved it so much, in fact, that he used it for most of the album.) As a 'dry run' prior to the making of their second album, the band had already worked with Launay to re-record 'Blind', a track from their debut 'Tomorrow' EP, for the soundtrack to the Jim Carrey vehicle *The Cable Guy.* Band and producer had understood each other from the start. The *Freak Show* deal was set in stone when, during pre-production in Newcastle, Launay drove the band around their hometown while they 'egged' the shopping centre. When Launay pulled over and tossed a few eggs himself, the band knew he was the right man. 'He slipped straight into our level,' Joannou said. 'He was as stupid as we were.'

Launay's musical background was in stark contrast to Shirley's, whose best-known work was with American arena-fillers such as Bon Jovi and Aerosmith. As a nineteen-year-old, Launay worked as a tape operator at London's Townhouse studio, learning the trade from his mentor, producer Hugh Padgham. During one session, a drunk John Lydon (then fronting Public Image Limited, but better known as Johnny Rotten of the

Sex Pistols) took a disliking to a hired engineer and locked him out of the studio. This gave Launay a shot in the engineer's chair, and he went on to produce one of PIL's best-received albums, *The Flowers of Romance*, its name taken from Sid Vicious's first band. Launay also worked with Killing Joke, the Nick Cave-fronted Birthday Party and Gang of Four, all highly credible art-rock, post-punk bands. After working on Midnight Oil's smash hit *10, 9, 8, 7, 6, 5, 4, 3, 2, 1*, he relocated to Australia.

10 ... 1, a revolutionary record for a band reared on Oz rock's dirty riffs, sold almost 250,000 copies in Australia alone, and was one of Johns's favourite albums. It was also a favourite of John O'Donnell's, as were the records Launay had produced for Public Image Limited and Australian band the Church, including 1983's *Seance*. O'Donnell would hire Launay to produce the debut album from Automatic, another Murmur signing. Ben Gillies voiced the band's approval of Launay in a conversation with the *Seattle Post-Intelligencer*. 'We talked to him [Launay] a few times on the phone and he told us some of the cool ideas he had. We thought, "That sounds pretty rad."' Johns also thought him 'rad': 'He's really open-minded. Anything we suggested, a lot of producers would have said, "Nah, you're seventeen, you don't know shit," but he'd listen to us.'

Gillies backed this up when he was asked about making their second album:

We spent a lot more time and were much more involved on this album. On the last record we were so young that we didn't know what was going on. Now that we were older, xve knew what we wanted, and we knew some of the basics to getting to that.

The band worked through their new songs in the Gillies garage, just as they'd done when they were nobodies.' In the end,' Launay said, 'some songs were drastically rearranged, while others remained untouched.' During these rehearsals, Launay also acted as chauffeur, picking up the band after school and driving them to rehearsals. This time he made sure there were no eggs in the car.

Of the songs shortlisted for the second album, several, including 'No Association', 'Freak' (the first single from *Freak Show*), 'Slave', 'Pop Song for

A NEW TOMORROW

Us Rejects', 'Learn to Hate' and 'Nobody Came' had been aired live in shows promoting *Frogstomp*. There was also a group of never-before-heard songs slated for the album. These included 'Abuse Me' (later to become the first American single from the album), 'The Closing', 'Petrol Chlorine' and 'Punk Song #1', which was renamed 'Lie to Me' during the *Freak Show* sessions.

Johns explained:

> We wanted to make the songs more extreme and different, so that means we made the fast songs harder and the slow songs softer. We also experimented with different styles and instruments.

It was hard to tell if it was simply teenage hubris or increased confidence in the band, but Johns seemed unfazed by the pressure of following up such a breakout hit as *Frogstomp*:

> If people don't think [*Freak Show*] is as good as the first one, or people think it's better, it doesn't really bother us. We don't feel any pressure. We don't really have a plan. We're just going to keep releasing music.

At the time, Johns was namechecking such hardcore American bands as Helmet, Tool and Quicksand as new influences. The Seattle heroes – Nirvana, Soundgarden and Pearl Jam – were relegated to the wastebin of 1995. Johns described the new album as 'more influenced by New York hardcore scene kind of stuff, but it doesn't really sound like that. It's just influenced by it. It's just a bit harder – it's just rock.' Though *Freak Show* would prove the distance between Seattle and Newcastle hadn't increased that much, it did deliver a few new musical twists – strings, Eastern influences, pop melodies. It was a stepping stone to a brave new rock and roll world.

Recording of *Freak Show* began on 30 May and ended on 16 July. (And the band's reason for choosing Festival studios again? 'It's got better Nintendo games.') On 6 June, Silverchair previewed some new tunes at the relaunch of Foxtel's cable music channel, Red, which later became Channel [V], In the crowd was crusty, behatted rock 'guru' Ian 'Molly' Meldrum, who flew in from Bangkok to check out the band. The faithful looked on in awe at their new idols, but the gig could have gone better

– the venue's power shut down during Silverchair's set when the combined needs of PA, lights, catering equipment and more kicked in. Silverchair retired to their trailer, taking solace in a rider fit for three kings.

Launay, meanwhile, was amazed by the band's energy in the studio. It appeared that they now had little time for slamming around the corridors, wrecking everything in their path, in between takes.

'Their enthusiasm is way more than any band I've ever worked with,' he told *Sonics* magazine.

> I said, 'Let's start at 1 1 o'clock.' I turned up at 10 o'clock and they've been there since nine, raring to go. It was like going in with a wild animal, trying to hold them back so we had enough time to put tape on the tape machine and push the red button.

The producer firmly believed they were a great live band, so he attempted to record them as naturally as possible, which would also keep them interested in what was going on. This wasn't some static, repetitive studio exercise – Launay was startled by how the band crashed around while recording, taking 'large, exciting jumps' while they laid down the tracks.

Launay did introduce some studio trickery. He squeezed Gillies's drum kit into a room 'about the size of your average toilet' to achieve a bigger drum sound, and used some backward recording techniques on 'Abuse Me', to which Johns responded: 'Bloody hell, it sounds like I'm singing in Arab[ic].' But in the main, Launay's plan was to get down on tape the raw energy of the band. In return, they were impressed with the man and his work. 'Nick's done some seriously weird shit,' Johns said, 'and if you saw him, he's like a praying mantis with glasses. He's like a mad scientist.'

One source of friction, however, was the band's concern that Launay was working too slowly. Watson had to take on the 'bad guy' role and tell the producer to pick up the pace, without letting on that it was the band who were actually doing the griping. Launay confirms that this did happen, but considers it a matter of 'perspective':

> Most LPs take about two months to record, but because Silverchair's first LP was recorded in a staggering seven days [sic], it may have

seemed to the 'young and restless' that *Freak Show* was taking ages. The reality is it took three weeks [five to six, actually], which is extremely fast, especially considering how elaborate some of the songs are.

On 18 July, Gillies, Johns, O'Donnell and Watson flew to New York to begin mixing *Freak Show* at Soundtrack studio with Andy Wallace, the most highly regarded mixer of the time, whose CV included work with Rage Against the Machine, the Smashing Pumpkins and Silverchair favourites Helmet and Sepultura. (The three loved Sepultura's *Roots* album so much that they'd often break the on-road monotony by chanting, 'Roots! Bloody Roots!' in the back of the tour bus.) Wallace mixed all of *Freak Show* except 'Petrol & Chlorine' and 'The Closing', which Launay worked on during an all-night stretch when Wallace was unavailable. This wasn't the only time Wallace's work on *Freak Show* was interrupted; the mixing stopped for a three-month stretch when he was occupied with Nirvana's posthumous live album, *From the Muddy Banks of the Wishkah*. 'Waiting three months for the mix to happen was really painful for everyone,' recalled Launay, who for the first time in his career wasn't mixing an album he'd produced. This time around, the Silverparents stayed at home. 'We didn't want any interruptions from anyone,' said Johns. 'There were really no visitors in the studio apart from our manager.'

While they all awaited the completion of the album, bassman Joannou, in an interview with Brisbane's *Rave* magazine, described how the band was growing up musically speaking:

> They [the songs] are a bit more mature. We have taken a fair bit more time in the way the songs have been put together. We had more pre-production time, just running over the songs and making sure they sounded right. All we had to worry about was playing it right and getting the good sounds.

But mixing those good sounds was a frustratingly stop-start process. Not only was Wallace occupied elsewhere but the band had to return to school – a key part of the juggling act that Watson, the band and their parents would struggle with throughout the *Freak Show* period.

Then Johns was the victim of another aggravating distraction, when he was accused of stalking by a Sydney prostitute, Paula Gai Knightly. She alleged Johns had begun following her in March, calling to her, 'I love you, Paula.' By July, Johns, allegedly, had begun warning her: 'I'm a natural born killer. I'm gonna kill you tonight and I'm gonna enjoy it.' Knightly took out an Apprehended Violence Order (AVO) against Johns on 24 July, and the formal application was set down for hearing. But before the matter could proceed, police withdrew it, as they learned that Silverchair weren't even in Australia at the time of the alleged stalking (in fact, they were working on the album mix in New York). Knightly returned to her native New Zealand soon after, but she had contributed to Johns's increased wariness of those who wanted a piece of him. (Johns was on the receiving end of another AVO three years later, this time from a Newcastle woman – known as both Emily Spencer and Jodie Ann Marie Barnes – who had a long history of mental illness. Her application was also dismissed, but not before a Newcastle newspaper ran a photo of Johns with the headline: 'He's Got a Gun!' When the case was eventually tossed out of court, Johns snapped back: 'I hope that the media covers the truth of this matter as prominently as they covered the lies.')

The band had an Australian tour lined up from 26 September to 7 October – during school holidays, naturally, just like most of the touring done for *Frogstomp* – with American alt-rockers Everclear supporting. Silverchair had quickly graduated to headliners, even taking the lead over an American band who'd done serious business with their 1995 album, *Sparkle & Fade*, led by the grunge-pop hit 'Santa Monica'. As the tour drew to a close, Johns and band put in a set at Brisbane's annual Livid Festival on 5 October that *Rolling Stone* magazine described as 'pure rock and roll'. Helped out by Everclear, Silverchair waged war on a cover of Black Sabbath's 'Paranoid', which closed their set. Then Johns and Joannou mooned the crowd, as all superstar teenagers should. Both the song and their support band left a lasting impression on Silverchair, because when they teamed up again in Europe, later in the year, members of Everclear wandered out on stage during 'Paranoid' with an inflatable sex doll, a banana tastefully inserted in what Gillies described as 'one of its three, uh, love entrances'.

A NEW TOMORROW

Silverchair's Sydney show on 7 October had been a fundraiser for the Surfrider Foundation – both bands had contributed a song to MOM (Music for Our Mother Ocean), a fund-and awareness-raising album compiled by Surfrider and released that year. The band's association with the foundation stretched back to 1994, when they had played a benefit show for the grand fee of one surfboard and wetsuit each. Later on, they would perform similar shows to raise funds for youth suicide prevention, as well as giving money and collectibles to organisations such as the Starlight Foundation.

Johns has aligned himself with many worthy causes, especially animal liberation groups – he often stated, prior to falling for Natalie Imbruglia, that his best relationship was with his dog, Sweep. His guitar was frequently decked out with stickers pledging his myriad allegiances. Though he was uncomfortable with being some kind of teen role model, Johns was finding a way of utilising his status. Whereas in the 1980s – the 'Me Generation' – being a rock star was statement enough, Generation Grunge had a different set of rules. Alt-rock heroes such as Eddie Vedder (who had donated US$50,000 to Surfrider in 1995) and Rage Against the Machine's Zack de la Rocha were proudly political, supporting mainly left-leaning agendas. Silverchair were now finding their own causes to believe in.

It was around this time that Johns became a vegetarian – later a vegan – a choice that his parents would also take up in 1999.' It's not any form of fascism or anything,' Johns told MTV, about his choice to go meat-free.

> It started pretty much with animal-related issues. It was just a guilt thing. I'm the kind of person, as soon as I get something in my head, I feel guilty about it, so I did it to get peace of mind. Once I was a vegetarian, I started to doubt whether I should be consuming any animal products at all, so I did the whole [vegan] thing.

Despite all their globetrotting in 1994 and 1995, Silverchair had stuck with the established music marketplaces of Europe and America, plus two quick shows in Tokyo and Osaka in April 1996. So manager Watson was surprised to get a call inviting the band to tour South America in November 1996. It was a sweet deal, too: three well-paid dates over a week, in Buenos Aires, Rio de Janeiro and Sao Paulo, the latter two as part of the Close-Up Planet Festival (Close-Up being a brand of toothpaste). Other bands on the bill included the reformed, we're-only-in-it-for-the-cash Sex Pistols, doped-up rappers Cypress Hill, Californian punks Bad Religion, and Marky Ramone with his new outfit, the Intruders.

Watson was surprised by the invitation because the band hadn't sold too many legitimate copies of their record south of the US border – roughly 5000 copies of *Frogstomp*. Their bootleg sales in that part of the world were strong, however, and the worryingly titled *Sounds Like Teen Screaming* – a recording of a set from Triple J's Live at the Wireless – had been doing some reasonable underground business. The recently established MTV Brazil had also placed 'Tomorrow' and 'Pure Massacre' on high rotation, and each had held down the Number One video spot on the cable network for five weeks.

The band travelled light: their party was made up of the three band members, Watson, Susan Robertson (Murmur's promotion manager), Peter Ward (who looked after the band's front-of-house sound), and production manager Bailey Holloway. As for chaperones, this trip was the mothers' turn. The band arrived for the Buenos Aires Festival Alternativo on 23 November, playing on the main stage between lipstick rockers Love and Rockets and expat Australian Nick Cave and his Bad Seeds. The sold-out event was held at the 25,000 capacity Ferrocarril Oeste. The Silverchair group kept some unusual company, sharing a hotel with former US President George Bush Snr, and the Reverend Moon, plus a gaggle of his followers. The band were getting their heads around how strange their lives as reluctant celebrities were becoming. By the time the entourage reached Rio de Janeiro for the 29 November show at the Praca Da Apoteose, word had spread as to where the band was staying. A small but dedicated posse of Silverchair-lovers chased them down: one female fan even had to be shooed off by Watson when she became amorous with Johns by the hotel pool. South America loved Silverchair, especially their blond and blue-eyed frontman.

Australian *Rolling Stone*'s then editor, Andrew Humphreys, covered the band's brief tour. The way he saw it, Gillies (whom he described as 'an exuberant, natural show-off') was the only band member really comfortable with the Silver fans:

> Gillies loves the attention and is in no hurry to go anywhere. Girls have begun to crowd the [hotel] pool's edge, and start quizzing Gillies as to his favourite bands. Before they go, he gives away a few strands of his hair, smiling broadly.

By this time, Johns and Joannou had long since returned to their hotel rooms. When Humphreys asked Joannou how the band reacts to fans, he shot back: 'Gillies is the man. If he wasn't in a band, he'd be a pimp, controlling the action.'

Silverchair's fanatical following in South America remains to this day. When they played dates there in 2003, pushing their fourth album, *Diorama*, the more hardcore fans would actually book rooms in the same hotel as the band just to be near their idols.

Keyboardist Julian Hamilton told me:

> One day we were relaxing by the pool [in Rio], and this young girl came up and explained that she didn't want to bother us, but she just wanted to sit nearby and watch us play cards. She just sat there, about ten metres away, and quietly sobbed until we finished our card game. She was so sweet.

Ben Gillies s natural charm extended to the stage, as well. When Johns had problems with his guitar at one show, the drummer stepped up to the microphone to give his rendition of 'Twinkle Twinkle Little Star'. Now that was one song the band had never covered, not even back in The Loft:

> I started singing and then I realised the whole audience couldn't understand what I was saying. So I said something really rude ['Fuck you,' as it turns out] and the whole audience started going, 'Fuck you! Fuck you!' I shouldn't have done that.

As Gillies sees it, at this point in his life, 'something just clicked' in his personality. He loved 'getting out there and talking to people and signing stuff. I was just having a good time; nothing more to it. [But] Daniel was never into it.' Joannou, meanwhile, shied away from off-stage flesh-pressing: 'I hadn't quite developed good people skills.'

Johns seconded Joannou's opinions, and also talked up Gillies's natural charm.

> He just loves talking to people and meeting people, [whereas] I just hate meeting people. I'm not very social and I'm really shy when I don't know people. I hate it. It's just weird. Especially when you know that they're not there to be friends with you. They're just there because you're in a band.

Within a few days, Johns's caution had turned into something closer to paranoia, a hint of what was to come in the future. 'You always think they're watching to see what you're going to do wrong or something,' he told Humphreys.

However, this insecurity didn't stop the band from playing some of the most ferocious sets of their short lives. In fact, maybe it was just the impetus they needed. At Rio's Sambadrome, before a crowd of 18,000, they came on after American rockers Spacehog and tore into *Frogstomp*'s 'Madman', sending the crowd into overdrive.

Humphreys captured the madness of the moment:

> The crowd goes fucking nuts. Girls in the front row are screaming hysterically as the mosh begins. Johns charges across the stage, feet shuffling, body shaking like an evangelical preacher possessed by the spirit of Jesus. Gillies's shirt is off, his long hair flying everywhere as he belts his drum kit and Joannou grinds into his bass. From the side of the stage, someone says, 'Fuck! They sound like Black Sabbath.' Silverchair drive the point home, launching into a cover of 'Paranoid'. The gig, as they say, went off.

As the band moved between Rio and Sao Paulo, the number of (mainly female) fans lurking in hotels and airports increased. It was obvious: Silverchair were now stars in South America. However, they were still very green. When Joannou spotted Nick Cave stumbling back into his hotel at ten one morning, seriously 'tired and emotional' and physically supporting violinist Warren Ellis, who was in an even worse state, Joannou turned to his bandmates and said:'He's just getting home? But it's ten in the morning!'

Silverchair wouldn't make it back to South America until January 2001, when they appeared at Rock in Rio, the world's largest rock festival. But the 1996 tour left its mark – record sales in Brazil, especially, skyrocketed. *Frogstomp* went on to sell 30,000 copies, *Freak Show* 38,000 and *Neon Ballroom* a whopping 116,000. (*Diorama* didn't fare so well, selling only 20,000.) No formal count of bootlegs exists, but it's fair to say you could double, maybe even triple, the official sales. Yet even though the tour was a raging success, the signs were there that the band – especially Johns – were becoming wary of the hangers-on and fair-weather fans they were meeting on the road.

Writing about the Rolling Stones' 1978 American tour, *Rolling Stone*'s Chet Flippo had precisely captured the weird dynamic that surrounds touring bands:

> The public does not really exist for the performers. The audience is an abstract, picked up and packed into the tractor-trailer trucks along with the lights and amps, and unpacked into the next hall. The audience exists only as box-office receipts, only as dollars passing through the gates.

Such things bugged at least two members of Silverchair, as they have many other young bands in this strange, unfamiliar position.

Life went into overdrive after South America. Three days after the Sao Paulo show, the band played a secret gig for American fan club members at the Troubadour in Los Angeles, billing themselves as the George Costanza Trio. Freed from the restraints of being 'the kids from Silverchair', they trashed their gear at the end of the set with a ferocity not seen since Nirvana's Kurt Cobain's legendary Fender-bendmg. There was another gig in Seattle, two days later, with a video shoot in Los Angeles for 'Freak' sandwiched in between, directed by Devo's Gerald Casale.

Johns was thrilled to work with Casale: he was a huge fan of art–pop oddballs Devo, best known for such left-of-the-dial bits as 'Whip It' and 'Freedom of Choice'. Johns also admired the clip that Casale had just directed for the Foo Fighters' breakout single, 'I'll Stick Around', where the band play on while what Casale described to me as a mutant 'Foo ball' – actually the visual representation of Courtney Love – attacks the band. Although Johns probably didn't realise it, he and Casale were from similar backgrounds: Casale was from the steel-town of Akron, Ohio, a city not unlike Newcastle.

Casale revisited the idea of the 'flying amoeba' in the 'Freak' clip, as various white-coat-clad scientists examine some weird life-form under a microscope. 'Viruses, disease and mutation are always there under the surface,' Casale told me via email, 'the ominous engines of change.' Casale could see the changes in Johns – the reasonably well-adjusted suburban kid was now, in the director's words, 'a very smart, depressed kid seething with contained anger.' (Court jester Gillies was the exact opposite: he turned up tor the first day of the shoot wearing a very convincing pair of false buck teeth that completely threw the crew, who began devising ways to hide him from the camera.) And how did the director respond to a song that roared into life with the rhyming couplet: 'No more babies / Your baby's got rabies'? 'Those are good lines for a fifteen-year-old,' he replied, 'who came of age post-AIDS epidemic.'

Casale, however, wasn't impressed by the final cut of the video – insisted upon by John Watson – which he felt placed way too much focus on Johns:

> I was happy with my cut; the label was happy, [but] the Aussie manager had it re-edited with 20 per cent more close-ups of Daniel. Anyway, he butchered the narrative and made the viewer sick of looking at Daniel.

(Casale would later direct the clip for Silverchair's 'Cemetery'. 'The song went nowhere, of course,' he added.)

Watson's take, however, is slightly different:

> I wanted more band footage. Gerry was great but like many video directors he was focused on telling his 'story' – that is, the old person getting

transformed by the lab workers. This is a very common issue with videos where people in my gig mainly want to see the band playing the song and the video director mainly wants to advance his narrative. Every single change that was made to the 'Freak' video was supported and encouraged by the band and the label, otherwise it obviously couldn't and wouldn't have been requested. The changes made the clip more compelling in the eyes of everyone except, apparently, the director.

Soon after the video was shot, the band struck trouble in Malibu, where Johns was arrested for driving a Mitsubishi Montero on Santa Monica beach, the same place where he had been hit by a bottle in late 1995. Acting on a pitch from Mitsubishi, Johns, Gillies and Joannou had joined Dave Navarro, then guitarist for the Chili Peppers and formerly of Jane's Addiction, to test drive the 4WD, with Navarro to write up the results for *Bikini* magazine. It turned out there was more than a little Newcastle left in the trio. Bored with doing laps of the beach carpark, Gillies steered the 4WD onto the sand and, once in motion, spotted the Mitsubishi rep running alongside the car:

> We thought we were in trouble. Instead he reached in and slipped it into four wheel drive. We went up the beach a bit; we were driving through volleyball games, everything.

Joannou then took a turn at the wheel, and Johns started to drive the car back to the car park. It was then that they heard the police sirens.

As Gillies tells it:

> This big black cop got out of the car – he was evil! He came up and screamed, 'Where's your licence, boy?' Daniel played dumb and told him that we drive on the beach all the time in Australia. [But] he took Daniel and threw him in the car. We were supposed to be going home the next day, but the cop was telling Daniel, 'You're going to juvenile hall, boy!'

After some fast talking from the band's American publicist, Johns was released and the charges were dropped. His first task, though, was signing autographs for the police chief's daughter, a massive Silverchair fan. Back at the hotel, Johns's mother was unaware of her son's predicament. (A poster made from a photo of the Malibu incident hangs in the Silverchair office in Sydney.)

A week before Christmas, the band shot another video in Sydney, this time for 'Abuse Me'. It was directed by Nick Egan, who'd worked with INXS, Alanis Morissette and Oasis. Then, as 'Freak' was added to Australian radio at midday on New Year's Eve, the band had ten days of R&R before starting their next Australian tour, this time in Hobart. And they had a new album to release, and the HSC to prepare for as well. While Gillies claimed they were having 'the best time of our lives', it wasn't so clear that Johns and Joannou shared his enthusiasm. They'd spend the next twelve months bouncing between school and the rock and roll highway.

Freak Show was finally released in Australia on 3 February (and in North America on 4 February), a lengthy seven months after recording had finished. Speaking with *Billboard* magazine, John O'Donnell explained the delay: 'The album was recorded in June, which essentially meant that we could have rushed to release it in 1996. [But] all around, the extra time has been used very well.' To which Epic Record's Jim Scully added: 'This is probably the strongest release for the [first] quarter [of 1997], and we wanted to make sure that we had enough time and energy to release it properly.' Of course it didn't hurt that *Frogstomp*'s sales were still going strong for most of 1996, as the album clung to the *Billboard* chart for forty-eight weeks — why release a new album when the old one is still selling well? That was elementary record company marketing.

Silverchair's second album documents a band in transition. As ever, they paid plenty of lip service to the moshpit marauders who loved nothing better than 'goin' off to the 'chair'. Songs such as the sludgy opener, 'Slave', and 'The Door' — a song with a riff so thunderstruck that Angus Young would have approved — were almost clones of the bulk of *Frogstomp*. These were fast, loud rock songs to be played at maximum volume and high speed. Gillies and Joannou, especially, loved playing these songs live.

But there was more going on in *Freak Show* than 'Tomorrow' and 'Pure Massacre' revisited. 'Cemetery' was the album's centrepiece. The band had originally planned to hire Led Zeppelin's John Paul Jones to compose string arrangements, but he proved too expensive. Jane Scarpantoni, who had played on albums as diverse as REM's *Green* and Sarah McLachlan's *Fumbling Towards Ecstasy*, was hired instead, and it was a savvy choice. Her sombre yet elegant arrangements (recorded in New York, at the Jimi Hendrix-founded Electric Ladyland studios) pushes Johns to new vocal heights. And the interplay of his acoustic guitar with her cello and violins makes for the most adventurous music the band had made. So what if Johns's lyric ('I live in a cemetery / I need a change') is barely high school standard; 'Cemetery' – a song that video director Gerald Casale called 'supremely morose' – showed the band how to make an impact using atmosphere rather than volume. And this was in spite of Johns's doubts about whether the tune fitted on the album, 'because it didn't really seem like a band kind of song'.

The song's evolution was unusual. While writing demos for the album, Johns had given Watson a cassette that included sonic sketches of 'Abuse Me' and 'Pop Song for Us Rejects'. Midway through the blank second side of the tape was a slow, sombre acoustic ballad, which Johns's parents had found and pointed out to Watson. Johns kept asking his manager to return the tape, because he didn't want him to hear what was a sketch of 'Cemetery'. But Watson knew the song belonged on the album, so at the Newcastle University show (the show where www.chairpage.com was conceived), he cornered producer Launay and told him about it, insisting that he should hear the song. He also told Launay that Johns didn't know he'd heard it. The producer agreed to go along with the ruse. (Watson remembers his response: 'OK, so I don't know the song exists but I have to ask him to play it for me. Cool.') Their ploy worked; Launay convinced Johns that if they included drums and strings 'Cemetery' would fit well on *Freak Show*, and the song was added.

Strings also left their mark on 'Pop Song for Us Rejects', in the form of understated violins from Ian Cooper and ex-Go-Between Amanda Brown. For possibly the first time on a Silverchair song, the guitars were crisp and acoustic rather than distorted and electric, while the song's very hummable melody proved that the 'pop' in the title wasn't ironic. Indian instrumentation – tambura, tablas and sitar – elevated 'Petrol & Chlorine', another serviceable Johns melody. The song is a handy reminder of how much Led Zeppelin the trio absorbed in their youth: Jimmy Page and Robert Plant loved nothing better than to drench their blues-based raunch in exotic Eastern sounds. Clearly, Silverchair were listening and learning. 'It's Led Zeppelin only and exclusively,' Johns confirmed, when asked about the track's roots. 'We really like that they mixed different instruments with rock music and we want to do that same kind of thing.'

Johns had told the producer that the song 'needs drums like they have on those documentaries on SBS' – that is, something with a world music flavour. Pandit Ran Chander Suman, who played tambura and tabla on 'Petrol & Chlorine', was tracked down by producer Launay by calling the Indian consul and the Ethnic Affairs department in Canberra. Suman left an impression on the band, especially timekeeper Gillies, who talked him up during a late 1996 interview:

> That Indian guy that was playing these really weird drums; we asked him how long he'd been playing for and he said something like sixty years. And he said he still hadn't learned everything about it.

The truth about that day, however, is somewhat different. None of the band could endure the session, which ran well into overtime. The Indian players worked to markedly different time structures, which slowed the recording down to a crawl.

Gillies recalled:

> We were all really excited that day they came in, but about an hour into it, you could see everyone going, 'Fuck, how are we going to get through this?' It was fun for a while; we all had a go on the sitar and checked it out. But after a while it was so frustrating that we had to leave.

Launay was left alone in the studio as the Indians droned on. 'He said it was one of the worst days he'd ever had in the studio,' said Gillies, although Launay now has more sanguine recollections (see separate interview, page 206).

Speaking with MTV News, Johns revealed that Suman was:

one of the guys who used to play with Ravi Shankar, who did some of the Beatles stuff. He has, like, a little group who he does stuff with and we've got some of that on the song and it sounds pretty weird.

This was true, although Suman didn't actually know of the sitar master's work with the Beatles – the Fab Four weren't really a band that appeared on his musical radar.

So *Freak Show* wasn't all about Daniel Johns's million-dollar riffs or voice. Ben Gillies's deft brushstrokes of percussion were a highlight of 'No Association', a song in which Johns neatly inserted a line about 'contemplating suicide' from the 1979 underground classic 'Shivers', by the Nick Cave-fronted Boys Next Door. In general, Johns had a lot to explain about *Freak Show*'s words. 'Freak', the album's debut single – which charted at Number One in Australia on 20 January 1997 – opened with the lines, 'No more maybes / Your baby's got rabies', that he still has to downplay today. But the song would become a live favourite of the band, along with 'The Door', another *Freak Show* cut.

Whereas Johns had dismissed *Frogstomp*'s lyrics as throwaway observations from the couch, the same couldn't be said of *Freak Show*. Even though he was still having some trouble articulating his feelings, there was enough fear and loathing here to scare off the late Hunter S. Thompson. When Johns wasn't ranting about babies with rabies, he was growling (during 'Slave') that the 'only book that I own is called How to Lose / Pick a chapter I know them all, just choose.' And 'Freak' came on like a taunt to those critics wanting to cut these tall poppies down after the madness of Silver mania. As *Rolling Stone*'s Humphreys wrote in February 1997, 'Silverchair have always been easy targets for the hipster crowd, a band that's somehow cool to hate, for no particular reason.' But it didn't help when Johns and Gillies told *Juice* magazine that 'Newcastle's the centre of a lot of fucking wankers.' The remark may have been taken out of context, but the backlash was immediate and it played on Johns's already fragile state of mind. No wonder he was the target of so much abuse in his hometown. As John O'Donnell saw it, 'Daniel was definitely venting; [the album] was definitely about him reacting to fame.'

There was another, more immediate part of life in the spotlight that Johns and the band were now trying to cope with: flying missiles. During 1996 shows at Livid in Brisbane and at the State Sports Centre in Homebush, Sydney, the crowd had tossed bottles and cans at the band, echoing the chaos of Santa Monica.

They dodged the missiles and tried to keep playing, but as Johns related, it was a strange way to show your appreciation:

> When it first happened, I was like, 'Fuck!' It's not that you're pissed off about getting hit with a bottle. It's more that you're pissed off because it fucks your show up. I don't get it, it's just weird. I guess it comes with playing in a band, that's what you expect. In the 1970s, everyone just spat on each other. I guess in the 1990s everyone throws bottles.

Although Johns stated he didn't 'really give a shit' about such things, his anger seeped through the lyrics of 'Freak'. 'If only I could be as cool as you,' Johns sneered, before declaring: 'Body and soul / I'm a freak'. There's even more self-flagellation in 'Petrol & Chlorine', where his world-weariness ('as my life just fades away / I wouldn't have a clue') is just plain worrying. Drugs and guns get a look in elsewhere, along with what could only be considered observations from Johns's herpes period. 'Your life's an open cold sore,' he yells during 'Pop Songs for Us Rejects', 'Got to get out the cream.' (It's a little known fact that microphones at festivals are herpes breeding grounds, so maybe the teenager had picked up his share of blisters over the previous couple of years.)

No matter how unintentionally comical much of this sounds, Johns's broody words were hardly what you'd expect from one of Australia's wealthiest teenagers. But Johns had sunk into what turned out to be the first of several depressions that followed the success of *Frogstomp*. When he was supposed to be writing new songs for *Freak Show*, he was holed up in his parents' house for a month, avoiding the world outside. Runaways would often turn up at their front door, asking for him. Tabloid reporters and photographers frequently cruised past the family home, hoping for a sighting – it became a ritual, of sorts, for snappers from the *Newcastle*

Herald to take up residency outside the Johns home. It was just as difficult for Gillies; his family were reluctant to change their home phone number because of their business, so they'd constantly be fielding calls from both fans and band-haters. But because of his more extroverted nature, Gillies seemed to handle the pressure better than Johns.

Much later, Johns said:

> I didn't want to go out and have someone go, 'That's the guy from Silverchair,' and fuck everyone else's fun up for the night, so I was just like, 'Fuck this, I'm just gonna sit in my room.'

It was a haven he would retreat to many times over the next few years. John O'Donnell, for one, noted how heavily it weighed on him:

> He wasn't the guy he used to be, hanging out with his friends. The tabloids started wanting pictures of him, people knew where he lived. We'd been telling the parents to get silent numbers, but they said no, it wasn't something people did.

Speaking on the *Denton* show in June 2004, Johns recalled how the constant presence of the press took away one of the few simple joys he had in his life – hanging out at Merewether Beach. The situation really got out of hand when Johns tried to hide away at the beach during one school holiday break:

> There were like fifty people around us screaming, and then people turned up with cameras and [the] paparazzi were there, and from that point, the beach wasn't such a tranquil and resting activity for me.

John Watson also remembers that time well:

> That was the month 'Israel's Son' was doing really well. Because I was really worried about Daniel, I had him stay at my house in Sydney for a while [on the suggestion of Johns's parents]. He was wrestling with the fact that he had become 'famous' and that life can be really strange sometimes.

What made it even more difficult for Johns was that he was seeking refuge with one of the people who were dependent on him for their livelihood. As a manager, Watson had the difficult task of balancing his and the band's career, as well as caring for their mental health. He wanted them to remain big-selling international artists, while keeping them relatively grounded as 'happy, healthy human beings'.

As he said:

From my reading of rock and roll history, most bands [from the Beatles down] end up frayed because they're caught in this crazy world, the tumble drier [ot rock and roll] – and then they turn on each other.

This juggling act would become even trickier for Watson in the future.

In January 1997, Johns said:

After *Frogstomp*, we were chased by the media and all kinds of people. That was weird. We needed a while to get used to it. I realise now that that attention goes with being in a band. [But] I don't feel like a rock star or anything like that.

Johns wrote most of *Freak Show*'s lyrics after the band returned from their second American tour, which ended on 18 December 1995, closing with a huge date at LA's Universal Ampitheater, alongside Radiohead, Bush and Oasis. The non-stop nature of the trip and the band's unstoppable success had been a lot for them – especially Johns – to take in.

As he noted:

I saw so much out there, so many weird things, that it really affected how I saw the world and myself. Some [lyrics] were actually changed because they were too personal. But they're a lot more real this time around.

On *Freak Show*'s release, Johns took to introducing 'Cemetery' as a song 'about a male prostitute', a not-so-subtle dig at all those who've profited from the band since 1994. 'There's a lot of good people in the industry,

'Johns insisted during an interview, 'and there's a lot of dicks. So you've just gotta live with the dicks and get on with the people that are all right.' Later on, Johns would admit that he was entering into a dark period in his life 'where I hated myself, and, you know, would have quite happily ended it.' One of his many problems was that he was simply unsure that Silverchair deserved so much success so early on in their careers; he was constantly reminded of the work that other bands put in to get even a whitf of success. 'I felt like I wasn't worthy of what had come to me at a really early age.'

In early reviews for the album, critics picked up on the band's lyrical SOS. The message was clear: they were having trouble adjusting to life in the spotlight. 'It doesn't take much scrutiny,' wrote Michael Dwyer of 'Freak' in Australian *Rolling Stone*, 'to reveal a metaphor for the dirty business which has already swallowed Silverchair up to their tender necks.' Writing in America's *Spin* magazine, Chuck Eddy echoed Dwyer's thoughts: 'If the whole world was gawking at my growing pains, I'd feel like a *Freak Show*, too.' Johns responded by sporting pierced eyebrows and make-up (though he never wore lipstick, as he'd later reveal to Andrew Denton); Joannou and Gillies, alternately, shaved their heads.

The upside of *Freak Show*, however, is that there were very obvious signposts – the lush 'Cemetery', the experimental 'Petrol & Chlorine' – that Johns was taking musical control of the band and pushing them away from the sludginess of Seattle. The next album, 1999's *Neon Ballroom*, was an even bolder statement, and as far removed from grunge as these three Novocastrians could manage. 'It doesn't sound like Seattle,' insisted Gillies, when asked about *Freak Show*. 'Now that we've travelled around the world, our music tastes have been widened immensely. When people hear the new album, they won't say, "That's a Pearl Jam clone."' Joannou, the kind of guy who could cut to the nub of an argument, figured that the only reason they were compared to Nirvana was 'Daniel's hair'. Many rock writers agreed. Murray Engleheart emphasised the band's movement away from grunge and declared that the album 'should knock on the head once and for all any lingering doubts that the band is operating squarely in Pearl Jam's shadow.'

Speaking just after the album was mixed in New York, Johns talked up the differences between *Frogstomp* and *Freak Show*. While admitting some songs were 'definitely heavier', he pointed to a more melodic direction, as well as highlighting the use of strings and sitar. 'It's got a bit more variety,' he said.' It's more complex than the first album.'

In the same interview, Johns seemingly opened the door for bassist Joannou to co-write songs. Up until this time, the bulk of Silverchair songs had emerged out of rehearsal room jams: Johns would lock into a riff, Gillies would work out a rhythm pattern and Joannou would kick it all along with some heavy bottom end. Then Johns would hide himself away to work on the lyrics. The bulk of the songwriting credits were shared by Johns and Gillies.' It's not like Chris isn't allowed to join in writing the songs,' said Johns. 'He just hasn't really come up with anything yet. Maybe on the third album – who knows?' It was an odd comment, considering that all Silverchair music for their next two albums would be written solely by Johns.

Clearly, Johns was moving away from his two band-mates and friends. Although he would talk *Freak Show* up as an album where they worked together as a unit, the amount of time they'd shared touring over the past two years meant they spent less non-Silverchair time with each other. Before the band made it big, they were mates who'd go to school together and then hang out at the Gillies home or go to the beach. They were tight; they were a unit. But now, when returning from a tour, they'd head in different directions – and the beach was definitely out of the question. Gillies and Joannou would hook up with their respective Merewether crews and party hard, while Johns went home, holed up with his dog, Sweep, and wrote more songs. It was at this time, too, that Gillies and Joannou would meet their first serious girlfriends: 'Before, every day, we used to go everywhere together,' Johns said. 'But because we've been touring so much together, I just wanted to be by myself for a long time.' At the same time Johns was turning inwards, Silverchair was becoming his band, the outlet for his songs and his feelings.

The critical response to *Freak Show* took a fairly predictable path. The Australian press praised it, the British panned it, and the American media sat somewhere between the two, confused as to whether the band were innovators or imitators.

Australian *Rolling Stone*'s Michael Dwyer was typically insightful, noting that:

> The casual sleeve peruser might conclude [from the song titles 'Slave', 'Freak', 'Abuse Me', 'Lie to Me'] that more bullshit than satisfaction had greeted Silverchair in their fast-track transition from Newcastle garage to international smash.

He went on to praise the band for its 'more melodic, diverse and generally satisfying musical agenda.' The American parent of the magazine didn't have the same homegrown agenda, but still praised the album's diversity and the way 'bursts of guitar blend easily with strings, acoustic moments and quasi-Indian elements.' Writing in the *Baltimore Sun*, highly regarded US critic J. D. Considine figured 'the album would stand as an impressive achievement of musicians twice as old.' It's a fair comment, too. Even today, listeners who overlooked the band during its first wave are amazed by the maturity of music on display on their earlier albums.

Like most reviews, the *All Music Guide* admitted that the band 'were slaves to their influences' on *Frogstomp*, but acknowledged that with *Freak Show* 'their own style started to break through.' 'Every once in a while,' wrote *The Buffalo News,* 'rock needs a jolt of youthful energy. While Silverchair has talent, it lacks originality.' *Spin* magazine, however, praised the album, noting its 'punkier speedups, fancier breaks and more dramatic climbing from quietude interlude to dude attitude.'

Most reviewers, however, couldn't resist such soft targets – if they were teenagers, went the standard line of thinking, surely they couldn't be originals. Typical was this review in England's *Metal Hammer* magazine:

> What exactly is it about this relatively unremarkable Australian trio that helped them shift so many copies of their debut album? They don't bite heads off pigeons [or] trash hotel rooms. *Freak Show* owes more than a drink to Nirvana . . . but just remember we're talking about Nirvana without the apparent depth, experience or, indeed, the heroin habit.

But then, UK critics were never impressed by the band – a dilemma faced by almost every Australian act except for AC/DC and Nick Cave, and sometimes justifiably so. And it showed in Silverchair album sales in the UK, although Watson, justifiably, puts that down more to a lack of radio airplay.

'That was never going to happen at the time,' he figured, because 'the whole country was into Britpop.'

> Back then, none of the US rock sounds were working in Britain, so acts like Bush and Everclear couldn't get arrested there, either. [And] very few Aussie rock bands are taken seriously there. They seem to think we can either do soap stars and novelty acts or arty stuff like the Triffids and Nick Cave. Apart from INXS, nothing else in the middle has ever connected in the UK.

'That's always going to be the British tabloid rock take,' David Fricke told me. 'Oh, they're Australian, let's trot out the kangaroo jokes. The fact is that they missed out.'

Freak Show, just like *Frogstomp*, did good business in Germany, France and Holland, but barely generated any commercial interest in the UK. But how to follow up the band's two million-plus *Frogstomp* success in the US? Manager John Watson was about to learn a lesson about dealing with the monolith that is the American music business, while the band was about to experience a little more controversy of its own.

Johns had announced, just before its release, that the album's title was *Freak Show*. As he explained, he likened life in a rock and roll band to:

> the old freak shows in the 1940s, just travelling around, doing your show and going to the next town and doing it again. We saw there was a similarity and thought it would be a good theme for the album.

Added Gillies:

> We reckon the music industry is like travelling freak shows. You meet all these freaks along the way. You meet good people, but you do meet a lot of idiots. I'm not mentioning any names.

A NEW TOMORROW

What Johns and Gillies didn't anticipate was the controversy the album's artwork would stir up. First the 'Israel's Son' court case, and now this. Throughout the band's life it seemed as though every album would be tainted in some way, whether it was by *Frogstomp*'s soundalike accusations or Johns's reactive arthritis that almost killed *Diorama*.

The nine images that decorated *Freak Show*'s sleeve – including a wolf man, a bearded lady and assorted circus sideshow weirdos – were found in the Circus World Museum, located in sleepy Baraboo, Wisconsin. The band stumbled across them in a magazine and immediately agreed they were perfect for the album. But with political correctness in full swing at the time, the band received some criticism of their artwork selection; many felt it was in questionable taste to highlight the physical deformities of these 'sideshow freaks'. The backlash was strong enough that their American label, Epic, had to issue a disclaimer insisting that the band 'are not in any way showing disrespect for the carnival performers of yesteryear. They simply think it's interesting that the human appetite for the bizarre seems to be timeless.'

It's more likely that the band just thought the images 'cool' or 'sick', but they had even bigger problems ahead. The American label had opted to lead with 'Abuse Me' as the album's first single, rather than their Australian Number One, 'Freak'. It was felt that a mellower song would sit more comfortably on US radio. That turned out to be a bad move. Looking back, manager Watson still believes this decision to be the key reason *Freak Show* sold only 620,000 copies in the US, after *Frogstomp*'s whopping 2,025,000. But more on that later.

What lay ahead for the band was one of the most restless years of their lives, as they tried to balance their last year of school with the demands of pushing their second album and keeping their respective heads together. Not only did they rack up more Frequent Flyer points than Richard Branson, but they started to understand what was required to make Silverchair more than a one-album fling: hard work, and shitloads of it.

* * *

JEFF APTER

Abuse Me: An interview with John Watson

John Watson has been Silverchair's manager since 1995, when he left his position in A&R at Sony to look after the band full-time. During more than a decade at the helm, he's done everything from lugging gear to acting as surrogate parent and negotiating multi-million dollar deals. The way he sees things, 'the nature of management is that you want people to love the artist – and if people have to hate the manager in the process, so be it.' Arguably the most powerful man in Australian music, he now oversees the careers of Silverchair, the Dissociatives, Paul Mac, Missy Higgins, Little Birdy, Wolfmother and Pete Murray.

Did you have a precedent for your plan when you signed Silverchair?
In terms of role models, we spent the first years of Silverchair's career trying to stop them becoming Ratcat. Ever since, we've been trying to stop them becoming INXS. I don't mean disrespect to either of those bands by that comment, I just mean that Ratcat exploded so big and so fast that everyone got sick of them within a year or two of *Tingles* [their 1990 EP, which contained the hit 'That Ain't Bad']. And INXS did an amazing job of breaking internationally but the price of those efforts was a backlash here at home. Having an Australian career was always important to Silverchair, so it was always important to them to keep the home fires burning – even if that meant doing less well in other countries. Given the fate of [2002's] *Diorama*, it's just as well.

Can you tell me about the band's signing with Murmur?
Had Sony not had Murmur, there's no way in the world we could have got involved with the band. Firstly, the nature of the deal we offered was one Sony would never have offered to an artist. Denis [Handlin's] brief was: 'Break all the rules.' A typical Sony deal would have been a worldwide deal for five or six albums with a pretty substantial advance attached to it and modest royalties.

The idea with Murmur was to give less on the front end but to provide more flexibility: shorter-term deals, higher royalties, in some instances give some artists the ability to get releases overseas if Sony passed. Given the generation of bands coming through, it was incredibly important, the issue of creative control and a dedicated team of people who were on your wavelength. [Silverchair left Sony in late 2000 and signed with Eleven, Watson's own label.]

How has your role as Silverchair manager evolved?
My role has changed a lot, but it's happened so slowly and gradually that it's only when you stand back that you can see it. The way I see it, it's best to think of your career as a truck going down a highway Some artists want to party in the back of the truck and don't care what the managers do as long as they keep the hookers and blow coming. Some artists want to drive the truck and would prefer to have the manager out the front as a bull bar. Other artists want to drive the truck and want the manager sitting next to them, up front, as a navigator, going, 'You really should turn left up here.' The manager's voice is the one you hear calling – as you go over the cliff– 'I told you you should have turned left.' The last metaphor is the one I've always felt comfortable with. But at the end of the day it's up to the artist.

In the early days, the band had strong ideas about what they wouldn't do – things were either hell or they sucked. The more interest they took in things, the more responsibility they took. They always had good instincts for what sucked. That's great, but it's only a part of the picture. Knowing the right thing to do is the next part of the learning. The dynamic is that I'm always the guy going, 'What if we get David Helfgott? What if we get Van Dyke Parks?' Ultimately the artist should pick and choose and that's how it should be.

Frogstomp cost just under AUD$40,000 to make and sold several million. How much larger was Freak Show's budget?
The figure has never been made public and I'd rather not say. [Watson has refused to divulge any album budgets, despite my numerous requests.] However, it would be safe to say that it cost a lot more than *Frogstomp* because we used Andy Wallace and a US mixing studio. And Nick [Launay] took a lot more time to record it. However, by the standards of bands who've sold a few million albums it was still comparatively cheap.

Was the choice of Nick Launay over Kevin Shirley, the producer of Frogstomp, made purely because Shirley went off to work with Journey?

Pretty much, although that sells Nick short. We were planning to use Kev but then he wanted to push Silverchair back because Journey was running over time. That was a concern because we originally wanted to have LP2 out by the end of 1996. That ended up becoming impossible when Wallace's time shuffled around. In the meantime, the band needed to re-record 'Blind' for the *Cable Guy* soundtrack and we used this as a try-out with Nick. It went well, so the transition seemed natural and unusually painless.

Was Shirley keen to do the second record?
Yes. They've worked with him since – he remixed a couple of songs for *Neon Ballroom* and mixed the TV audio of Rock in Rio [where Silverchair performed in 2001], as he happened to be down there already. Nick, meanwhile, was tailing over himself to do *Freak Show*. He almost felt it was meant to be, having heard that early demo [of 'Tomorrow'] under such unusual circumstances.

Was Steve Albini on the shortlist?
Not really I think Daniel loved the sound of his work and would have loved to make a record with him. But his association with Nirvana would have just invited more of those comparisons which everyone – particularly Daniel – wanted to avoid. When [Brit grunge wannabes] Bush used him, too, that really sealed it.

Was anyone else on the Freak Show *shortlist?*
Not that I recall. Andy Wallace was the dream candidate at the time because of his work with Helmet. That's why the guys were willing to wait for him when his schedule shuffled around. He'd come to the show in New York [10 December 1995] and expressed interest in the band, so he was always in the mix for LP2, if you'll excuse the pun.

Wallace took a three-month break during the mixing of Freak Show. *What happened?*
There was a bunch of stuff, including the Nirvana live CD, although the main thing, weirdly enough, was a band who he actually produced from

scratch. They were called Cola and had been signed in a big bidding war, so everyone was touting them as the next big thing. My recollection is that it was the only thing he'd tracked from scratch since [Jeff Buckley's] *Grace*, but I'm not sure about that. He spent most of the gap recording and mixing their album [*Whatnot*, which was released in 1997].

How radically did marketing plans have to be rewritten when that delay happened?
Marketing plans were never written for a late 1996 release, as we knew by June-ish that we weren't going to make it by Christmas. If I may be allowed a sidebar here for a second, I still think that *Freak Show* was the best set-up I've ever seen for an album. We had all the marketing and promotional tools – new photos, bios, press kits, interview CDs, artwork files, EPKs [electronic press kits], a video, preview samplers, stickers – manufactured and delivered all around the world a full ten weeks before the release. This probably doesn't seem like much but given how important set-up is to the fate of a release, it's extraordinary how often things run late. This means albums are often compromised.

What I'm saying is that *Freak Show* really benefited from the extra set-up time caused by Wallace's delays. This is part of the reason it did so much better than *Frogstomp* in Europe because we came out of the gate with a bang that made people pay more attention.

Was Nick Launay ever a possibility to mix the whole album?
No, although he was there for all of the mixes and added quite a lot. The combination of him and Andy [Wallace] was a great yin/yang thing because Nick always wants to keep polishing and loves to use lots of effects, while Andy likes to keep things fast and simple. Either of them would not have got the sounds you hear on that record.

There were a few name changes on songs from Freak Show, *right?*
Yes. 'Punk Song #1' became 'Lie to Me' and 'The Closing' started out as 'Cat and Mouse', while 'The Door' was originally called 'The Poxy Song'. As you might guess from that title, they originally didn't like that one. In the weeks before recording started, I was nagging them to try and come

up with a couple more tunes. They only had about ten songs they liked at that stage and that didn't leave any breathing room if one of those tracks didn't turn out well in the studio. So they doubled the tempo of 'The Poxy Song' and decided they liked it after all.

What do you think prompted Epic to choose 'Abuse Me' over 'Freak' as the first Freak Show *single in the US?*
Oh boy. That was a big, big issue and is still at the root of the band's post-*Frogstomp* situation in the USA – along with releasing it into the wind of the pop revival, of course. The promo department at Epic felt that 'Freak' was too heavy musically and too young lyrically – 'No more maybes / Your baby's got rabies' – to get played across the board on all US alternative stations. If this happened, then the song would not have charted very well on the US airplay charts and they thought the limited exposure would hurt initial album sales. This would have meant that the album would quickly have been pegged as another 'sophomore slump' and the band would be assumed to be one-hit wonders.

What was your take?
Our view was that 'Freak' was a song that would mobilise the younger fans who liked Frogstomp. These people usually don't listen to radio during the day, anyway. As such, we felt that we'd be better off having half as much airplay on that tune because we believed it would connect better with the band's core audience – and sell enough records to avoid any perception of a 'sophomore slump'. We thought the more melodic 'Abuse Me' would appeal to a more mainstream audience who were unlikely to rush out and buy a 'Chair album. As a result of all this, we – that is, the band, me and Murmur – were all strongly of the opinion that if it came first, the alternative music fans would think that the band had 'gone soft'.

At what stage did all this take place?
Well, it was only when the music reached the promo department that the issue raised its head. By then it was quite late in the piece, around November 1996. It really threw a spanner in the works. We fought them [Epic] for several weeks and there were many memorable conversations.

Eventually it turned into a complete stand-off, with both sides honestly believing they were completely right.

We were therefore in a no-win situation. If we forced the pronao department to work 'Freak', then they would have egg all over their faces if they made it work. This hardly provided an incentive to get them to get it played on the radio. On the other hand, if we reluctantly agreed to let them work 'Abuse Me' first, then they would look like idiots if that song didn't work. So they had a powerful incentive to get that song lots of airplay.

How involved were the band in this?
I distinctly remember discussing this with the band. We had a conference call – I was overseas – during which the final decision had to be made. Daniel said, 'Well, it's just a question of doing what sucks the least, isn't it?', which summed it up perfectly, I think.

So, what next?
What then happened was those promo people – many of whom were tremendous supporters of the band and honestly thought they were doing the right thing – got massive airplay for 'Abuse Me'. In other words, they were right that the song was well suited to what radio was playing at the time. However, we were right, too – the song didn't mobilise the band's fanbase in the numbers you would normally expect from that kind of exposure.

This meant that the album started to lose heat and each week it slid down the charts, creating momentum – but it was all going backwards. By the time Epic got to 'Freak', radio programmers had the perfect excuse: 'We played the last song a lot but it didn't really connect with listeners – so why should we play this one which is less accessible?'

And the end result?
I should point out that the 'Freak' CD single sold three times as many copies as 'Abuse Me' in Australia, even though 'Abuse Me' was their first song – and only song, apart from *Neon Ballroom*'s 'Miss You Love' – to ever get significant daytime airplay on mainstream stations. So that showed we were right – 'Abuse Me' had broader appeal but 'Freak' was more appealing to the band's audience.

One other important point is that Epic's last-minute change of heart on the singles' order really compromised the video for 'Abuse Me'. We had everything planned perfectly for *Freak Show* and the 'Freak' video was no exception. That clip was all very well set up and still looks great [see director Casale's comments on page 124]. However, the 'Abuse Me' video was thrown together far too quickly and the result is probably the worst video the band ever made.

How did the band come to choose the images for Freak Show's *cover?*
I read a story about the Lobster Boy in a magazine while the band was on tour. It was an amazing tale. There's also a cult paperback about him. He was one of the last superstars of that world, but he became an abusive alcoholic who was implicated in several murders. Then he was murdered by his own family who couldn't take any more of his abuse.

I showed the story to the band and they thought it was amazing, too. The thing we liked about it was how things are actually a lot different from how they appear on the surface. I guess that fitted well with many of the lyrics on the album, which were about the perversions associated with attention and about how things can seem great on the surface, but there's a lot of trouble underneath.

That idea was carried into the album art. The cover image of his boyish face seemed really angelic, then when you opened up the album and took out the disc you discovered his disability. You might then have felt compassion for his condition – unless and until you found out what kind of person he became. So your outlook twists a few times over the course of looking at one image.

The whole 'freak' theme was triggered by the song, initially, but kind of took on a life of its own as we kicked it around more and more. Just one of those metaphors that works at lots of levels.

CHAPTER FOUR
SO WHERE'D THAT YEAR GO?

> It wouldn't bother me if *Freak Show* sold half as many copies [as *Frogstomp*], but got treated with a little more respect.
> Silverchair manager John Watson, 1997

If the band had lived the two previous years in top gear, 1997 was twelve months spent in overdrive. Their first date for the year was in Hobart on 10 January, and their final show was on 20 December at the Perth Entertainment Centre. In between they played a hundred gigs, toured the US and Europe three times, and completed four Australian jaunts, as well as playing shows in Canada and the Philippines. Just as it was for the Beatles thirty years earlier, the Philippines show was a first – and a last – for the band, as out-of-control fans kicked in doors, inflicted US$10,000 worth of damage on an orchestra pit hydraulic system, and drifted into the unpatrolled backstage area to meet their idols. It was a long way from the military precision of Madison Square Garden.

The year had some particular thrills. They opened the ARIAs with a blistering version of *Freak Show*'s 'The Door'. They toured with such multi-platinum peers as Bush, the Offspring and Collective Soul, and had a song featured on the soundtrack of *Spawn*, the film of the hugely popular Todd McFarlane action-adventure comic book series. Epic promoted *Freak Show* in the US with a toll-free number that played grabs from various songs. And, finally, they graduated from high school, an event they celebrated with a tour that they still regard as a career high: the 'Summer Freak Shows'.

But there were also endless days of promo for radio, print and TV. Some of these were exciting: they did a midnight m-store signing at Blockbuster Records in Atlanta, performed at Virgin Records in New York's Times Square, attended the MTV awards, and appeared on the hugely influential *Late Show* with David Letterman. (Gillies told one reporter: 'All our friends love Letterman and all of them have been, like, "Fuck, you're going to meet Letterman!" It's going to be pretty cool.') Yet these were exceptions; the usual media grind of quickie interviews and smiling on cue for photographers was a serious drag for these hyper teenagers.

Silverchair had a lot to prove with their new record. By 1997, the bands that had heralded the arrival of grunge and generation alt-rock – Pearl Jam, Nirvana, Soundgarden, the Smashing Pumpkins – had either split or started exploring new musical sensations. Instead, it was punkish acts such as Californians the Offspring that were shifting serious numbers of units in the album charts, as the boundaries continued to come down between the mainstream and alternative worlds. It was also the year that 'rocktronica' (aka electronica) – a flashy fusion of rock attitude and dance beats – was declared the future of music, thanks mainly to career-making albums by the Prodigy (*The Fat of the Land*) and the Chemical Brothers (*Dig Your Own Hole*). Silverchair were out to show that they could still satisfy the fans, still cut it live and that they weren't 'one-zit wonders', as one wisecracking writer put it.

But first up, Silverchair had an album to launch. They did it in style in the Circus Oz tent in Sydney's Moore Park, on 20 January. The venue made perfect sense: the album was called *Freak Show*, after all, and the three had regularly been comparing life on the road to a travelling circus. More than a thousand people, including high-profile media from *Spin* magazine, MTV and elsewhere, either squeezed onto the wooden benches around the tent's edge or into the moshpit, to check out the band's fifty-five-minute long, eleven-song set. The stage was decorated with cut-outs of the muscle men and circus oddities from the album's cover that had caused such a fuss in America. In the crowd looking on was Snazz, the tattooed man from the 'Freak' single cover, who'd also appeared in the 'Abuse Me' video.

When the pre-show murmur died down, a shirtless MC appeared on stage and introduced the opening act, a fire-eating sword swallower. Once he'd done some freaking of his own, the lights went down and the band appeared on stage, as if out of nowhere, Johns wearing a T-shirt that proclaimed 'Nobody knows I'm a lesbian', which was subsequently auctioned for charity and raised over $1000. The new album's first single, 'Freak', turned up early in the set, along with a mix of five more *Freak Show* tunes (the Indian-ised 'Petrol & Chlorine', however, was deemed too tricky to recreate live) as well as *Frogstomp* standards 'Pure Massacre' and 'Tomorrow'. Then Gillies and Joannou disappeared in a puff of smoke, leaving a solo Johns to strum his way through the sombre 'Cemetery'. Despite the heavy-handed, parallel-import-themed speech from Sony head Denis Handlin that closed the night, the launch was a success. The band proved to a tough local audience that they had the presence – and the tunes – to be a worthy headliner. Tall poppy syndrome be damned.

While launching the album was the band's immediate priority, Watson and the band's parents had an equally challenging task. They were trying their best not only to keep the band in good mental shape but also to ensure they didn't miss too much school. Typically, teen stars would drop out of the formal education system, preferring to use on-the-road tutors, thereby capitalising on the chance to squeeze every last drop out of what could be a short-lived career. (And whatever happened to Hanson, by the way?) But this wasn't the case for Silverchair. While the band did rely on a tutor at times, those close to them knew that attending school as often as possible would keep them sane and grounded. And the trio's schoolmates were always there to keep their egos in check, something they didn't get when dealing with the music business. They were about to enter their final year of high school, and had committed themselves to finishing it, even though they'd now dedicated themselves to careers in music. This was standard working-class thinking: always have a back-up in case the bottom drops out of your dream.

Watson found himself turning down more requests for interviews and photo shoots than ever before; he figures he rejected up to 90 per cent of requests during the *Freak Show* phase. He also made sure that while touring overseas the band never performed more than five shows a week (most bands averaged at least six), at one point turning down a six-figure-fee show at Wembley Stadium so the band could swing an extra two days at home. On another occasion, they spent AUD$40,000 on airfares to get them back to Newcastle for a welcome six-day break between gigs.

As they'd proved with their Surfrider shows and various other acts of charity, Silverchair didn't consider the rock life to be just about the cash. Before accepting any offer, the band's parents had to sign off on the deal first. Thanks to the runaway success of *Frogstomp*, the band were financially comfortable and had more control of their career choices. While these self-imposed restrictions may have contributed to fewer sales for *Freak Show* in North America – along with Sony's hotly-contested choice of lead single – the challenge now was to hang onto the joy they felt when playing and recording music. Which, in the end, was what they really desired.

While the gloss was starting to wear off their very atypical teenage lives, there was the occasional golden moment. At the band's 24 February show at the Palace in Los Angeles, Ozzy Osbourne turned up with his daughter Aimee, whom Johns would date for a short time. The band coped well with playing before one of their (and their parents') idols, dedicating their crashing cover of Black Sabbath's 'Paranoid' to the man known for allegedly biting heads off bats, who was soon to reinvent himself as the accidental star of a reality TV program. Sammy Hagar, occasional Van Halen vocalist, was another Silverchair convert, fronting at a show and asking to have his photo taken with the band. Even porn star Ron 'The Hedgehog' Jeremy showed up backstage at one show. After dates in Europe during March, with their tutor Jim Welch in tow, the band breezed through Australia for four dates, releasing 'Abuse Me' on 24 March as the second single from *Freak Show*. It went gold soon after. (The album had sold gold in the US in late February, after four weeks in the charts.)

It was after their 30 March set at Melbourne's Offshore festival, alongside Blink-182 and Tool, that drummer Gillies took the drastic step of getting rid of his hair, which he'd often vowed to grow down 'to the crack in my arse'. He'd complained to Johns that his unruly mane was restricting his playing, so Johns shaved Gillies's head, almost to the bone. 'I'm a gimp,' Gillies laughed afterwards, to which his father, David, added: '[He's] bald as a baby's bum – just like Yul Brynner.' Gillies premiered his clean scalp a week later at the Surf Skate Slam Festival on Sydney's Maroubra Beach. The band then disappeared for another two months of touring, this time swinging through most larger North American cities, before more European festival dates. *Freak Show* may have gone gold (500,000 copies) in the US, but its sales still didn't match the frenzy that had surrounded 'Tomorrow' and *Frogstomp*. Still, Silverchair had reasonable pulling power, all but filling the Plaza of Nations in Vancouver, packing Chicago's Aragon Ballroom and drawing 6000 punters to Arrow Hall in Ontario. The latter show grossed a handy US$89,000, while the Aragon Ballroom set and a show in Worcester, Massachusetts, also grossed more than US$50,000 each. Later in the year they truly hit paydirt with a show in The Woodlands, Texas, which grossed a very useful US$185,808. A bunch of hopefuls going by the name of Matchbox Twenty opened the show for the Newcastle three. Admittedly, the band's pre-tax share of receipts was about 25 per cent, but they were very clearly on a commercial roll.

If Frequent Flyer points were a reliable predictor of record sales, *Freak Show* was set to outstrip even *Frogstomp*. But as the *Toronto Sun*'s reporter shrewdly observed when reviewing the album, *Freak Show* was 'a stronger and less popular album' than its predecessor. Johns realised this, too, but stuck to the party line that 'as long as you keep writing good songs that people like, and that you like, 1 think that you can just keep going for as long as you want.' With one eye always on the larger picture, Watson even admitted he'd trade reduced record sales for more critical kudos, which would ensure a longer life for the band. 'It wouldn't bother me if *Freak Show* sold half as many copies [as *Frogstomp*],' he said, 'but got treated with a little more respect.' (Watson's request was granted – *Freak Show* shifted 1,414,000 units, just under half of *Frogstomp*'s 2,898,000.)

Despite the work they were putting in to promote *Freak Show,* and reviews that were, in the main, more positive than for their debut, the album wasn't a breakout success. Although it debuted on the *Billboard* album chart at Number Twelve, it slipped away quickly. Of course it would reach the top spot on debut in Australia (which it did on 10 February), while in Canada it debuted at Number Two, in Germany at Twenty-eight, France at Twenty, the UK at Thirty-eight and New Zealand at Eight. But these were good – not great – figures, in regions where sales were measured in thousands, not millions. Yet although the band's established markets reacted with some caution to *Freak Show,* no doubt exacerbated by the misstep with the first US single, there was a sharp rise in sales outside North America. Such new(ish) Silverchair fan bases as France, Holland, Germany and South America started buying their records in good numbers. The band were going global.

But their excellent rock and roll adventure was starting to become, well, not so excellent. While non-stop international travel was a dream come true tor these Novocastrians when 'Tomorrow' blew up, they were now several international tours down the line. The idea of racing around the corridors of five-star hotels in the middle of the night, knocking on strangers' doors and running like hell, as they'd boasted of in the past, had lost its appeal. As Johns had made quite clear with *Freak Show*'s title and many of the songs' lyrics, the band were having some trouble adjusting to the leeches and star collectors that frequent the music industry, and the personal cost – his first major depression – was a clear sign that he mightn't have the right stuff for this life.

As one writer observed, 'Daniel, almost eighteen now, looks shy and vulnerable, his eyebrow pierced and wearing silver-glitter eye shadow, his fingernails painted with half peeled off nail polish.'

Another writer, on the road with them in LA, noticed how swiftly Gillies and Joannou tired of hijinks – while Johns didn't even bother getting involved:

> Their devilish grins fall away, replaced with bored expressions similar to the one worn by Daniel Johns, who is staring out a window. There they sit, three antsy teen rockers in skate-rat duds, trapped in a fate about as fun as spending a Saturday night with the parents.

The band were also losing patience with one of contemporary rock and roll's necessary evils: fencing inane questions from VJs and DJs, designed to generate the snappiest 'grab' – usually just a few seconds long – for a short-attention-span marketplace, all in the name of flogging the product. When promoting *Frogstomp,* Gillies, Johns and Joannou cheerfully played bullshitters, talking up invented pasts and twisting answers to the same questions into any number of different responses. But now that they believed more strongly in their work, they found little opportunity to speak with even a little intelligence. Their conversation with Modern Rock Live (MRL) typified the dumbing-down approach they found so frustrating.

MRL:

I actually read in an interview, I don't know if it was you, Daniel, or Chris, or Ben, I don't know who mentioned that the last record you did, after listening to it . . . you guys weren't particularly happy with it.

Daniel:

Um, no, we're happy with it, it's just that we're more happy with the new album. The first album had three or four songs on it which we didn't particularly like but that we had to put on to make up an album's worth of songs. But we're as happy as you can be with the first album.

MRL:

Well, I can tell you, I've listened to the new CD and it's amazing. I mean you guys have definitely . . . for a band that had a quick turnaround between two albums you guys seem like you were very focused in the studio. I mean is that how you went into this record, going, 'OK, this is our second album, we have to be really focused?'

Chris:

Um, it was kind of ... we had a bit of time off in between and we thought, 'Let's work a bit harder on this one.' It took three weeks instead of nine days and we sorted out a lot of sounds and just made everything better.

Equally vacuous were the obligatory caller questions. 'Does one person write the songs, or do you collaborate?' asks one, who obviously hadn't bothered to check their albums' liner notes. 'I was wondering', asks another, 'what are your views on musicians and their drug addictions and stuff? 'Cause you guys are real famous now and are you, like, into that stuff?' A third rings in to ask the band if they ever felt nervous on stage.

In a discussion with *TV Hits*, Gillies was asked: 'Would you agree that your audience is still pretty young? Is that what you're into – screaming teenagers?' You can almost feel Gillies cringe, before he politely replies: 'I think we've got the weirdest crowds in the whole world. Sometimes teenage girls, older girls, young guys and older guys and sometimes you have forty-year-olds.' Gillies's permanent grin must have been stretched just that little bit tighter when the next question posed to him was this: 'So it doesn't bother you that your audiences on the *Frogstomp* tour mainly consisted of teenage girls?' Then came the topper: 'Are you in search of a typical or original sound?' 'Through gritted teeth, Gillies replies, 'This album is close [but] I think the third album will be the real Silverchair sound.' Another interviewer asked Johns: 'When you're on tour, do you get a lot of older women coming on to you?' Johns snapped back: 'We wish.' It was a frustrating time for a band that was doing their best to prove they were a serious rock and roll force, not some disposable music biz creation.

During the course of early promotions for *Freak Show*, the question, 'How does it feel to be Seattle clones?' was asked repeatedly, like some kind of mantra. Initially, the question was fended off, but the more it was repeated, the feistier the band's responses became. Speaking with the *Edmonton Express*, Joannou laughed it off, stating: 'That's kind of worn off now, because the whole Seattle thing has kind of quietened down a bit. It's not as full-on as it used to be.'

But Gillies snapped at a similar question from *Request* magazine's Jon Weiderhorn, describing people who compared them to Nirvana as 'hill of shit' and elaborating that:

> We don't listen to Nirvana. Personally, I don't really even like Nirvana. The thing is, people don't realise that Nirvana was influenced by old 1970s bands like Led Zeppelin and Deep Purple and Black Sabbath.

Johns also found himself playing down more soundalike accusations when he spoke with the *Orange County Register*. 'You can always hear a band's influences on the first album,' he said. 'It's that way with everyone. We're over it.'

Johns was seriously understating Silverchair's case. When *Frogstomp* went mad, everyone recognised their musical roots, but still wanted a part of them. They were fresh-faced, they were new, they were from regional Australia, for God's sake. There was a story here. Now, with *Freak Show*, they were constantly defending themselves against the same Seattle soundalike accusations, even to the point of having to give music writers lessons in the history of rock. The band was getting to understand how shallow the rock and roll world could be. 'If people can't take us seriously,' Johns told the *Denver Post*, 'they're never going to.' He amplified the response when speaking with the *Toronto Sun*. 'It's good to be able to say "fuck you" to everyone who said we weren't capable of producing a second album.'

Australia, nonetheless, still loved the band, despite the frequent criticism. Back home in June for one-off shows in Brisbane and Darwin, they set new sales records when the tickets for their Brisbane Festival Hall show sold out within a day, a feat they'd repeat six years later as part of their 'Across the Night' tour. (Both tours were helped no end by www.chairpage.com announcing the tour dates just prior to their on-sale date.) It was the first time in the venue's history that an Australian band had sold out their 4000-seat venue so quickly. Their concert at Darwin's MGM Grand Casino also set a new ticket sales high.

Yet in spite of the thumbs-ups that *Freak Show* had been receiving at home, and the occasional high such as the album launch, the tough mixture of touring, studying and being teen role models was causing the band some real trouble, especially the vegetarian Johns, who had now been meat-free for a year. 'Johns is slim to the point of thin,' wrote the *Sydney Morning Herald*'s Bernard Zuel in April, 'his jeans and shirt hanging loosely from him.' Not long after, Microsoft's *Totally Live News* noted that Johns looked 'dangerously emaciated'. Frustrated by the impositions his stardom was placing on his family, and feeling as though his life was out of his control, Johns was slipping into the first of several serious depressions, one that was manifesting itself in his sunken features and rake-thin physique. It was almost as if he were trying to physically disappear.

Even the laddish Gillies admitted he was having some dark days of his own, trying to cope with the mix of rock and study. 'Sometimes, you just kind of get so sick of it you don't want to do it any more,' he said.

It's like, 'This isn't worth it.' Then in the end, if I didn't do all the bull, I wouldn't be able to travel around the world. It kind of makes it worth it in the end.

Johns wasn't so taken with the glamour of globetrotting. 'I just enjoy being at home,' he said at one point, mid-tour. 'I just sit at home with my dog and watch telly. I don't know if sitting home every day is normal, but that's what I do.'

In Sydney on 2 June, the band spent a day in the now very familiar Festival studio, this time with engineer Wayne Connolly, cutting the song 'Spawn' for the soundtrack of the same name. (A reworked version of the song would reappear on *Neon Ballroom* as 'Spawn Again'.) The 'Spawn' track was to be remixed by UK whiz kid Vitro, for a soundtrack of unusual collaborations: nu-metal angst-merchants Korn with the Dust Brothers; speed-metal screamers Slayer teaming up with Atari Teenage Riot; Filter joining forces with the Crystal Method, and so on. *The Spawn* album epitomised a moment when hard-rock acts were hoping to grab a little of rocktronica's cool. 'If anyone heard the song without the techno remix they wouldn't think it was us,' commented Gillies. 'One section of it has a riff like Sepultura. It's real heavy.' It was the second time one of Silverchair's full-throttle rockers had been electronically tinkered with. (Paul Mac's remix of 'Freak' was a bonus track on the 'Abuse Me' single.) At the same session, Silverchair also thrashed out a cover of the Clash's 'London's Burning', which was destined for a Clash tribute disc featuring Bush, Rancid, the Mighty Mighty Bosstones and Moby. The band were starting to develop a taste for crossing over into unfamiliar musical territory. It was an area Johns would explore even further, a few years on, when he collaborated with Mac for the 'I Can't Believe It's Not Rock' EP.

After more European festival shows, the band made it back to Sydney for a surprise gig at Luna Park on 26 July. The audience was made up of 200 Triple J prizewinners, while the show was a benefit for the Reach Out appeal, which raised cash and awareness for youth suicide prevention. The live video for Freak Show's final single, 'The Door', was taken from this one-off show. The band's set was revealing. Such firestarters as 'Slave' and the obligatory 'Tomorrow' set the moshpit alight, but Johns's wayward behaviour was leaving its mark, too. He dabbled with an instrumental version of the national anthem, 'Advance Australia Fair', between songs, and introduced 'Abuse Me' as 'a song about masturbation'. Johns's attitude mattered little to their fans, however, as 'Cemetery', the third single from *Freak Show*, raced into the Australian charts at Number Five on 7 July. Each of *Freak Show*'s singles had blitzed the ARIA Top 10.

Alter two weeks of school, the next stop for the band was Europe. But as they rolled through Sweden, Holland, Germany and Austria during August and September, as well as playing a handful of Canadian and American dates, what they really needed was a break. Badly. That finally came in October, after the band had performed 'The Door' at the ARIAs. By the time the three were announced winners of the Channel [V] award for Best Australian Band – which they would win so often that there should have been talk of renaming the award in their honour – Johns was long gone. Claiming an asthma attack, he was halfway back to Newcastle, with his father at the wheel, when the envelope was opened.

Apart from the Australian release of 'The Door' on 6 October – *Freak Show*'s fourth Top 10 single at home – much of October and early November was absorbed by the HSC exams, which they completed on 14 November. It was a burden the three were desperately keen to get out of the way, partly in the hope journalists would finally drop it as a point of discussion. The three realised their career paths were already laid out before them, but figured they'd gone this far with school, so they might as well graduate. And at least school gave them a much-needed break from the spotlight.

Johns, as he frequently and freely revealed, was fast becoming the band loner. He told *Hit Parader* magazine:

> After spending so much time on the road over the last couple of years, and being surrounded by so many people all the time, it's good to be able to get away for even a few hours with just your dog. You get time to think a little and get a hold on everything that's happened. You can always trust your dog.

The band said goodbye to school with their first major Australian tour, the 'Summer Freak Shows'. Strangely, while they'd covered much of the planet promoting their first two albums, they'd rarely toured Australia beyond the capital cities and larger regional centres; it was almost as if they were working in reverse. Now they were set to play twenty shows over five weeks, commencing on 21 November and swinging through the capital cities and such less-visited towns as Mackay, Ballarat and Dubbo, where they played in a spicier-laden aircraft hangar on the RAAF base. Magic Dirt – whose lead singer, Adalita Srsen, would become Johns's occasional girlfriend and, allegedly, the woman who freed him of his virginity during this tour – opened these all-ages shows. (Srsen declined the offer of an interview for this book.) It was the last time Australian audiences would see the band for a year.

The 'Summer Freak Shows' was the Australian rock event of 1997. Now chaperone-free – all the band members had turned eighteen – and without their on-road tutor (who had been given the choice position as head of band security), the trio started to cut loose. While their peers were in the midst of Schoolies Week, the traditional drunken post-exams blast, the band were busy with their own version of this teen rite of passage. Sure they had to work, but there was plenty of downtime and the shows were a (well paid) riot. This was the end of the *Freak Show* road, which had begun back in Hobart in January. The band remember it as a career high, probably the most enjoyable tour of their lives. 'Yeah, that was a peak,' said Joannou. 'We'd finished school, we were without our parents, we were playing all different-sized venues; it was so much fun.' Gillies's recollections are a little foggier: 'It was drinking galore, freedom, lots of fun. We let our hair down and had a good time.' Mind you, drinking only took place after the shows. The band had a firm 'no alcohol before shows' policy (although that had changed considerably by the time they came to tour *Diorama*; during one European show they were 'blind' onstage, according to Joannou).

At the Melbourne Festival Hall show in mid December, Johns was torn between darkly comic monologues about his lifetime loser status ('I was only a seconder at scouts – I mean, imagine that, I was even coming second in scouts, for Christ's sake') and playing the full rock dude. He flicked plectrums into the crowd and stopped at one point to try on a bra thrown from the moshpit. 'How do you put these things on?' he pondered out loud. 'Don't know much about them.'

Writing for online site *Addicted to Noise*, Andrew Tanner saw the changes in the late 1997 version of Daniel Johns:

> Johns, who only a year ago was the most diffident of front-men, now prowls the stage with growing confidence, his long blond hair fashioned into a mane of spiky dreadlocks. He looks sort of like a younger, leaner Johnny Lydon.

As he became even more withdrawn off-stage, this teen loner was undergoing a transformation – once he plugged in, he became physically assertive and could whip a moshpit into a frenzy. It was in direct contrast to the *Frogstomp* model. Johns wasn't just a more imposing presence on stage: he was getting mouthier.

During the Melbourne show he fell into a rant about critics who figure his dark emotions couldn't ring true:

> The people who say stuff like that are just dumb old fucks who can't remember what it's like to be young. Just because you're a teenager doesn't mean you don't have those emotions. Those people are just jaded, silly old cocks.

Gillies and Joannou looked on as Johns, sans guitar, threw himself into the Paul Mac remix of 'Freak', which closed most shows. (Mac even joined the band on-stage at their Sydney University show on 8 December.) Then Gillies – sporting a mohawk – stepped from behind his kit and whaled on some tom-toms and a gong bass drum as 'Freak' built to its climax. Crowds would erupt as the band freed themselves from their regular Silver-roles, losing themselves in the heavy rhythms. 'We were trying to do something different,' says Gillies, 'We were playing along to a tape but we didn't care – and the audience didn't seem to, either.'

Johns explained:

We wanted to do something really different in our set that no one would expect. We've been toying with the idea of doing the 'Freak' remix for a while now. It seems to be going down really well.

The *Freak Show* campaign ended in Perth on 20 December, and Silverchair's hectic year was over. But instead of winding down, Daniel Johns was about to disappear into some of the darkest days of his life.

* * *

Silverfan: An interview with a Silverchair obsessive

Twenty-seven-year-old Sydneysider Phil McConville is known as the biggest Silverchair obsessive to walk the earth – and that's quite a statement, given the level of hero worship the band inspires. And to think that it all began with the seemingly innocent purchase of a poster in a record store. 'My Dad is OK [with my obsession],' says McConville, a single man who's training to become a teacher, 'although really deep down he probably thinks I am nuts.' His mother seems happier with his musical addiction; after all, she did finance the Silverchair tattoo on McConville's upper right arm.

What and when was your first exposure to Silverchair?
Well, I was at a friend's BBQ back in '94, and some mates were running around singing 'Tomorrow', and I was thinking, 'Man, that song is awesome!' I couldn't really get it out of my head. Someone said that these dudes are 14 and are from Newcastle. I was like, 'Shit, I am 14 and from Sydney – they are from my state and are my age!' I couldn't really believe it.

Was there a key gig or song that turned you from a fan into an expert-cum-obsessive?
I don't necessarily think it was a gig or a song, but I remember the time was around late '95. I was in Sydney with my mate Kane and we were in Utopia, a record store on George Street. There were these posters and I was tossing around the idea to buy them, like, man, I *want* to buy it, but I don't know. I don't know really why I was thinking that; maybe it was

only having $20 a week to spend on whatever! He was like, 'Mate, they will probably be gone next time you are here.' And from that moment on, when I bought those two *Frogstomp* posters, my life would never be the same again. Every bit of spare money I had was spent on 'Chair memorabilia. Yes, I am comfortable about being known as the authority on the band; I actually love it more then anyone could ever know. To have the respect from every person I meet is the greatest feeling in the world.

How many shows have you seen and what type of collectibles do you own?
I've really lost count of the amount of shows I have seen. Collectables I have range from records from all over the world, ranging in different colours, including the first *Frogstomp* promo pack; animation cells from the 'Luv Your Life' film clip; an apple, which is from the *Neon Ballroom* recording sessions; signed ties, jumpers, beer coasters; singles from around the world; articles from all over the world; signed setlists; film clip extras. Whenever Silverchair appear on the front of a magazine I buy it three times: one for the display table and the other for back to back [storage]. I could really keep going. I had to move my bedroom downstairs to the garage to fit everything.

Is your dedication to the band unconditional? Have you been OK with the band's shift in direction over the years – and do you have a favourite period / recording?
For sure it is. Man, we are growing up and experience more feelings than angst. Tunes and tastes change, so if fans don't like them for doing what they do, I think it is pretty lame. It would be pretty fucking boring doing the same stuff every day for, like, four years – let alone 12 years! Definitely my favourite music is the *Diorama* sessions; the music is like the movie *Fantasia* – totally mind-blowing! I still get goosebumps listening to all their albums, but *Diorama* is fucking out of this world. Live, the *Freak Show* times were hardcore heavy; awesome energy. 'The Door' is still one of my favourite live tracks; 'Emotion Sickness' is also out of this world live. And from the *Frogstomp* days, 'Israel's Son' – man, what a song! And *Diorama* live is just body-tingling music.

Do you have the same level of devotion towards any other bands?

No, not at all. But I do thank Silverchair for making the music that I love more than anything, because this has let me love so many bands and appreciate good music. I have helped out a few bands with promotions, marketing, etc., and my love of music came from Silverchair, which has resulted in music becoming a huge part of my life.

Are you part of a sizeable community of Silverchair obsessives? What is it about the band that attracts such a hardcore following?
I know most of the Silverchair obsessives from all around the globe. I tend to take as many people as I can to Silverchair gigs and talk about Silverchair as much as possible, and let them enjoy it and take the journey. Then they can see why I talk about them nearly every day of my life. I talk to a lot of people – friends, family, anyone who I meet – and I read a lot, check out stuff online, have people send me stuff from around the country and the world, all about Silverchair. For my 21st, my cousin made me my own Silverchair throne. I love it – and no one would have anything like it in the world.

The band attracts a hardcore following for many reasons. First and foremost, for me, the reason I love Silverchair so much is that their music is so fucking amazing, mind-blowing, life-changing – it's the greatest music ever. When I have kids, they will talk about Silverchair like people talk about the Beatles. You can see that the guys put their heart and soul into what they do. Their live shows are without a doubt the most amazing, breathtaking, energy-filled events that most people would have ever witnessed in their lives. It doesn't matter if you are 7 or you are 70, your life will never be the same.

Is there a hardcore group of Silverchair nuts that you spot at most gigs?
Yes, there are Silverchair-ists that I do see at gigs but, like I said, I love to take as many new people as I can to watch them. My friends and family totally understand where I come from, and it is cool to see them enjoy the experience, too. Some 'Chair fans are very competitive and try to outdo people, but I don't see the point of that shit. No matter what type of fan you are, it doesn't matter. Enjoy it, love it, live it.

How many times have you met the band? What's your take on each member, and have you had any embarrassing/unusual Silverchair encounters?

I've really lost count on how many times I've met the band. Firstly, they are all awesome dudes: Chris is a champion, really cool and easy to talk to and have a laugh with. Daniel: yeah, really, really awesome, such an awesome fella. He makes you feel really at ease and chilled. I kind of didn't want to wreck my tie that he signed, though. I was like, 'Man, this is a really cool tie – are you sure?' Ben is also really cool. A funny story – after the *Diorama* launch, I was talking to him and Sam Holloway, and he was bagging me out about my [Silverchair] tattoo, saying it is forever and things like that. And lo and behold, the next time I see him who has a giant James Brown tattoo [on his arm] and Led Zep tattoo on his neck? Mmm.

Are your friends/family understanding about your enthusiasm towards the band?
For sure. Well, this is going to sound like a Grammy speech, but my Mum is the greatest and she loves it; really, I think she does! I have lent CDs to her friends and am pretty sure they then went out and bought them. My Dad is OK, although really deep down he probably thinks I am nuts. But I know he supports me in every way. My sister and brother love it, I think. My friends, like my family, see it as nothing but positive. To see how happy I am when I listen, talk and watch the mighty Silverchair means nothing but good times. They encourage it and try to find out stuff and quiz me or SMS me when the band are on the radio; to have this kind of support from friends and family makes this so much more enjoyable. I meet people at parties and around – some of them are, like, 'Man, you are the Silverchair guy.' How cool is that?

What's the most extreme thing you've done in order to maintain your Silverchair obsession?
I have a Silverchair tattoo, and the day I have kids I want to call them Daniel John, Chris and Ben. What do I love about the band? Their integrity, honesty and their 'never give up' attitude, while lately it's been watching the guys have a fucking blast on stage. There's also the pride that comes with them being Australian, and the way they influence so many people – from everyday people to rock stars. Last but not least, their mind-blowing music.

How do you respond to critics who've given the band a hard time over the years?

JEFF APTER

I have always wanted to give a big FUCK YOU to all the critics and tall poppy fuckers who cut down the mighty Silverchair, as they are without a doubt the greatest band to come out of Australia. They have changed millions of people's lives – and their music is still getting better with age, like a fine wine.

Chapter Five

BALLROOM BLITZ

> We went through the whole being-famous-and-going-through-adolescence thing together, and came out the other side complete opposites. I've no idea how it happened.
>
> Daniel Johns

Coming off the long and winding road that was the *Freak Show* promo trail, Daniel Johns was exhausted. Mentally and physically drained, he was in dire need of some serious downtime. Joannou and Gillies were also feeling some pain, but they recovered through travel. Joannou and his girlfriend headed off to Thailand; Gillies and his partner travelled to North Queensland and Byron Bay. When they returned, both kicked back in 'Newie' with their mates, 'surfing and hanging out' and doing a whole lot of nothing.

'It was such a luxury, just hanging around at home,' Joannou said, of the first half of 1998. 'Beforehand, you'd be carted off all the time; it was nice to sit around at home.' But it wasn't always easy for him to adjust; he admits that some nights he had to stop himself when he reached for his bedside phone and started placing a wake-up call, as he would each night while on tour.

As he recalls:

> For seven days a week you had an itinerary. It felt funny, at first, being alone, because you'd been in this group of ten, twelve people for so long, travelling around all the time.

Unlike his bandmates, as Johns readily admitted, he was no 'social butterfly'; he much preferred holing up in his parents' Merewether house with his dog and his guitar.

'I was pretty lonely,' he remembered, when asked about life after *Freak Show*.

> We'd just left school and all our friends were going to university. Ben and Chris were going out with their girlfriends, doing their thing, and I was living in a house by myself, just writing.

Just like Joannou, Johns had also locked into the touring mindset, as he would later explain to me – and now that school was out, he was also having trouble adjusting to his new life:

> That [time] was so fucking hectic. We'd go to school during the week, play shows on the weekend and then tour during the holidays. None of us wanted to be dumb; we wanted to pass the HSC, we were trying our asses off. As soon as we ended school it became a thousand times harder; we found out that school was an escape. I started to realise, 'Fuck, this is my life, this is all I've got.'

By early 1998, the pressure was on Johns to generate some new tunes for the band's third album. The stop-start nature of touring prevented him from writing on the road; the demands of playing live, travelling and doing press were intrusive and cramped his songwriting style. In the past, many of the band's songs had emerged from jams; now Johns wanted to write alone. He was taking over as the band's main songwriter, and his only chance to write was when the band returned to Australia.

At the same time, Johns's musical mood was changing. While still deeply enamoured of the red-meat rock on which he'd been raised, the positive response to the more pensive, orchestrated songs of *Freak Show* ('Cemetery', 'Abuse Me') had opened his ears to a whole new world of sound. Gillies's tastes were changing, too; he was opening up to dance music, a form which had previously meant nothing to him. Johns wanted to create music that wasn't dependent on volume and his full-throated roar to express what he was feeling. He was also underwhelmed by the type of music American radio had opted to play instead of *Freak Show*, especially such bland, corporate rock acts as Matchbox Twenty and Third Eye Blind. The way he saw it, Silverchair needed a serious musical makeover, not just to survive but to thrive.

But Daniel Johns had more immediate problems. The past four years had taken their toll. First there was the massive hit of 'Tomorrow' and the band's rapid ascent in America and elsewhere. Then there was the pressure of hitting back after such a huge first-up hit, as well as the Apprehended Violence Order, the 'Israel's Son' controversy, graduating from school, becoming a public figure and teen role model and the obligatory backlash – it was a lot to digest. It was easy to forget that he was all of eighteen when *Freak Show* ground to a halt in December 1997.

Johns felt he had lost control over his life; instead, it was in the hands of people in the music business. As he told me several years later, he was also growing apart from his bandmates:

> When we started out at thirteen or fourteen, we were exactly the fucking same. But as we grew up and went through the same kind of experiences, it's interesting how it affected us and shaped our personalities. We went through the whole being-famous-and-going-through-adolescence thing together, and came out the other side complete opposites. I've no idea how it happened.

He'd even thought about splitting up the band at the end of the *Freak Show* tour; it was a low point he would revisit a few years on, after the global tour to promote *Neon Ballroom*.

'We were either going to stop or keep going,' Johns told *Kerrang!* magazine.

> I decided that music's always been my dream since I was a little kid, and to throw it away would have been something that I'd regret when I was thirty years old. I'd look back and go, 'Fuck!'

(There is more to this, of course: it turns out that Johns had issued the band an ultimatum about their direction. But more on that later.)

By now, Johns's parents had convinced him to start seeing a psychotherapist to help him cope with the type of pressure most eighteen-year-olds aren't exposed to. Johns later said that he saw the therapist to 'learn to associate with people', although he stopped the initial treatment after two months. By that time his participation in consultations consisted of him walking into a room, sitting down and saying, 'Just give me the tablets and I'm going.' He didn't take well to the idea of being picked apart by someone who didn't know him; he'd already had enough of that from the media. One piece of the therapist's advice he did take, though, was to move out of his family home – he bought a two-bedroom home near Merewether beach, with an uninterrupted view of the ocean. The house's interior decorating style was best described as spartan: it comprised a couch, a television, a bed, a stereo and not much more. Johns only stepped outside to walk his dog, Sweep, see his therapist, or hit the video store (where he quickly racked up a $1600 bill, renting 'anything to pass the time and help me get through another day'). But for a teenager seeking some privacy, Johns could have chosen a better location: he lived near a public carpark, which was usually occupied by hopeful Silverchair-watchers or Friday night yobbos. His always-supportive parents looked after his groceries and any other day-to-day needs, while keeping a watchful eye on their oldest son. As Johns later revealed, he was sinking deeper and deeper into a funk of alienation and depression. And then he stopped eating.

'As our popularity grew, so did people's expectations,' Johns admitted.

When you're a guy in a band, everyone thinks you should be happily swimming in girls. But it's just not that way unless you're a really confident person to start with. Every time the crowd got bigger, I felt more empty when I walked offstage. Towards the end of 1997, I gradually began to feel more and more alienated from people.

And after moving into his house by the beach things took a turn for the worse:

The psychological problems that surfaced on tour intensified and my view of reality became distorted. I began to feel really anxious and paranoid. I couldn't leave my house without thinking something terrible was going to happen, whether it was getting beaten up or being hounded by photographers. I was really freaked by phones. When mine rang, I'd have to leave the room to get away from it.

Johns figured that the only part of his life he could take charge of was his food intake. It was his way of controlling 'the chaos I was feeling inside'. He had hit on this 'solution' to his psychological problems as early as 1997, but now he started to push himself, trying to discover how little he could eat and still get by. He saw it as a personal test. Quickly, he was down to eating two or three pieces of fruit a day.

He said afterwards:

The only way I can describe it is to say that it felt comforting to be in control of something, like I hadn't totally lost it. The problem is, you think you're gaining control over something, but in reality you're losing control over the functioning of your body. Within a few months it got to the point where I was eating just so I wouldn't collapse. If I felt like I was going to black out, I'd eat a piece of fruit or a cup of soup. At the time, my parents and my brother and sister were the only people I trusted and could see without feeling anxious. Of course they were all worried sick about me, but I couldn't really see how bad it was.

Johns was so self-deluded, in fact, that he was convinced that 'every chef in the world wanted to poison me' and that even a harmless apple contained razor blades. Even when he looked in the mirror, and could see the obvious physical changes he was undergoing, he'd shrug and figure that somehow his clothes had increased in size since he last wore them. As he explained to Andrew Denton in 2004, 'I (didn't] understand how all my clothes [had] stretched and I still looked the same.'

In the midst of this self-deprivation, Johns found himself unable to shake a cold, which was hardly surprising given his diet. He visited his family doctor, who gave it to him straight: if he didn't start eating he was going to die. What he'd done was seriously damaging his immune system. Being a vegan – and suffering paranoid delusions that his food had been poisoned – didn't help Johns's decline.

'When I was about seventeen, I had this great phobia about different foods I couldn't eat because I thought they'd cut my throat,' explains Johns.

> It seems silly when you look back on it, but at the time it was scary to eat cereal because I thought it was sharp and it would cut my stomach.

Johns's doctor went on to explain that he was already displaying the physical signs of those with advanced eating disorders: receding gums, exposed teeth, protruding bones and sunken cheeks. That was a turning point.

By this stage, Johns's weight had slipped to under fifty kilos. His doctor prescribed Aropax, an anti-depressant that would mollify his anxious state of mind. Johns moved back in with his parents to start his physical and mental recovery. (The move might have been coming anyway. Johns's neighbours had started complaining about his barking dog and his tendency to play loud music late into the night. However, he still owns the now-empty house on the beach.)

What Johns didn't realise was that the anti-depressants he'd been prescribed were just as effective at blocking out the rest of the world as locking himself away in a beachside house or giving up food. While Gillies and his father swam laps in the local pool every morning, and Joannou kicked back at his parents' home, Johns was sinking into what he would later call an 'anti-depressant haze', a wobbly state of mind that it would take him three years to shake off. As much as his bandmates wanted to support him – Gillies had even helped him move into his house by the beach – Johns had shut off the world. His bandmates felt frustrated by his inertia.

'I saw him a few times,' says Gillies.

> I was friends with the guy, but when all he wants to do is sit around all the time and do nothing, after a while you go, 'Fuck, this is boring, let's go and do something.' But if you did go out, someone would say something [to Johns], It was frustrating seeing a friend go through it. We'd achieved so much and we could have done anything we wanted – and then that happened to him. You care about the guy, but there's nothing you can do. All you could say was, well, I hope he works it out.

Manager Watson was also relegated to outsider status. 'He made it pretty clear that he didn't want people to contact him. He wanted to be on his own,' Watson recalled. Nonetheless, Watson was getting updates from Johns's family and felt very concerned: 'We had a lot of pretty intense conversations.' Several years later Johns explained that his condition was 'too personal' to share with family and friends. And although he insisted he wasn't suicidal at the time, 'When I was really bad with the eating disorder, I thought that I might die and I think everyone that knew me thought I might die if I kept going.' He would never sink lower, although his bout of reactive arthritis in 2002 came a close second.

While Johns may have been slipping away from his family, his bandmates, and the world in general, he had started to write the songs that would form *Neon Ballroom*. Initially, however, he wasn't writing songs per se (there was too much pressure to write songs), but poems: reams of poems, over a hundred in total, scribbled on scraps of paper. He had no music to accompany his words, which was in complete contrast to the band's songwriting methods of the past, which had typically begun with jamming in the Gillies garage, followed by Johns writing lyrics to fit the music. But now Johns was the main songwriter – and if this approach worked for him, so be it. Writing these poems provided an emotional outlet for Johns; the process allowed him to slowly come to grips with his insecurities and his depression. What better way to understand your problems, especially for an introverted loner such as Johns, than to write them down? His next step during the early part of 1998 was to take all the poems he'd written, cut them up, and make a collage of the words that made the most sense to him.

Johns explained it this way:

> With the previous two albums, the music was written first and then I just went home and wrote lyrics. I didn't ever want to get too poetic with lyrics in the past, because lyrically I've been very influenced by old-school punk bands like Minor Threat and Black Flag. [But] with this album I wanted to really focus on what I was feeling at the time. I really wanted people to focus on the lyrics and what I'm trying to say in the songs and then focus on the music, rather than the other way around.

The poems were never intended to be lyrics for Silverchair songs. 'It was just basically a form of expression. [But] I liked the words so much that I changed it to a more lyrical format and put music around it.'

As *Rolling Stone* magazine later noted, Johns's lyrics – derived from these poems – were 'full of sickness, needs, obsessions, uncertainties and pain'. Rather than rely on the atrocities he saw on the six o'clock news, as he did for the songs on *Frogstomp*, rant how 'baby's got rabies' or decry the machinations of the music industry, as he did during *Freak Show*, Johns now had some deeply personal, real-life pain to document. Not surprisingly, this would make for some of the most powerful – if self-indulgent – songs of his brief songwriting career.

Growing in confidence, Johns felt he was finding his own songwriter's voice with these songs:

> On the second [album], I got into this mind frame where if it's too melodic, that's too wimpy. I didn't want to be perceived as too feminine because people always thought I was gay. I was self-conscious about that with the second album. With this album [*Neon Ballroom*] I just said, 'Fuck it, I'm just going to do what I want to do.'

As the songs slowly came together for the album, Johns was putting all this personal baggage into the most poignant lyrics he'd ever written. Interestingly, neither Gillies nor Joannou would ask Johns about the meaning of his new, anguished songs when the band finally reconvened in mid 1998 for the *Neon Ballroom* recording sessions. To them, that was Johns's job, to write the words – analysing them was for the critics and fans. 'I don't think we've ever picked through his lyrical content,' Gillies told me. 'It's been more, "Cool, let's play."'

'Ana's Song (Open Fire)', the second single from the album and one of the most stirring (and richly melodic) songs Johns would ever write, emerged from his six months of isolation. The song wasn't just a metaphor for anorexia, although Johns quite blatantly roars the words: 'Ana wrecks your life / Like an anorexia life', as the song builds to its climax. 'It was the first time I exposed my eating disorder to anyone,' Johns said.

> The lyrics of 'Ana's Song', particularly 'In my head, the flesh seems thicker', are about my desire to see how far I could take it. I'm sure the reason some people get eating disorders has to do with a distorted body image, but often it has nothing to do with looking a certain way. It's about gaining control over a part of your life. It's about an obsession, whether it's an eating disorder or whether it's a distorted image of one's self.

Pointedly, Johns then revealed a home truth about his adolescence that few people knew. It would explain a lot of the thinly veiled anger in many of his songs, both old and new: 'I've always had a fascination with the darker side of life. I'm a bit fixated on it,' he said. He would repeat this in 2001, telling me, 'I've always had an obsession with death. Love and death, I'm always thinking about those two extremes.' One reason, he had suggested, was that he had gone through a hard time in high school.

This was news to most people, because the party line was that the band fared well enough at school, even if Gillies and Joannou sided more with the sporting jocks than the lean, blond, more creatively inclined Johns. Former Newcastle High principal Peter McNair strongly believes that the band members were treated well at school by their peers; any problems Johns experienced happened outside of school hours.

'When we started playing at thirteen, I was called a fag and beaten up,' Johns explained.

> Even though Ben and Chris were in the band with me, for some reason they weren't subject to the same ridicule. Probably because I was the lead singer and they played relatively masculine instruments.

Joannou and Gillies understood this. 'I suppose with him being the frontman, it was unavoidable,' said the drummer.

In another interview from the period, this time with *Juice* magazine, Johns described how this hassling intensified:

> I was getting beaten up, constantly being called a faggot, people throwing shit into our pool and hassling my family. That was really

hard. There was a point during *Freak Show* that Silverchair was about to end because I didn't want to inflict anything else upon my family.

Johns had been through a lot of teen trauma, but now he was developing the songwriting confidence to let out his anxieties and aggression. Unlike most teens, he actually had a very public outlet for his pain. Accordingly, the songs for *Neon Ballroom* had just started to flow as the band convened for the first time in two months, on 22 February, to record a song with Nick Launay for the *Godzilla* soundtrack. The song, 'Untitled', was an old tune; it had first been recorded for the *Freak Show* album, but didn't make the cut. It had then been considerably reworked for *Godzilla*. The session was the first time Johns, Gillies and Joannou had been in the same room since 20 December of the previous year, but Johns wasn't ready to debut any new material to his bandmates. Not yet, anyway.

Just as they had given producer Launay a 'dry run' with 'Blind' prior to recording Freak Sho*w*, the band were now testing themselves: Could they record another album? Were they comfortable together in the studio? Reassuringly, making music still felt right and the session, although brief, went well. The next four months were consumed with Johns's slow recovery and the gradual development of songs for *Neon Ballroom*. Launay was locked in to begin pre-production in early June, so Johns had a lot of fine-tuning to do, which he did in isolation, transforming his scraps of poetry into full-blown rock and roll anthems.

Four months since they'd last plugged in together, Silverchair finally got back together in June, in a Newcastle rehearsal room. They chose this space over Ben Gillies's parents' garage (even though The Loft was now seriously soundproofed) so they could better amplify Johns's vocals. Producer Launay, who since *Freak Show* had worked on albums by Semisonic (*Feeling Strangely Fine*) and Girls Against Boys (*Freakonica*), was again staying at the Johns family home. He convened this first band meeting. With the exception of the one-off 'Untitled' session, Johns hadn't spoken with his bandmates for six months. There was a lot of bad feeling at the time, especially between Gillies and Johns. The drummer felt rejected by his close friend, who'd shut him out during his breakdown, while Johns, despite the confidence he was showing as a songwriter, was worried that Gillies would reject the style of the new, deeply personal music that he was writing. He just wasn't sure that this music was right for Silverchair. And, as Launay points out in a subsequent chapter, Johns wasn't the greatest communicator on the planet.

Johns's reservations about premiering these new tunes to his bandmates made some kind of sense. While they were written with rock's basic guitar/bass/drums/voice format in mind, the emotions in the songs ran much deeper than, 'Come on, abuse me more, I like it'. And some of the songs, especially 'Emotion Sickness' and 'Steam Will Rise', were far more restrained than the riff-heavy rock of *Frogstomp* and *Freak Show*. Johns could hear strings in many of the songs – they were way more cinematic than anything he'd tried writing before. An uncertain Johns even had vague notions to hang onto these tunes for a solo album (a planned project that has reared its Head several times since). 'I was really nervous,' he said, after he'd finally played the songs to Joannou and Gillies. 'I didn't know whether or not to keep them and do a solo album or whether to show them. I thought they'd go, "What the fuck is that?"'

To Johns's way of thinking, Gillies was the true rock dog of the band; he figured he'd reject these songs as 'too wimpish'. 'I thought Ben would be like, "No, man, metal! We want metal!"' But as Johns played the songs to the band on an acoustic guitar, with Launay looking on, Gillies started suggesting rhythmic ideas and Joannou quickly jumped on the bass. It was a flashback for the band – after all their globetrotting of the past three years, they were almost back to where they first started, when life seemed a hell of a lot simpler. All it would have taken was for Gillies's mother to tell them to turn it down and the scene would have been complete.

Later, Johns explained to *Rock Sound* magazine that some of the more restrained passages in his new songs did throw his bandmates, just a little, but added:

> They could see that these ideas were going round in my head and that there was no other option. Ben and Chris are enormously alike – they have the same interests and the same view of the world, whereas I'm different. But I respect them, you know? They're my friends. Our

temperaments are at odds with each other but that's OK. We complement each other, which is the essence of Silverchair.

Gillies had brought one song, entitled 'Trash', to the pre-production sessions for the new album. It was a throwaway he described as 'heavy, fast, punky'. But it didn't make the final cut for the album, though it did appear later as a B-side. Joannou had also tried to write music, but as he admitted, 'It really sucked.' With the exception of 'Spawn Again', co-written by Johns and Gillies, a track resurrected from the soundtrack for *The Cable Guy* (where it was simply called 'Spawn'), the songs on *Neon Ballroom* were all Daniel Johns compositions. For the band's next two albums, Johns would be the songwriter, which didn't sit well with Gillies's mother, for one. She was hoping some of her son's tunes would make the final cut, as they had on the first two albums, thereby generating songwriting royalties. But that's not how it panned out.

After the near-breakdown he'd experienced at the end of the *Freak Show* tour, Johns was finally straight with Gillies and Joannou. He told them that the only way he could continue as part of Silverchair was to write all the band's music. He had conceptual ideas for their future recordings, and these couldn't come out of the type of jams that had produced the bulk of their first two albums. Joannou and Gillies didn't think about it for too long – they were too enamoured of playing in Silverchair to shoot down Johns's plan. It turned out to be the smartest move the band could make, as their music matured greatly, even if the perception of Silverchair from then onwards would be as 'The Daniel Johns Band'. Despite the freedom this deal gave him, Johns still had some emotional baggage to work through. He still felt like a prisoner of Silverchair, albeit one who had been granted creative day release.

Unlike famously fractured trios, such as the Police and the Jam – bands divided by the usual 'creative differences' cliches – Silverchair had come up with a design for survival. Johns was the creative force, frontman and loner, Gillies and Joannou were both the band's musical engine room and good mates. They each had their place in the band, onstage and off.

'Emotion Sickness', which was to become *Neon Ballroom*'s mood-swinging, richly evocative opening track – and Johns's favourite cut on the album – was a vivid snapshot of his fragile state of mind. He explained it as being 'about any kind of mental disorder or problem', but the finished version of the song is proof positive that he connected deeply and emphatically with the song. David Helfgott's mad-professor piano heightened the song's white-knuckle intensity.

'It's about depression or anxiety or anything like that,' Johns said. 'It's about trying to escape it without resorting to an anti-depressant or some kind of pill.'

'Paint Pastel Princess' was another lyric from Johns's darkest days. It was a metaphor for Aropax, the antidepressant that his doctor had prescribed. 'The song's about how taking that type of medication prevents you from feeling highs or lows – every day is the same,' he explained, likening Aropax to Prozac, which 'keeps you on the same level, but at the same time they numb you. Unfortunately, I need them, but it doesn't mean I have to like them.'

'Anthem for the Year 2000', a riff-crunching rock beast – which would become *Neon Ballroom*'s lead-off single – was another song to emerge from this frenzied song-writing period between the 'Untitled' session and the recording of *Neon Ballroom*. But whereas 'Ana's Song' and 'Paint Pastel Princess' were deeply felt lyrics about the trauma Johns was going through, 'Anthem' came from somewhere else entirely. A dream, in fact.

It was also one of Johns's fastest turnarounds, as he told *Guitar* magazine:

> I had a dream we were playing at this huge stadium, and we had no instruments because everything had broken. Thousands of people had their hands in the air, clapping. And I started singing, 'We are the youth, we'll take your fascism away' over the handclaps, in order to compensate for the lack of instruments. So I woke up and straight away wrote [the song], I did it from start to finish in, like, five minutes. It was the quickest song I'd ever written, and the first verse starts with drums and vocals – just like the dream, only with the handclaps.

'I wanted to write a stadium rock song,' Johns told America's K-ROQ radio station. 'I want it to really rock.' He was correct on both counts. (In a curious footnote, the band approached AC/DC rhythm guitarist Malcolm Young to add guitar to the track; although it was an inspired choice, he politely declined. Elsewhere, a proposal to use indie-pop piano Ben Folds on some tracks was shut down by Johns.)

Although Johns had been downplaying the political nature of his words – despite such titles as 'Israel's Son' and 'Pure Massacre' – 'Anthem for the Year 2000' was overtly political, if a little glib. The song's social conscience was something he couldn't deny. He even drew links between its theme and the outbreak of One Nation and Hansonism that was creeping into Australian politics and society at the time.

'I think the government treats us like shit,' Johns said.

They think the youth is a bunch of people who are wasting their lives on drugs and loud music. The song draws a parallel between politicians and how they view youth and how they put certain restrictions on them. It draws a parallel between that and the record industry and taking away from young stars and using young people – and taking their innocence.

On closer inspection, maybe 'Anthem' wasn't just a political rant – it was closer to Johns's current state of mind than even he knew at the time.

Just like 'Anthem', 'Satin Sheets' – another song from Johns's hermit phase – wasn't as deeply personal as the bulk of *Neon Ballroom*; it was more observational. He described it as a comment on class, taken from a time when 'die yuppie die' was a counter-culture catchphrase. It was about 'the corporate world looking down on people'. 'If I walk into a restaurant or something,' said Johns, 'there's this whole yuppie mentality of people who think I shouldn't be there because I don't brush my hair. But I've probably got more money than them.' Clearly Johns hadn't quite shaken off the anti-everything stance to which the band blindly swore allegiance back in 1994.

'Miss You Love' and 'Black Tangled Heart' were other poems-cum-songs written during band downtime. But they reflected a different Johns trauma: his inability at the time to form a lasting relationship.

'I've had girlfriends, but I've never had a relationship that's lasted longer than a month,' Johns admitted.

I think I've got some kind of phobia [a word Johns would repeat endlessly when talking up *Neon Ballroom*], I'm scared of getting too

> attached to someone. Just when someone gets close to my heart, that's when I cut them off.

As Johns freely and frequently admitted, the bulk of *Neon Ballroom* was personal, not political. He didn't picture himself as some kind of youth spokesman, even though he'd been burdened with that tag, very much against his will.
He explained:

> I find it a lot more creatively satisfying to express myself the way that I feel inside my head or inside my heart, rather than focus on things that are more political. Because I don't know about political issues – I just know what I feel strongly about.

By 23 June, the trio were finally back in Sydney's Festival Studios, where both *Frogstomp* and *Freak Show* had been recorded. But for the first time in their lives, Silverchair entered the studio with a set of songs that felt honest and real and not in any way related to grunge. Despite the emotional baggage they were carrying, they'd never been so prepared to make an album.

'The first two albums were traditional hard rock music,' Johns said when the band began the *Neon Ballroom* sessions.

> This album's a lot more ambitious. You have all your bands and they're either pop or rock or whatever and they always stick to that. [But] we didn't want to be labelled as a certain kind of style. We wanted to change and try different things.

One constant, however, was their choice of producer Nick Launay. Before agreeing to go with Launay, Johns had called him at home and talked for an hour, running him through the new songs and what instruments and production techniques he felt would bring them to life. Launay was in full agreement. 'Nick's really good because he's really willing to listen and doesn't try to dominate the sessions,' said Johns. 'A lot of days, me and him just sat around fiddling with effects units and effects pedals and different miking positions and stuff.' It was clear that Johns was learning to love the studio. This would prove handy, because the singer/guitarist was about to share the studio with a string section, a choir, various non-Silverchairists – and he was also about to go head-to-head with *Shine*-man, pianist David Helfgott.

Though they might have resided in completely different musical universes, Helfgott and Johns had more in common than they knew. Born in 1943, Helfgott had been a teen star, winning the state finals of the ABC Instrumental and Vocal competition six times. (Coincidentally, Johns and Silverchair had also come to prominence through the ABC, of course, via massive airplay on Triple J.) Just like Johns, Helfgott suffered terribly from the impact of being a teen prodigy. After a complete emotional breakdown, he disappeared from view in 1980. He staged a comeback a decade later, which culminated in an astounding recording of Rachmaninov's Third Piano Concerto and sell-out shows around the world. His wild ride of a life story had been documented in Scott Hicks's 1996 film, *Shine*, which featured Geoffrey Rush in an Academy Award-winning role as Helfgott. Johns's life story paralleled Helfgott's in intriguing ways.

For his part, when asked about their connection, Helfgott joked that he and Johns shared a lawyer, although he did admit, when we exchanged emails in 2006, that 'I felt a strong bond with him [Johns]. He was extremely kind and sharing; it was a great experience for me.'

The day before Helfgott's arrival at Festival had been adventurous enough: the NSW Public School Singers choir had been brought in to add their voices to 'Anthem for the Year 2000'. Conducted by George Tobay, the young voices gave the song an eerily similar mood to Pink Floyd's 'Another Brick in the Wall'. The next day, 19 August, was Helfgott's turn in the studio; he was scheduled to add piano to the epic 'Emotion Sickness', which would become *Neon Ballroom*'s opening track.

During pre-production, when he presented the song to the band, Johns figured it needed a 'manic kind of piano part', designed to 'exaggerate its sadness'. On Watson's suggestion, it was decided that Helfgott was the right man for the job. The band agreed after a meeting at Watson's house during which Helfgott, at one stage, excused himself so he could slip upstairs and brush his teeth – with Watson's toothbrush. Throughout the meeting, he kept putting his arm around Gillies and muttering, 'Very different, very different.' The drummer didn't know quite what to make of the wildly emotional piano man.

Then the band met with Larry Muhoberac, who was writing the piano part for Helfgott. While Johns lay on the floor shouting out the notes he was imagining Helfgott would play, Muhoberac – a renowned player who was once Elvis Presley's pianist – made sense of the songwriter's untrained stream of consciousness. Strangely, it worked. As for Helfgott, he came into the studio well prepared. 'I spent a lot of time preparing for the recording,' he told me, 'as it was a challenging piece. But [it was] great to do it.'

In the studio, Helfgott behaved true to character. He hugged and kissed anyone who came near him, while mumbling all the time. Unable to keep still – and needing the same kind of affection that he generously gave – Helfgott had trouble settling down sufficiently to record the part. Eventually, Muhoberac shared his piano stool, hugging Helfgott with one arm and pointing to the musical score with the other, while Launay talked the pianist through the recording process via his earphones.

Helfgott clearly connected with Johns, too. At one stage he reached across and quite innocently grasped the singer's crotch. 'There was one time he grabbed my dick. He didn't know that he was doing it,' Johns said. 'He just has to be intimate.'

Johns – as documented on Robert Hambling's *Emotion Pictures* documentary, which was shot as the album progressed – clearly fell under the spell of the unstoppable Helfgott.

'David was great,' Johns said after the session.

> It was the first time he'd ever played on a song that wasn't really classical, so it was an interesting experience for all of us, I think. David played his piano part like a classical composition. Then he started improvising around what he felt, which was exactly what I was looking for. Only a pianist as inspired as he is could have managed what he did.

Producer Launay was another Helfgott convert, describing the session as 'probably the most amazing day of our lives'. And true to character, Helfgott had the final word: 'The prodigies are alright, it's the parents who need advice,' he mumbled. 'I have plenty of emotion sickness myself.' He would later reconnect with Johns when he was invited to his 2003 wedding, an event Helfgott described as 'very beautiful'.

The band's only regret was that they weren't able to capture on tape the words 'Here we go into musicland' that Helfgott muttered each time he began to play. ('Sounds like me, so I guess I did say it,' Helfgott later confirmed.) It would have been the perfect opening line for an album where the band proved there was more to Silverchair's music than screaming riffs and hammer-of-the-gods rhythms.

As the *Neon Ballroom* sessions continued into the first week of September, more guests added their parts. The album's liner notes will attest that Paul Mac 'attacked' the piano on 'Anthem', 'Spawn Again' and 'Satin Sheets'. (Mac hit the keys so hard that during recordings for their next album, *Diorama*, a piano tuner was needed after every session he worked on.) Midnight Oil's Jim Moginie, who was to become a Silverchair studio regular and actually ended up on a shortlist to produce their next album, added what the band fondly dubbed 'keyboards Mogenius' to 'Anthem', 'Ana's Song', 'MissYou Love', 'Dearest Helpless', 'Do You Feel the Same', 'Paint Pastel Princess' and 'Point of View'. Sydney musical journeyman Chris Abrahams played piano on 'Black Tangled Heart' and 'Without You', a track that would finally appear, in an updated version, on 2002's *Diorama*. Jane Scarpantoni, whose string arrangement on *Freak Show*'s 'Cemetery' was the centrepoint of that album, added various arrangements to *Neon Ballroom*, along with eight other violinists and cellists. And Johns's long-time companion, his dog Sweep, howled during the album's closer, 'Steam Will Rise'. It was every bit the team effort.

Johns was particularly engrossed when working with Scarpantoni. Whereas 'Cemetery' had been written as a ballad and only had strings added as an afterthought, Johns was now writing with strings in mind – especially strings as arranged by Scarpantoni:

> She was classically trained but had a rock mind. She understands my language; I describe things more as scenery or pictures, and she latched on and got the right kind of mood.

Not that Johns completely understood her language. There's a priceless moment on Hambling's *Emotion Pictures* when she mentions the classical term 'legato' (which is translated in layman's term as 'smoothly') to Johns. He mugs for the camera, replying, 'Yeah, right, more "legato".' But you sensed that Johns was storing the information away, as his musical vocabulary increased day by day. The studio was no longer somewhere to bash out songs and then rattle around the corridors on trolleys, as he, Gillies and Joannou had done in the past. There were no girlie mag centrefolds decorating the vocal booth this time around. Now it was a place where Johns could give some life to the musical pictures in his head. This was serious business.

Despite being 'smoothed out' by the anti-depressants he'd been prescribed, Johns was at his best in the studio. He was learning that the thrill he'd lost in performing had been substituted by this new kick. It was now more of a home to him than the stage or even The Loft in Gillies's garage. A significant shift had occurred in Silverchair's world – the band renowned for 'going off' live were becoming studio craftsmen.

Johns reasoned:

When I first started, it was more about playing live and everything was about energy. Everything was about being really loud and playing live. [But] the thing that keeps me doing it is just creating music and exploring different elements of musical and lyrical angles.

Yet in spite of their musical progress, and Launay's success at defusing some inner-band tension in the rehearsal room during pre-production, the *Neon Ballroom* sessions were still the most taxing of the band's recording life.

Johns was recovering from his eating disorder, and Gillies and Joannou could sense the discomfort that permeated every session. Said Gillies:

It was like this elastic band of tension was pulled tight around us. It was everything – Daniel wasn't well, we were having to do another record, thinking whether this is what we really wanted to do. We were also thinking that if our lead singer's not well and doesn't really want to do it, well, then, shit, I don't want to do it.

Launay's studio perfectionism – he'd often ask for twenty or more takes of individual parts – didn't make the situation any easier.

'Ana's Song' was the last track recorded, and it took some hard talking by Johns to convince everyone else that the song belonged on the album. Johns hadn't revealed the song to Watson until late in the sessions, when they were doing string overdubs at Sydney's Paradise Studios. Watson recognised that it was the ideal second single, but after a few listens to the song, knew that its anorexia theme was a major controversy just waiting to happen. Watson put in a call to John O'Donnell and told him to drop everything and get down to the studio. When he heard the song, the Murmur boss agreed that it was a great song but also agreed there was no way it could go on the album. As an ex-journalist, O'Donnell could visualise the headlines that a song like this would generate.

Watson and O'Donnell put in a call to Johns. 'We told him he had no idea of the scrutiny this would subject him to,' says Watson.

> He was just coming out of a dark place – he didn't want to be thrust back into it. Particularly not as the single that's meant to sum up the whole album. Which, of course, it does.

But the song's lyrics were simply too personal, too close to what Johns had (just) survived while he was writing the album, for it to be excluded. He told Watson and O'Donnell that he wanted to make an emotionally true record, and in order to do that, the track had to stay. 'Because it was so honest as a song,' Johns said, 'I didn't want to censor myself at all.' It was a wise move. 'Ana's Song' stayed.

After almost two months of recording – a far cry from the rushed sessions for *Frogstomp* and the stop-start creation of *Freak Show* – *Neon Ballroom* seemed ready to throw open its doors. But Johns and Launay discovered one final hitch. Having just spent a week in Mangrove Studios laying down vocals and various other music (mainly provided by Midnight Oil's Moginie), they detected a strange, muffled quality to Johns's vocals, which in playback sounded as if a sheet had been laid across the speakers. It was never determined what the exact cause was, but his vocals had to be re-recorded. (By the time of their next album, the studio had been rebuilt.)

A genuinely pissed-off Johns took a fortnight's break to regain his physical and emotional strength. In those two weeks 'there was a lot of smashing things because of the frustration' but Johns felt gratified when his vocals were finally done. 'All the struggles were worth it. We've made an album that combines lots of different sounds and instruments that you don't usually hear together,' Johns commented at the end of the recording sessions. Then he, Watson and Launay got ready to decamp to Los Angeles for three weeks of mixing, where Launay would mix every track bar 'Miss You Love' and the single version of 'Anthem for the Year 2000', which were presided over by Kevin Shirley.

'We wanted to carve our own little piece of turf, blending futuristic noises with more classic influences,' Johns said as he left for LA.

Then he added, in a telling kiss-off to grunge:

We're fed up with all the usual comparisons that people keep making about our music. I wanted to make guitar [rock] pretty much a non-issue. I wanted us to make an album that was different from everything else that's out right now.

Neon Ballroom hit the Australian stores on 8 March 1999. As statements of musical independence go, it was a success. Though not shy of Johns's trademark force-ten riffs, it broke the band out of the grunge ghetto that had characterised *Frogstomp* and *Freak Show*. The opener, 'Emotion Sickness', set the tone for the entire album. Instead of a monster riff to open the disc, there's a neo-classical orchestration, introducing a tense, terse psychodrama enhanced by Helfgott's piano interlude and a surging soundscape. Johns's voice drifts for much of the song, floating, until he suddenly bursts into life, screaming, 'Get up! Get up! Everything is clearly dying,' as if they were his final words on Earth.

Daniel Johns (right) and Ben Gillies in The Loft above the Gillies family's garage. All the Silver-parents were hugely supportive of their kid's chosen career, although Gillies's mother would sometimes ask them to turn down the volume. (All photos by Tony Mott, except as otherwise noted)

Johns, Gillies and Chris Joannou (from left) during the photo shoot for the 'Tomorrow' EP. (Gillies is wearing a T-shirt celebrating their recent win at Youthrock.) 'They were absolutely dreadful,' a grumbling resident told the *Newcastle Herald* after witnessing the band at a Newcastle street fair. 'The music was amplified, it was loud and it was really bad.'

The raw appeal of Johns, Gillies and Joannou (from left) was obvious, especially to someone like Sony's John Watson. 'When you're that age you don't make music to get laid or to make money,' he said. 'You like the noise you make when you bang on your guitar. All great music is born from that.'

Johns learned early on that his guitar was a handy billboard for his preferred band, or cause, of choice. Here he pledges his allegiance to nu-metal heroes Korn; at other times he would give props to Fugazi, Animal Liberation and many others.

A NEW TOMORROW

Silverchair cleaned up at the 1995 ARIAs, winning gongs for Best New Talent, Best Debut Single. Best Australian Single and Highest Selling Single ('Tomorrow'), as well as Best Debut Album. To end their night of nights, they jammed Radio Birdman's 'New Race' with You Am I's Tim Rogers (second from right, bottom photo), another of their heroes. 'Shit, it was funny.' Johns recalled. (Top photo: Newspix/News Limited)

JEFF APTER

Another album, another trophy for the mantelpiece. A cross-eyed Gillies, a mildly impressed Johns and Joannou (from left) with their gongs from the awards hosted by *Hot Metal* magazine, circa *Freak Show*.

Joannou. Johns and Gillies (from left), circa *Freak Show*. 1997. Compared to their debut LP, the record was a Failure in North America, but it still shifted more than 500,000 copies. 'They were growing as players and I think Daniel was really growing as a songwriter.' said *Rolling Stone*'s David Fricke.

A NEW TOMORROW

Joannou, Johns and Gillies (from left) prior to launching *Freak Show* at the Circus Oz tent in Sydney's Moore Park, 20 January, 1997. The band kicked out the jams during their 55-mimite set, but Johns's on-stage T-shirt – which read 'Nobody knows I'm a lesbian' – left the crowd scratching their heads.

Johns rocking Luna Park, 26 July 1997, at a fundraiser tor the Reach Out appeal. The live video for their single 'The Door' was taken from tins set, which was played in front of Triple J prizewinners.

Johns revealed a darkly twisted sense of humour during the Freak Show dates in 1997. He would dabble with 'Advance Australia Fair" between songs and took to introducing 'Abuse Me' as 'a song about masturbation'.

Abuse me: Despite the best efforts of manager John Watson and label head John O'Donnell, the band became tabloid newspaper fodder, being on the receiving end of AVOs from women they'd never met and facing accusations of providing the soundtrack to murder. The May 1999 Australian *Rolling Stone* cover story, where Johns came clean about his eating disorder, grabbed both headlines and newsstand sales. It became one of the magazine's best selling issues ever. (Cover courtesy of Australian *Rolling Stone*)

Johns was still struggling with the aftermath of life-threatening anorexia during the sessions for 1999's *Neon Ballroom* LP. 'I [didn't] understand how all my clothes [had] stretched and I still looked the same,' he would admit afterwards. He also feared that his food was being poisoned; eventually he reduced his food intake to just an occasional piece of fruit. (Courtesy of Eleven)

A NEW TOMORROW

While touring the *Neon Ballroom* album, Johns started to notice how far he'd drifted from Gillies and Joannou, his childhood friends and bandmates. He considered splitting up the band at the end of the tour. 'Ben and Chris are enormously alike.' he said, 'whereas I'm different. But I respect them, you know?"

JEFF APTER

The band cleaned up at the 2002 ARIAs, and *Diorama* raced hack into the local charts.' We've [always] been told [of] the importance of promotion.' Johns said afterwards, 'and we've gone "bullshit". Now all we did was turn up ... and sell all these fucking records!'

Although fit at the start of the *Diorama* recording sessions. Johns's health deteriorated with the onset of chronic reactive arthritis. His meat-tree diet didn't help. 'He was starting to get these rashes,' said producer David Bottrill, 'and I said to him. "Don't just eat the fruit plate!" ' (Photo: Adrienne Overall)

A NEW TOMORROW

Johns (far left) plants one on Van Dyke Parks, while producer David Bottrill (far right) and Gillies look on during the *Diorama* sessions, 2002. 'I know there s a lot of dark meat on that bird,' the legendary US arranger said of Johns, who he likened to Brian Wilson, 'but lurking in there is the voice of the human spirit.' (Photo: Adrienne Overall)

Johns recently slammed a tabloid report that his marriage to Natalie Imbruglia – they wed in Port Douglas on New Year's Eve 2003 – was on the skids. 'Those things give me the shits. We heard about it and just went. "Who is this source?" Time will tell if our marriage is on the rocks.' Here they play tourist in Pompeii. Italy. September 2005. (Photo: Lucky Mat/Getty Images)

157

WaveAid, held at the SCG on 29 January 2005, marked the reawakening of Silverchair. 'Watching Midnight Oil,' Johns admitted, 'we figured we only had one opportunity to be a great, great band. The great ones are the bands who have been together since they were kids, sorted out their shit, and kept going and twenty years later they were still killing it.'

A NEW TOMORROW

Johns and Paul 'Yoko Quo' Mac, raising the roof on Sydney's Gaelic Club, March 2006. 'It had to be better than a T-shirt that read Linda [McCartney] or Courtney [Love],' Johns said of the cheeky slogan on his piano man's top, which featured the name of the woman who allegedly split up the Beatles.

Johns, Mac, Gillies and Joannou (from left), Gaelic Club, March 2006. Gillies, for one, found this small-scale gig one of the most nerve-racking of the band's career.' I was scared shitless.' he confessed, 'because we knew everyone in the crowd and were worried they'd be judging us.'

A NEW TOMORROW

Spurred on by their blazing Gaelic Club set – 'I just walked on stage and immediately felt comfortable,' Johns said – Silverchair also burned brightly at the Great Escape, held at Homebush on 14 April 2006. Johns slugged lustily from a bottle of bourbon throughout the set.

Johns on the mic during sessions for their fifth album, *Young Modern*, March 2006. 'I want it to be sprawling and unpredictable,' he said of their new LP. 'If people like it, they like it. I know I'm going to like it.'

Gillies (left) and Joannou during the *Yonng Modern* sessions. March 2006. According to Gillies, 'I honestly believe that if you put us in a room with any of the top ten bands in the world, we could take them. It's not arrogance, either.'

A NEW TOMORROW

Chris Joannou. Ben Gillies and Daniel Johns (from left), 2006. 'To be honest, over the years, even after *Freak Show* and *Neon Ballroom*, we've always taken time off after the record and didn't really know where we were going to go.' said Gillies. 'But I always knew in the back of my head that none of us were going to let Silverchair go.'

The song's selection as the album's opening track was a smart move on the part of Johns (and manager Watson), even though Launay and several of those at Epic weren't so sure. If *Neon Ballroom* had opened with 'Anthem for the Year 2000' (already a Number Three hit in Australia by the time of the album's release), it would have been seen as an entirely different album, as many reviews are dictated by an album's opening cut, which typically establishes the mood of what's to follow. Johns realised that, but boldly went with his instinct.

And the contrariness of the move must have appealed to him, too:

We were warned not to do it, because it would alienate and confuse people, and turn them off the album. But I found that really intriguing. As soon as someone said that to me, I said, 'Yeah, I'm definitely going to do it.' It shows the ambition behind the record and sums up what I was trying to do.

'Ana's Song (Open Fire)', the album's third track, drove home the point that this was a new Silverchair. With Jim Moginie's keyboards adding woozy texture, Johns worked his way through his troubled year as if he were on the analyst's couch. Gillies's powerhouse drumming and Joannou's solid bottom end left their mark, but it was Johns's searing honesty that elevated this track, as it did the bulk of *Neon Ballroom*.

Johns's personal anguish was underscored on several tracks by Scarpantoni's classical leanings, which meshed perfectly into the lush 'Paint Pastel Princess', the turgid 'Black Tangled Heart', and 'Miss You Love', a gentle, waltz-like ballad with a dark underbelly. 'I wanted to write a song that people could dedicate to their lover on the radio or dance to,' Johns confessed, when asked about 'Miss You Love'. But this was a love song with a twist, according to Johns. 'It's actually about not having love and not being able to find love, and being lonely.' If there was one track on *Neon Ballroom* that summed up Johns's tortured soul, this was it: an anti-love song, combining a gorgeous melody and a perversely glum lyric.

However, the band still had a moshpit – their established fanbase – to satisfy. Tracks such as the pure punk fury of 'Spawn Again' and 'Dearest Helpless' were throw-backs to the simpler times of their first two albums.

A NEW TOMORROW

Although neither track was a standout on *Neon Ballroom* – 'Spawn Again' was actually pretty dreadful – they both packed a kick like a mule, bound to send bodies flying live. Still, you couldn't help but think Johns was paying lip service to the fans who had snapped up *Freak Show* and *Frogstomp*. These songs were for them, not for him.

But how much musical experimentation could Johns get away with before his audience started looking elsewhere? It was a conundrum that marked much of *Neon Ballroom*. If anything, *Ballroom* adequately managed to fulfil Johns's need to scratch his creative itch without alienating the band faithful. For every lush, near cinematic mood piece there was a raw, bleeding rocker. As each-way bets go, the album was a winner. But with the benefit of hindsight, perhaps Johns was selling himself just a little short, even if the album does contain the best songs he'd written to this point: 'Miss You Love', 'Emotion Sickness' and 'Ana's Song (Open Fire)'. *Neon Ballroom* may have been an album of both killer and filler, but it was a necessary stepping stone for the epic, ambitious sprawl of 2002's *Diorama*.

Astute local critic Barry Divola, writing in *Who* magazine, got it right. He described *Neon Ballroom* as 'an experiment that didn't quite have the *cojones* to back up the vision'. However, most critics acknowledged *Neon Ballroom*'s broader vision. *Massive* magazine, for one, took a vive la différence approach: '*Neon Ballroom* is different, Silverchair is experimenting and the results are awesome,' they reported. Craig Mathieson, a close follower of the band, gave it a four-star review for Australian *Rolling Stone*: 'It's an ambitious, varied record, one brimming with intelligent ideas – some not always realised – but worthy nonetheless.' He then added that '*Neon Ballroom* is a sustained, adult work . . . The musical sophistication takes Silverchair beyond being a [typical] three-piece.'

Most overseas press also praised the band's ambition, if not always the mixed bag of an album it had produced. American *Rolling Stone* awarded the record a three-star review, but measured their praise. 'The problem is that the kids can't decide what they want to do when they grow up,' wrote a mildly condescending Neva Chonin. The review softened up, though, finally admitting that, '*Neon Ballroom* is what you'd expect from a young band going through its awkward stage.' (In their 'feedback' section, most Silverfans disagreed. One disgruntled fan fired back: 'This album was the best thing to come out of one of the worst times ever for rock.' In fact, it was a generally awful time for music, a year when the charts were dominated by a resurrected Cher, teen queen Britney Spears, the Goo Goo Dolls and Latin himbo Ricky Martin.)

Similarly, Ken Advent in the *Cleveland Free Times* wrote that:

> Silverchair is making a concerted effort to stretch the band's musical boundaries... When Silverchair is on top of their game, there are flashes of a visionary band like Pink Floyd filtered through the heavy guitars.

Johns's development as a songwriter was often singled out. *Electric Music Online* praised the album's 'some oomph' but added that:

> The biggest credit has to go to Daniel Johns. His song-writing skills have improved out of sight – no longer is he simply copying his peers and influences, [he's] writing songs with their own structure and sound.

New Zealand's hard-rock mag, *Rip It Up*, which gave the album a mixed review, admitted that 'all the time you know Daniel Johns's songwriting skill has progressed beyond playing three chords and shouting very loudly.'

As the reviews started filtering in, Silverchair's attention turned to their upcoming tour. In order to recreate the lush, orchestrated sound of much of their new album, they spent two weeks at home, in late November 1998, auditioning keyboardists. The band had tried out half a dozen players before settling on Sam Holloway, late of moody Melburnians Cordrazine, whose first (and last) album, *From Here to Wherever*, had brushed the Australian Top 10 before the band imploded. Not only was Holloway classically trained, but he also looked good on stage and had a laddish nature that sat well off-stage with Joannou and Gillies. They admitted that Holloway's 'good blokiness' was as big a factor as his keyboard skills when it came to their final decision.

After the Christmas and New Year break, the band began rehearsing with Holloway in Newcastle on 4 January. His first public appearance with Silverchair was on 21 January, but the show was so low-key that only the truly faithful chairpage addicts knew about it. Billing themselves as the Australian Silverchair Show, the now four-piece shocked locals at

Newcastle's Cambridge Hotel as they aired new songs and dusted off early standards. 'We just thought it would be a fun, low-pressure way to kick off a tour,' said Gillies. 'We've got a lot of new songs, so we wanted to try them out in front of a real crowd.' It was their first public appearance for over twelve months and the last time for a couple of years that they'd get to play such an intimate, low-stress gig. From now on in, every show would be about selling the product.

The next day, the revitalised band was in Sydney, shooting an anarchic clip for the album's first single, 'Anthem for the Year 2000', with American director Gavin Bowden. He'd shot videos for MTV darlings the Red Hot Chili Peppers, Live and Rage Against the Machine, which definitely gave his CV the right kind of buzz. After all, Silverchair's career needed a kick-start after the moderate performance of their second album in the US. In keeping with their new 'keep it different' policy, the band had sent out invitations via their fan club and chairpage, again, inviting anyone interested to come and get involved in the massive crowd scene that forms the heart of the video. On the second day of shooting, 1200 hopefuls turned up in Sydney's Martin Place, transforming it into a seething mass of Silver-madness. Johns had expected 300. 'Anthem' blared repeatedly through an outdoor PA during the shooting, as the army of extras staged their scripted riot and were sprayed with industrial-strength hoses.

Another feature of the clip was a cameo from Australian actor Maggie Kirkpatrick, best known as 'The Freak' from Australia's long-running 1970s TV drama *Prisoner*. In the clip, Kirkpatrick plays a robot, a Pauline Hanson-like figure that serves as a visual metaphor for the song's 'authority sucks' message, a sentiment Johns described as 'youth rebelling against people who are supposedly more important'. It turns out that Kirkpatrick shared more with the band than even she knew: not only was she a Novo-castrian, but her niece and nephew were schoolmates of the band.

'My first reaction was, "Why me?"' she told the *Sunday Herald-Sun*.

I later found out that the boys were from Newcastle, and being an old Newcastle girl myself, I was more than prepared to help them out. I encourage anyone from my own town.

Not that Silverchair had much time to swap hometown stories with the TV star. By the time the water cannons had been shut down and Martin Place had been dried and cleared, the band were on a plane to Melbourne, en route to a headlining spot at the Peaches & Cream Festival. Ahead of them lay another heavy year's worth of travelling, playing – and messing with their audience's heads.

* * *

The Peacemaker: An interview with Nick Launay

British-born, LA-based (and occasional Sydney resident) Nick Launay produced *Freak Show* and *Neon Ballroom,* as well as Silverchair's latest album, *Young Modern.* In the process, he coped with inner-band tensions, argumentative Indians and a sweet, strange genius named David Helfgott. His subsequent production credits include Lou Reed's *Animal Serenade,* Nick Cave & the Bad Seeds' *Abattoir Blues/Lyre of Orpheus* and the Living End's *Roll On.*

How did you first become involved with the Innocent Criminals?
Robert [Hambling] rang me about 'Tomorrow'; this is before either of the two Johns heard it. He said, 'You've got to hear this tape; it's amazing, I want your opinion.' He was working for SBS. They were inundated with tapes and CDs [for the *nomad* competition] but hadn't determined who was going to listen to them. He volunteered, and got it down to two or three – at the top was the Innocent Criminals. He played it to me and I was blown away by a couple of the songs.

What was the reaction of the other judges?
The SBS people didn't like the Innocent Criminals because it was too aggressive, too whingy.

What happened next?
Robert called Daniel's phone number and got his mum, who said he was at school. Robert assumed that Daniel was her boyfriend or her husband.

Once he realised the age he went back to the SBS people and said, 'This is insane; these people have got to win.'

How did you react to 'Tomorrow'?
To me it was the most tuneful song, the most memorable song on the tape. I spoke with Robert and suggested quite a radical rearrangement. He called me back the next day and asked if I could chop it up. I wasn't working at the time, so I edited it on my two-track. I did a cassette of it, gave it to Robert, he took it back to them. By then I was really into it and played it to three record companies – and Robert played it to I don't know how many No one bought it. They [the SBS staff] then asked Robert if he could ask me to go into the studio with them. I said, 'Absolutely, yes,' but I was leaving the next week to go to America. Then I got horribly ill; I couldn't get out of bed, I had to leave for America late, still ill. So I got on the phone to Phil McKellar, who did a great job. He was the Triple J guy, and the free Triple J studio time was part of the prize. I told him what I was going to do – add a guitar solo, that kind of thing.

When did you next hear 'Tomorrow'?
When I came back from America, on Qantas, I heard this song which I thought I really knew. It sounded like something I'd done or been involved with but I could not work it out. Then I looked at the magazine and it said 'Silverchair'. I thought, 'Who the hell is Silverchair?' When I got back home I finally worked it out and found out it had been Number One for seven weeks.

Did you want to produce their first album?
I wanted to work with them when I started editing the [demo] version – and told everyone that. By the time I got back they were already in the studio. I wasn't offered the job because I was out of the country. I honestly thought, having taken the demo of 'Tomorrow' around to record companies and having it rejected, that I could have taken it around after I got back and got them a deal. But it happened much quicker than that, which never happens.

What did you think of Frogstomp?
I think it was perfect. It was done quickly, it was done with Kevin Shirley, who's very 'get them in, bash it out', which is very different to what I do. I would probably have worked on getting better takes, getting into sounds. I wouldn't have necessarily made it less raw, but I would have worked longer on it. Maybe two weeks [laughs]. The band's attention span then was very short. When I worked with them a year later, when they were sixteen, it was still very short.

So what happened then?
When it came to doing *Freak Show*, I'd met up with them a few times, but it didn't click with them at all that I was the guy who did the edit on 'Tomorrow'. I think halfway through doing *Freak Show* the conversation came up and the penny dropped. They had no idea. Anyway, I was about to go to America again and John Watson called me and asked would I like to do the next Silverchair record – and he said to bear in mind that Andy Wallace was going to mix it. I said, 'Well, that's not a bad thing.' I was about to go to America and meet a band and see if I wanted to work with them. That definitely wasn't as exciting as working with Silverchair, so I came back.

What went on during pre-production?
I went up to meet them [in Newcastle] and it was the funniest thing. I arrived there by train. I brought with me, from America, a big snare drum that I'd bought that used to belong to Soundgarden and I thought it might sound good on their record. I'd talked to Ben a few times and told him that if he really liked it he could buy it, which he did. So I arrived with this really heavy thing – it's made out of sewer pipe, solid steel and it's eight or nine inches deep. I'm outside Ben's house and I saw these kids on skateboards. It's stupid, I know, but it's only when I got up close to them and they're going, 'You Nick?' that I realised they were really so young. It was really bizarre to me – they were such a great band and they were so young. Nothing was serious.

You were their chauffeur, right?

A NEW TOMORROW

Well, then Ben came up to me and said, 'You got a car? You wanna go for a drive?' And I said, 'Yes, but I came by train.' And he said, 'No, I've got a car.' And I was thinking, why was he asking me this? Then I realised they were so young they had to go with an adult. So we went into the garage and he's got this big, powerful car. And they jump in, all excited, when out jumps Ben's mum. She said, 'Hang on a minute, where are you going?' Then she pointed at me and said, 'Young man, can I have a word with you inside, please?' And she said, 'They're young, they're impressionable and they're hoons. You're the adult, you've got to be responsible.'

I got back in the car, feeling like I've been told off. I told the band and they just went, 'Yeah, yeah, yeah,' and as soon as we were around the corner Ben floored it. It was just insane; they're all laughing their heads off. Then we went up this hill and there were all these girls coming back from school. The guys slowed down – and then the girls suddenly realised it was Silverchair. Off we took, with girls running behind. Then we drove around Newcastle and they showed me the sights. It was hard for me, because I didn't want to come over like the adult but at the same time I had to be careful because an accident could have happened at any time. I had to tread a very fine line.

What's this about you going 'egging' with the band?
We went in and rehearsed and played a few songs. That lasted about half an hour, given their attention span. I said, 'Can I hear another one?' They said, 'Nah, that's the lot.' I said, 'Well, that was three songs, not enough for an album.' So I think I squeezed six songs out of them. Then we went for another drive. They said to me, 'Have you ever been egging?' I had no idea what that was. So they stopped at the gas station and got some eggs, and they were driving around egging things, which I thought was just insane. But the excitement level ... I was a bit of a kid, too, and still am. I guess they thought I was OK, because I got the job.

How did you connect with Johns?
I relate to him very well – we're both arty, skinny types. We're not blokey types. Newcastle is a pretty blokey type place, which isn't Daniel.

How did the Indian ensemble come to play on 'Petrol & Chlorine'?

Daniel said to me that he didn't think there should be drums on the song. It was quite a shock. Ben was like, 'What?' I asked whether he meant it should just be guitar, vocal and bass, and he said, 'No, but I don't reckon it should be drums.' I asked what he wanted for percussion – shakers, that type of thing? He said, 'No, no, no hippie shit. I reckon it should sound like one of those docos on SBS.' The next day I brought in some CDs of Indian music and African music and Latin American music and played them to him. When I played the Indian CD he went, 'Yeah, that's it.' It was a tabla he was hearing. Then I thought that I should play him some Beatles stuff – I played him 'Within You Without You' and he heard what we thought was a sitar. He thought that was cool.

I ended up calling the Indian Consulate who had a list of musicians. One of them was a guy called Pandit Suman. I went out to Bankstown; he had a studio where he taught traditional dance. We got talking and I played him what we'd recorded of the song. He picked up a tabla and started playing and it was absolutely perfect, spot on. I complimented him and he told me that he used to be in a band in India. He showed me a picture that had three or four musicians in it. He pointed to one and said, 'This man is called Ravi Shankar.' I thought, how about that? I'm in Sydney, Australia and the first guy that I find has played with the guy who played with the Beatles. But he hadn't heard the Beatles song Shankar played on. I played it to him and he identified the instrument, which I thought was a sitar. It's a one-stringed instrument [the tempura] that follows the vocal. I said that's what we wanted and he said he'd organise everything.

Tell me about the day in the studio.
The day came and we realised we needed someone to go there and pick them up. I called John O'Donnell and the only, car Sony had was a limo. So we sent a stretch limo to pick them up. Two hours later all these Indians, in full dress, arrive in this big stretch limo. It was hilarious.

So they came in, but they'd never used headphones before and we found out that their timing is different – they don't count in fours at all as we do. They work out the metre and then go from there. I didn't know this at the time. Daniel was dying, he was going nuts – this guy can't count! It was a combination of hysterically funny things; they even started arguing in [an] Indian [language] at one point. In hindsight, if I'd got Silverchair to play live with them, it would have been much quicker. But the basic recording was already done. It worked out, but it took a few hours.

A lot had changed within the band by the time of Neon Ballroom *– could you see that?*
There was a lot going on. The first album, they had all the songs, they went in and played it and bashed it out in seven days or whatever. The second album, one half was rock songs and half was experimental, where they had no idea what was going to happen. I think they found that fun, they were more curious about how things worked. *Neon Ballroom* was a completely different thing. That whole thing about being so famous and not being able to go outside had really hurt Daniel, plus he'd started on his not eating thing. He didn't hang out with Chris and Ben at all. He stayed in his room, didn't go out. Everyone was worried about his mental state.

How did you convince Daniel to play his new songs?
No one knew what songs he had and he was convinced the songs he had weren't right for Silverchair and that was it. He had a lot of pressure on him from the record company to make another Silverchair record, which he didn't want to do. He'd been listening to a lot of different kinds of music. He didn't relate to Ben and Chris – and he's not a communicator, he wasn't about to get on the phone. He didn't know how to deal with this.

I went up there, lived in his parents' house for maybe a week, got him to play me the songs. Then I went to Ben and Chris. Chris was no problem, he had a very good view of it, he accepted that if Daniel didn't want to make an album, that was it. But he wanted his friend back. Ben was different. He's a tough kid. He said he didn't know what was going on, why wasn't Daniel talking to him, he thought they should make another album, blah, blah, blah.

What do you think was really going on?

The more I got into it, it became very personal, and Ben was really, really upset that his friend hadn't called him. I told him that I thought that he was Daniel's best friend in the world. I told him: he doesn't believe you'll like any of his songs and he doesn't want to play them because he's scared you'll reject them. He told me he wouldn't do it, he likes what he does and he didn't want to do a rock record, anyway.

Ben was listening to dance music; they were all growing up. Chris was great; he was like the glue between them. He told me where Ben's head was at. So what I proposed was a day of rehearsals. They'd go in, Daniel would play them the songs and then they could tell him what they thought. It was really emotional; on-the-point-of-crying kind of stuff. Basically, we went in, Daniel sat on a chair, with no eye contact with either of them, and went, 'I've got this song.' He played it and of course it was a beautiful song.

Then Ben would go, 'I reckon that's heaps good – what if you put a beat to it?' Ben, of course, is one of the best drummers in the world, so he started playing this beat to this song that Daniel felt shouldn't be a Silverchair song – and it worked. Before you know it, they're all laughing and talking. I remember turning to Chris and saying, 'Will you look at these two? They should give each other a hug.' I don't think they did, but it was a major turning point. Over the next week we found out he had a whole album's worth of songs, half of them rock songs, half of them not, and everyone loved it.

Do you think Ben felt rejected because none of his songs made Neon Ballroom?
I think he did and does from an artistic expression point of view, but from an ego point of view he doesn't. I think the tension about that kind of issue came from their individual managers – that is, their mums. And I don't mean that in a nasty way; it was just a concern thing. They look after their own son's interests; all mums do. I think that was something Daniel was aware of and that's why he was very resistant to showing these songs; he didn't want to upset Ben. It was a caring thing – it wasn't a case of, 'My songs are better.' This tension has happened with every single band I've worked with.

On Neon Ballroom *you had a memorable experience with David Helfgott. What was the genesis of that?*
It started when we met Larry [Muhoberac, who composed the arrangement for 'Emotion Sickness'], me, Daniel and [John] Watson. He was perfect, because he understood rock music and classical music. Larry would say to Daniel, 'Well, what do you think should happen?' And I remember Daniel being in this huge almost fluorescent green beanie – he looked like an alien – saying, 'Oh, I dunno, you know, kind of, Bling! Bling! Bling!' And Larry asked him [how] these blings should go. And Daniel would tell him in the funniest way – he'd dance around the room, doing it with these great gestures. And Larry could actually do it. Daniel turned around and went, 'That's it.' And they went through the whole song.

The stuff he was coming out with was brilliant – and I don't think Daniel realised. He'd never done anything like this before. I really do think that these two songs ['Petrol & Chlorine' and 'Emotion Sickness'] are the beginning of what he would go on to do. This was definitely a turning point. He realised that as long as he could articulate the music he was hearing to talented people, he'd be OK.

Was it difficult to record Helfgott's part for 'Emotion Sickness'?
Difficult? Yes. The biggest problem was that, again, like the Indian musicians, when he plays, everyone follows him. But with Silverchair he was listening through headphones and playing along, which is something he hadn't done. So we had to do it line by line. With his kind of piano playing, it's extremely fast – he plays so many notes in one run. We had to work out how we'd get this crazy guy to do it.

He doesn't stop talking; he has no inner voice, everything he thinks, he says. When he met Ben, he was going, 'Ah, Ben, Ben, the timekeeper, very strong, he's the man with the beats.' Then he met me and said, 'The decision maker! The decision maker! Where would we be without the decision maker?' He hugs you while he talks to you. He's very tactile. A beautiful person. He kept saying how angel-like Daniel was – 'You've been sent to sing to us like an angel.' [And] that's exactly what it's like to work with Daniel.

How did you keep him in check?
He couldn't sit still at the piano unless someone was hugging him; he also needed Larry to be near him to tell him what came next. The end result was this crazy thing of me playing one part of the tape, him and Larry sitting on a bench at the piano with Larry hugging him with one arm and pointing with the other, saying, 'OK, David, now we're going to play this part,' and talking him through it.

As Larry explained this to him in a very schoolteacher way – because you have to – David would be saying, 'Very exciting! Like this bit!' When he was being counted in he said he was going to be like a racing car, waiting for the start. Just as I'd count to four, David would shout, 'And here we go!' Then he'd slam this poor piano, and as soon as he'd finish the last note he'd shout again, 'There she goes! It's a good one!' Could you imagine doing that for three hours?

It took a long time to do the song, and we had to be very patient, but we did it. Then we had to take the tape and put it through Pro Tools to get rid of all the talking. It was a wild experience for all; I left the studio that day with my mind blown. I was very lucky to have been in that room. He's unique – an amazing musician and an amazing person.

What are your memories of the Neon Ballroom *sessions?*
Very comfortable. Compared with other bands, it went extremely smoothly. When you're making artistic stuff – be it painting, making music, whatever – and you've got more than one person, friction is what makes it great. The closest band I can think of [by comparison] is Talking Heads. In my mind there's no doubt that those musicians are the best musicians David Byrne could work with. But he was so close to it he couldn't see it. It's the same with Daniel; Ben and Chris are the best musicians he could work with. Whether he sees that, I don't know. It's a tricky thing.

Chapter Six

CAN I GET A HALLELUJAH?

> OK, listen. We spent several fucking hours signing hundreds of CD covers and it was all for you. They're fifteen bucks – over there.
> Daniel Johns charms another American audience, 1999

'Oh shit, we're all going to die really, really dramatically.'
A nervous Daniel Johns was sitting in Sydney airport, alongside Gillies and Joannou, looking out at a threatening sky. Those were the first words he uttered when the band convened to begin the Australian leg of their 1999 world tour, promoting *Neon Ballroom*. It was 2 March, and the trio were en route to Brisbane – and then much of the Western world – as the story of Johns's near breakdown started to become public knowledge. After some pre-release album promotion with one-off shows in London, New York and New Orleans, this was the start of the real grind.

When they arrived at Brisbane's Dockside Apartments, prior to their 3 March show at the Tivoli Cabaret, Gillies, Joannou and new boy Holloway hit the pool, as a rainstorm burst through the 98 per cent Queensland humidity. Johns was holed up in the hotel with a journalist, talking about himself, a situation that would be repeated throughout this year of touring.

The Australian *Rolling Stone* music editor at the time, Elissa Blake, was travelling with the band, writing a cover story for the magazine's May 1999 issue. But what she thought would be a typical band-on-tour piece quickly changed into something radically different and far more serious. Johns needed to spill. He felt it was important – almost a community service, in fact – to let Blake know exactly what he'd been through during 1998, prior to the recording of *Neon Ballroom*.

Almost nonchalantly he turned to Blake:

A lot of people have been very worried about me.
Do you want to talk about it?
Yeah, I do.
What was going on while you were writing this album?
I was dealing with a lot of psychological things. I cut myself off from everyone that I knew for about six months.
Was it depression?
It was associated with depression. I started getting really bad anxiety trouble. I ended up getting medication because every time I left the house I'd be really badly shaking and sweaty.

Johns then proceeded to detail his season in hell: the isolation, the panic attacks, his eating disorder, his fear that in the midst of his breakdown he might actually die. He even showed his medications to Blake – nine sheets of coloured pills, including two different varieties of sleeping pills. 'I'm just trying them out,' he said casually, as if he was talking about his favourite sweets.

Johns had spoken to a newspaper staffer two days earlier, and the morning after the first Australian show of the tour the local media had picked up on the story. 'Eating Disorder Rocks Teen Star', was the *Courier-Mail* headline that manager Watson read over his bacon and eggs. He was livid. Once again his band was front-page news for all the wrong reasons. Watson was especially livid that he'd been deceived into arranging a photo of a gaunt Johns, thinking it would be used to run with a live review of that night's show.

But Johns had willingly chosen to share his problem with his audience. Possibly, among his millions of fans, there was someone who could benefit from knowing that even Daniel Johns suffered typical (albeit extreme) teenage problems. Once Watson had calmed down, he began to accept what his youthful charge was trying to do by being so frank with journalists. 'I have a great deal of concern for Daniel as a human being,' he told Blake, explaining that 'he wanted to help other people and now we just have to do our best to help him.'

When Blake's story was published, Australian *Rolling Stone* was flooded with responses. Many were written by teenage girls with similar eating disorders who felt comforted by Johns's revelations. They wrote that they were relieved; they didn't feel alone anymore. Some even sent poems to Johns via the magazine. The volume of letters was so overwhelming that Blake forwarded many to John Watson, who then relayed them to Johns. It was the strongest response to a story that the magazine had ever had.

More was happening within Silverchair than the frontman's very public personal problems. Things had begun changing onstage, as well. It was as if by turning inwards offstage, Johns enabled himself to suddenly explode when he plugged in and played the band's new material. Six weeks earlier, at Cobram's Peaches & Cream festival, on the first official date of the tour, he turned up in a spangly, glittery top found in a Newtown op shop, which would become standard stage-wear during the *Neon Ballroom* tour. The old cargo pants and band T-shirts were dumped in the bottom of his closet. In the same way that his deeply felt songs were now the focus of the band, Johns had become the centre of attention on stage, slashing at his guitar and windmilling his arms like a young, blond, even-scrawnier Pete Townshend. The band chaperones were gone, school was out, and Daniel Johns had morphed into a seriously watchable, albeit unpredictable, rock star. In part, he was giving his fans exactly what they craved: a wild-haired, electrifying frontman. But Johns also knew there was a big difference between 'person' and 'persona'.

This inner conflict was astutely noted by *Rolling Stone*'s Craig Mathieson, who spotted the differences between 'Daniel of" Silverchair' and Daniel Johns:

> It's a complicated relationship. Daniel from Silverchair puts Daniel Johns in the public eye, where he feels uneasy. But Daniel from Silverchair also sells the albums, which satisfies Daniel Johns's self belief in his songwriting and quietly fierce ambition.

Not long after taking the stage in Cobram – a show watched by Sarah McLeod from the Supeijesus, who was soon to become Joannou's live-in partner – Johns launched into a barely decipherable tirade, one of dozens documented during the tour.

'Right,' he yelled:

> Put your hand up if you had a stage in your life where you felt alienated from the rest of the world. OK, yoga is for you. It stretches the mind and everything is about spirituality. Spirituality or drugs. You're gonna take your pick, right? Or Jesus, but Jesus at times can be very stressful. Because you don't know whether to read the Old or New Testament. Two different stories; it fucks me up.

You could hear a collective sigh of relief from the crowd when he ended his rant by screaming 'Are you ready to rock and roll?' as the band crashed into 'Pure Massacre'.

What this audience – and most other crowds during the almost one hundred dates Silverchair played during 1999 – didn't know was how hard it was for Johns to get on stage at all. While he might have been busting some of the most outrageous moves of his life while playing – roaring at the crowds, playing, as one review described, 'as if the power chords had taken over his body' – Johns was in the midst of a serious prescription-drug dependency. He needed pills to help him play, pills to help him come down from the show, pills to help him sleep. Every day was a variation on this medicated theme. Joannou, Gillies and Holloway were becoming tight; on tour they were often found together at the back of the bus bellowing such classic rock tunes as 'Sweet Home Alabama' at the top of their lungs, or checking out local hotspots. But Johns would be a million miles away, staring out of the window as the road flashed past him. Looking back, Gillies and Joannou agree that there were many moments on the *Neon Ballroom* tour, as there were during its recording, where 'you could just feel this tension in the air.'

Johns's manic onstage persona didn't help. His live raves took any number of perverse variations. In London, he responded to an audience taunt by referring to himself as 'a lesbian wanker'. In New York, before a crowd that included *Neon Ballroom* collaborator Jane Scarpantoni and *Rolling Stone*'s David Fricke, Johns fell into a rap about becoming Posh Spice, 'because I'm a bitch and I'm gonna be married to a famous soccer player'. At a key LA showcase, watched by startled Epic A&R staff, he gave an impromptu Bible reading. In Chicago he declared the Windy City 'my favourite city in the whole world. Favourite people, favourite neon lights, favourite balconies, favourite people on balconies'. In Melbourne he tried to explain to the sold-out crowd that eating a beaver saves trees, because 'Beavers eat trees, right? So the more beavers there are, the less trees, right? So, save the trees by eating the beavers – then there'll be less of them to eat the trees.' Sometimes it seemed as though he was disgusted by his audience, who he figured just wanted to hear 'Tomorrow', which Johns now played solo, in a truncated, acoustic version, and bang their heads. At other times it was as if Johns was playing some kind of macabre joke on himself and the concept of 'rock star'. (Looking back, he laughs long and hard about some of the peculiar statements he made on stage.)

Johns had also begun to talk to himself, frequently, between songs. Almost like a tennis player he was urging himself on ('I can do it'), or screaming obscenities. 'I hate you, I fucking hate you,' he yelled at himself in Minneapolis, before telling the crowd, 'OK, listen. We spent several fucking hours signing hundreds of CD covers and it was all for you. They're fifteen bucks – over there.' While the rest of the band played on, Johns was coming on like a bizarre cross between rock and roll madman and stand-up comic. Not surprisingly, Chinese whispers circulated that Johns was taking something stronger than anti-depressants, even though he's never owned up to indulging in anything heavier than pot and the occasional vodka tonic.

The fans were starting to notice how lost the frontman seemed. A German fan, writing on chairpage about Silverchair's Dusseldorf show on 4 April, noted that 'there was almost no contact between the band members', comparing the show, negatively, with the first time she had seen the band, in 1996, when 'they were three funny young guys who just had fun playing music.'

Two nights after the Dusseldorf show, back in the UK, Johns actually stopped the band's set midway through 'Pure Massacre' when a stage-diver was kicked by a security guard. 'Hey, what the fuck do you think you're doing, man?' Johns drawled, as the band crashed to a halt. 'You don't go kicking people like that.' Johns then led the band back into 'Massacre' as if nothing had happened. There was a similar incident in Vienna in mid

April, when a stage invader was dragged away by security in the midst of 'Anthem for the Year 2000'. 'Fuck the security!' Johns screamed. Then he repeated his antagonistic refrain, before returning to the song. Now it seemed as though both audiences and security were getting under Johns's skin. And the tour still had eight months left to run.

The notices for the tour were as mixed as Johns's attempts at humouring himself and his audience. Reviewing their 4 March Sydney show, the *Sydney Morning Herald* noted that 'what was meant to be a triumphant kick-off for the world tour was largely a forgettable evening.'

Shrewdly, reviewer Jon Casimir wrote:

> Johns increasingly appears to be fronting another band. While his colleagues cling to casual (almost invisible) stage behaviour and costume, Johns is now resplendent in spangly shirt and shiny eye shadow ... he has also acquired the full catalogue of rock god poses. There is a distance between the band members . . . Johns seems self-conscious, as if age and experience have leached some of the raw joy from the job of performing.

Writing about their Melbourne Forum show in *Inpress* magazine, Greg Cormack observed not only that 'Johns was definitely running this show,' but that 'not a smile, not a high five or even a word seemed to be exchanged between the three throughout the set.' Daniel Johns was experiencing the odd sensation of emerging from his shell onstage and yet feeling something close to contempt towards his audience. The antidepressants weren't helping his confused state.

The band were in Chicago on 15 March when *Neon Ballroom* debuted at Number One on the Australian album chart, repeating the runaway success of *Frogstomp* and *Freak Show*. It went on to sell 204,000 copies at home. The album was also released that day in North America, making its debut on the US charts a week later, at Number Fifty. It was certified gold (sales of 500,000) by the first week of April and would spend thirty weeks on the *Billboard* Top 200 chart. In Canada the album entered the charts at number five, while the album's European chart debuts were the best of their career: twenty-nine in the UK, thirteen in Germany, and twenty-three in France. *Neon Ballroom* marked a strong turnaround for the band's commercial wellbeing.

In America, *Neon Ballroom* achieved roughly the same sales as *Freak Show* – 633,000 to *Freak Shows* 620,000 – not a notch on *Frogstomp*'s two million-plus sales, but a none-too-shabby effort when you realise that the charts that year were dominated by apple-pie pop from Britney Spears, Christina Aguilera and the way-too-cute Backstreet Boys. Rock radio, meanwhile, was dominated by the austere Creed, U2 without the songs or the charisma. Yet sales of Silverchair's third album increased elsewhere. It sold 101,000 copies in Germany, compared to *Freak Show*'s 68,000; 116,000 in Brazil, compared to its predecessor's 38,000; and 25,000 copies in Sweden, which was 8000 more than the previous two albums combined. On 10 May, when 'Ana's Song (Open Fire)' debuted at Number Fourteen on the Australian singles chart, it became the band's eleventh consecutive Australian Top 40 single. Silverchair had become the most successful Australian chart performer of the 1990s, even outshining golden boys Savage Garden.

The returns for their North American live shows were consistent, even though they were playing smaller venues than in 1997. During a run of dates in March, they filled the Roxy Theater in Atlanta, and the Vic in Chicago. In Cleveland they sold out the Odeon, while in Canada, with fellow Australians Grinspoon along for the ride, they packed the 2345-seat club the Warehouse in Toronto and the Le Spectrum de Montreal. In another case of choosing a support act who'd soon blow up – as Matchbox Twenty had since the band's last US tour – po-faced plodders Nickelback opened for Silverchair at their next date, when they filled Vancouver's Croatian Cultural Centre on 26 March. Not all of their shows were so successful: only 800 punters fronted in Columbus, Ohio, while the 2460-seat Boathouse in Norfolk, Virginia, wasn't even half full when Silverchair plugged in on 2 June.

And still Silverchair kept touring – and Johns continued to behave in occasionally comical, sometimes bizarre ways. At times it seemed as though he had moved beyond his audience, who still bayed for such older songs as 'Tomorrow' and 'Pure Massacre'. On other occasions he was quite clearly playing up his role as frontman: why not give the crowd some razzle-dazzle to go with the rock? In Tampa, Florida, on 2 May, Johns tried out his rock and roll evangelist persona again. 'Can I get a hallelujah?' he asked the crowd at the worryingly titled Rockstock festival. 'Let's hear it for Jesus!' he yelled. 'Let's hear it for Satan! Let's hear it for sex, drugs and fucking rock and roll!'

His bandmates were uncomfortable with his strange turns. Joannou felt that Johns was challenging himself by digging a metaphorical hole on stage and then seeing how he could pull himself out.

But it wasn't something the bassman enjoyed watching, especially when Johns turned abusive:

> Sometimes you thought, 'This is good, he's becoming his own person.' Other times you thought, 'Oh boy, where is he heading tonight?' There was definitely a case of, 'Just three more months, just three more months.'

Gillies, meanwhile, maintained his 'man of the people' role, signing autographs and chatting with fans at shows long after Johns had left the building. He figured it was a fair trade-off for not having Johns's responsibility as band mouthpiece. And he didn't mind the attention, either. A writer I spoke with who'd spent some time on the road with the band, who preferred not to be named, recalls once watching Gillies actively pursuing a 'tattooed rock chick', a roadie for LA punks Bad Religion; women were never far from the drummer's mind.

Another sign of Johns's increasingly unpredictable behaviour was the way that he vented his frustration towards his audience. If he wasn't grumbling about their lack of response, he was lecturing them on the subject of animal rights. In St Louis, after trying on his combination of 'Do you believe in Jesus?' and/or 'Do you believe in Satan?', he turned on the crowd at Pointfest (another cringingly titled summer free-for-all).

'You guys are too quiet!' he yelled.

> I've tried but you aren't saying anything. We're going to play now so you shut the fuck up and we will play. Just sit there like you are and rock out like you fucking should!

Then during 'Freak', he gave the crowd the finger, and changed the lyrics to 'Body and soul / Suck my dick'.

Johns's onstage behaviour just kept getting stranger and angrier. In Boston on 30 May he posed the question: 'Do any of you believe in shooting ducks?' Clearly, not many in the crowd knew they were being addressed by an Animal Rights advocate (the band set up an Animal Liberation stand in the foyer at their Australian shows, and Johns even got himself an Animal Liberation tattoo). When they replied in the affirmative, Johns shot back: 'Anyone who answered "Yes" is a fuckwit.'

In Atlanta three nights later, a protest group calling itself Be Level-Headed picketed the Hard Rock Fest '99, where the band was playing, citing 'Suicidal Dream' and 'Israel's Son' as 'particularly offensive'. The band dropped both songs from their set, acquiescing to a request from the event organisers. Nonetheless, Johns stopped the show midset to point his finger at the church-related group that accused them of promoting violence: 'That's what we do with our music, we promote violence, according to the church. The church is always right. So we promote violence, sorry. Can I get a halle-fucking-lujah?' Johns then jammed 'Advance Australia Fair', a tune completely lost on the southern crowd.

Occasionally, Johns would slip up and hint at the source of his irritation. 'Thanks, that's our only hit,' he said after playing a desultory 'Tomorrow' in Denver. 'That's when we were an Australian teenage grunge sensation. Now we're just a rock band, according to the press.'

Despite Johns's wayward behaviour and the sometimes indifferent responses to the shows, the band was still an A-list attraction. In Vancouver on 14 July, Johns got into a shouting match with a surly punter while Hole's Courtney Love and Samantha Moloney looked on. In San Francisco, he remained uncommunicative throughout the band's set as Limp Bizkit's Fred Durst stood at the side of stage, mouthing most of Johns's lyrics like a star-struck fan.

It was still unclear whether Johns loved or hated his audience. When he wasn't getting into verbal sparring matches, he was inviting them up on stage to join in. He tried this out in Dallas in early June during 'Anthem for the Year 2000'; by tour's end in Australia it became a regular feature of a night with Silverchair. Once Johns had assembled a choir onstage, he would encourage them to chant 'We are the youth' at the top of their lungs. The lucky ones stood on a specially prepared choir stand, while wearing T-shirts printed by the band. It was anything-goes chaos.

But despite the many faces of Daniel Johns – rock god, crowd-baiter, blasphemer, hit-and-miss comic, evangelist, choir master – he was still alienated from both bandmates and crowd. While Gillies, and sometimes Joannou and Holloway, were signing autographs and posing for snaps with fans after their shows, Johns would either be holed up on the bus or safely back in his hotel room.

In Australia during July, Johns encouraged another onstage invasion during 'Anthem'. 'Listen to me now, I am the boss,' Johns told the audience and security staff. 'Don't listen to anyone else!' But when one female fan tried to get too close to Johns, he freaked. 'Let go of me now,' he said. 'I've dealt with psychos enough this week.' As it turns out, Johns wasn't blowing smoke – a few days earlier, on 26 July, Johns had been cleared of an allegation of harassment filed by one Jodie Ann Marie Barnes, another Silverchair obsessive.

There was another lap of Europe, supporting old buddies the Red Hot Chili Peppers, and a final fling in America, before they were ready for an album-closing circuit of Australia, in late November and early December. The sometimes bizarre, physically and emotionally draining *Neon Ballroom* tour ground to a halt in Sydney's Domain on 11 December, when the band headlined the annual Homebake festival, a locals-only bash that had developed in the mid 1990s as a sort of 'all Aussies Big Day Out'. With Triple J having gone nationwide, and TV shows such as *Recovery* spreading the word about homegrown music, it was a good time for local bands – many of whom were inspired by Silverchair's success.

Silverchair had already announced that the Sydney Homebake show would be their last for at least a year. They were exhausted after the past five years, and needed a break from music, the road and each other. In an interview just prior to the show, Johns dreamed out loud of 'seeing friends and not being tied to a schedule. Stuff that doesn't involve promoting the band or being Mr Silverchair.' Backstage, the rumour doing the rounds was that this was it, the band was breaking up. Side stage, Natalie Imbruglia looked on, alongside her sister Laura. The pop star (and former *Neighbours* actress) had hooked up with Johns two months earlier at the ARIAs, where their relationship had blossomed as they locked into a serious conversation in the Gazebo Hotel, the location of the after-party for her record label, BMG. In fact, they were still talking the next morning, when they were spotted at a Kings Cross bar. The couple had met in London a year earlier, but this time their connection seemed much deeper.

As Silverchair took the stage at Homebake after such bands as Powderfinger, Jebediah, Eskimo Joe and Deadstar, the sight of Johns in his amazing technicolour rocksuit – a purple, spangled, mirrored, custom-made rocksuit, no less – sent the Domain crowd nuts. Despite the success that many of the acts on the bill had experienced, none boasted a star like Johns. The band understood the significance of the event, too, so they'd invested more money in lights and visual effects. While playing festivals in Europe earlier in the year, they had seen how big bands incorporate spectacular light shows into their performances. Silverchair wanted some of that, especially knowing that they'd be off the scene for some time. 'We spent a lot of time on the lights because we wanted it to be remembered,' Gillies said afterwards.

Liberated by the fact that this was the end of the tour – and thrilled to be back in front of an Australian crowd – the band shed the year's baggage like an old skin. They poured themselves into 'Israel's Son', with Gillies – introduced to the crowd by Johns as '154 kilograms of glory!' – taking the lead, pounding his drum kit like it had done him wrong. Johns called for some 'hallelujahs' before the band unleashed the see-sawing 'Emotion Sickness', with keyboardist Holloway doing a fair take on Helfgott's frenetic piano part.

By the time the band reached 'Miss You Love', the Domain had been transformed (as reported in *Rolling Stone*) into 'stadium rock proper, from the single spotlight on Johns for the first verse to the background drench of red in the chorus and the rapturous crowd singalong.' Not long after, Johns – as he had done frequently during the *Neon Ballroom* shows – turned on the charm, riffing on Lou Bega's 'Mambo Number Five' and Christina Aguilera's 'Genie in a Bottle', before tearing into 'Freak' and 'Anthem for the Year 2000'. He, Gillies and Joannou then ran off stage, with the thunderous roar of 20,000 fans ringing in their ears.

'We're not supposed to do an encore,' Johns told the masses a few minutes later, 'but we'll do it because we love you.' They brought down the curtain on the night, the tour and the album – and, some thought, maybe even their career – with a roaring 'Spawn Again'.

'That show had a special chemistry,' Gillies said afterwards.

> It was really the icing on the cake for the past six years. It was a new millennium, it was the end of *Neon Ballroom*, and it had been a really long haul and we all made it. It was like a celebration.

Joannou captured the band's mood and mixed emotions perfectly: 'As soon as we did the Homebake show and said "Thank you, goodnight," we went, "Hang on." It was weird. It was over too quickly.' Despite spending much of the tour wishing he were elsewhere, suddenly he didn't want it to end.

As the band drove back to Newcastle, they were readying themselves for a whole lot of nothing. While they settled back into their domestic routines, unsure whether the band would tour or record again, Daniel Johns got busy writing a rock and roll opus.

* * *

Emotion Sickness: An interview with Elissa Blake

In 1999, Elissa Blake wrote the controversial and frank *Rolling Stone* cover story that revealed, in intimate detail, Daniel Johns's eating disorder. She was also the first journalist to cast eyes on his amazing swag of prescription drugs.

How long have you spent with Silverchair, and in what kind of situations?
My first contact with them was through a handful of phone interviews when I was a news reporter at the *Age* in Melbourne. It was around the time *Frogstomp* started to take off in America, and the band seemed genuinely shocked by their success. I think we were all shocked. It wasn't that they lacked talent or didn't deserve it, but success like that happens like a tidal wave. It's sudden and huge and somehow starts to be larger than the band itself.

Talking to Daniel and Ben in those days was like talking to your kid brother. They sniggered at the questions and answered with an 'I dunno'

A NEW TOMORROW

or 'it's all so weird'; that kind of thing. But I remember they were always so polite and grateful for their opportunities. They were never snotty.

Some of those stories went on the front page of the *Age*. They had the 'gee whiz' factor. The senior editors thought they were a novelty story because they were so young and Australia hadn't had a big chart success in the US since INXS.

What came next?
After that, I met them briefly at the ARIA awards, but didn't have closer contact until 1999, when I was writing the *Neon Ballroom* feature for *Rolling Stone*. By then, Daniel had started to look and behave like a troubled rock star. There was a lot of speculation within the Sydney music industry that something serious was happening with him. He looked dangerously thin and he seemed to be pulling away from the other band members. Chris and Ben seemed to be regular knockabout blokes who laughed a lot, had long-term girlfriends and surfed most days. Daniel had started wearing eye make-up, had gone vegan, seemed to be withdrawing emotionally, and was rumoured to be in an on-again-off-again relationship with Adalita from Magic Dirt [who was several years older than Johns]. Adalita had talked about her own drug use, and now the media were starting to wonder if Daniel was using some kind of hard drug. Most suspected heroin.

The other huge rumour doing the rounds was that Daniel was gay and was either trying to hide it or was about to come out – either way, the rumour was that he was struggling with his sexuality. God knows where that rumour came from. All I know is the morning I went to the airport to fly to Brisbane with the band, I had in my mind that I had to ask Daniel about his sexuality and/or his heroin use, and I had no idea how I was going to do that.

What was your initial reaction when Daniel Johns started revealing the details of his eating disorder?
I was really shocked. I had never suspected he had an eating disorder. When you see a painfully thin rock star you tend to think drugs, not anorexia. It was incredible, and I was trying to hide my surprise so that he didn't get self-conscious and stop talking.

The topic came up when I asked him to talk me through each of the songs on *Neon Ballroom*. He told me the first track, 'Emotion Sickness', was about trying to maintain a normal state of mind to avoid the need for mood-altering medications. He was talking about depression within the first five minutes. I was surprised, but it seemed like he'd made a decision to talk openly; it was almost confessional. I abandoned my list of questions and just listened. Whenever he paused for a while, I just asked him to keep going. He didn't volunteer any personal information, but when I asked how he was feeling, he answered freely. I could have asked more, but I could see he had limits and wasn't about to spill all the details of his life – and nor should he have. He talked in a stop-start kinda way, making direct eye contact every now and then. He was gauging my reactions pretty closely, which is unusual in an interview. I'm sure he'd decided that week that he was going to talk openly to journalists about his depression and anorexia.

So you think it was premeditated?
He seemed resolved to speaking about it, and had obviously thought through it. 1 don't think it accidentally started spilling out in that interview. Some have said that maybe this was a calculated move, to spill all and sell more albums. But I don't think he had a choice. So much of the album was about his personal experiences, how could he not talk about it in interviews? I guess he could have made up stories to hide what the lyrics were about, but that would have been unsustainable. If he really wanted to keep it private, he'd have written a different album altogether. He said he wanted to express his feelings in his music and he wanted to help other teenagers who might be going through the same thing. It sounds idealistic, but I believe his motives were genuine.

This sounds ridiculous, but we were sitting in a hotel coffee shop doing the interview when this enormous late afternoon storm started blowing in across Brisbane. Daniel would say something really important about his thoughts on suicide and then a clap of thunder would break over our heads. It was creating a really weird atmosphere and we both knew it. At the end we were able to laugh about it. The mood couldn't have been more dramatic – it was almost silly.

Can you describe your reaction when he whipped out his stash of prescription drugs?

That was the most surprising moment. About an hour after our interview was over and we were just getting ready to get in the car to go to the soundcheck, Daniel suddenly pulls all his tablets out of his bag to show me. I hadn't asked for that; it was totally out of the blue. I wondered if he was trying to shock me – he had a smile on his face. But I think he himself was amazed by the number of tablets he was taking. It was like, 'Hey check it out!' I didn't know what to say. I mean, really, what are you supposed to say in these circumstances? He'd put them away in a flash, so it wasn't really discussed. I'd asked what they were all for and he claimed not to know. I don't think he wanted to discuss it any further.

He told you his eating disorder wasn't 'a reaction to fame or the pressure', but didn't actually reveal a root cause. Any theories?
I don't like to speculate. From my limited understanding, anorexia is often an attempt to control something when everything seems out of control. Daniel says he was simply trying to push how far he could go with it, like some weird not-eating experiment. I suspect that's a flippant answer and not the whole truth. I've heard anorexics say that at least they can control their bodies and have some order over what they do and don't eat. It's an area where no one can tell you what to do. But it can also be a lack of care for yourself, that you don't care about yourself enough to eat properly. Almost a rebellion against yourself. Sometimes someone feeling that way can be living so much in their heads and emotions that they neglect their bodies or don't care about them, as if eating is an annoying chore. It's hugely complex and different for everyone. Only Daniel knows what was really going on.

Is it typical of the man, from your perspective, for him to be so frank?
Daniel had always been pretty open in interviews. He'd never refused to answer a question or given a deliberately unhelpful answer. He seems to take interviews fairly seriously, as part of his job. I reckon he's the kind of guy who prefers to tell the truth and doesn't think he should have to hide things. Having said that, he rarely starts telling personal stories voluntarily. Like most musicians, he prefers to keep his private life private. But in this instance, it really seemed like he had something to say and he

had to get it out. His music has become increasingly personal so we may hear him continue to talk openly about his life or he may choose to let the music do the talking in future.

Listening to Neon Ballroom *before your interview, did you get a sense that he'd been through something very heavy? Did you view the album differently after the interview?*
It was strange, because the lyrics seemed dark but his singing voice was so beautiful. I was really struck by the risks he was taking with his voice, really singing those high notes rather than the screaming style he used on the earlier songs. So it sounded like he was working some stuff out and things were shifting. The album had a lot of drama in it. After the interview, I was able to hear how delicate a lot of those lyrics were underneath the heaviness of the sound. I think a lot of people were touched by that.

Could you sense a distinct difference at the time between the personality of Johns and those of Gillies and Joannou?
Yeah. I think at that time Daniel was trying to get back in touch with his sense of humour. Chris and Ben are such jokers and Daniel had been part of that, mugging at the camera and saying stupid stuff. But around that time, he seemed so much quieter, but as if really wanting to get that humour back. He's not the kind of guy who is deliberately dark or wallows in his darker emotions; he seems to prefer a happier state – you can hear that on *Diorama*.

Daniel is more introverted than Ben and Chris, and I guess you could say he has that artistic temperament where he can disappear into his own headspace. But that doesn't mean he's weird or reclusive or especially different. All three of them are pretty sensitive, funny guys.

Do you think that Johns would have this kind of fragile mental state, regardless of what he did for a living?
Again, it's impossible to say. He's definitely a man unafraid to express his emotions and he's highly creative. I think those qualities, and all the highs and lows that go with them, would be part of his life no matter what he was doing. Maybe if he'd had less pressure at such a young age he may

have felt more in control of his life. But depression affects people in all occupations and at all different stages of life, so it's hard to say. He may have felt worse if he didn't have a creative outlet. He talks about music being a life force, so he's lucky he's found that.

Were you surprised when he fell ill, again, not long after making Diorama?
Yes, I was surprised. It seems incredibly unlucky. I wonder if he puts so much into his creative work that his body tends to pack it in if he doesn't get enough rest. That's pretty common. It just seems so extreme in Daniel's case. But I guess if he was just a regular person we wouldn't hear about his health; he's very much under the microscope.

From a [former] magazine editor's perspective, what's your take on the Silverchair phenomenon?
I think they had great songs at the right time when they first started out. They have consistently struck a chord, lyrically and musically, with other young music fans. Add to that a teen idol quality in Daniel – girls love him. That can't be ignored but it doesn't belittle the quality of the band's records. Also, Daniel's openness has brought about an incredible loyalty from Silverchair fans. He's a survivor, and fans love that about him. I think they also appreciate his growing writing ability and the risks the band take on each new album. This isn't an arrogant band just trying to make money or have as much fun as possible. There's something musically exciting about them.

Chapter Seven
DRAMARAMA

> All of a sudden I started appreciating the ups,
> which I hadn't felt for such a long time.
> Daniel Johns weans himself off anti-depressants, 2001

In 1994, Daniel Johns pointed to the row of houses on a hill overlooking Merewether, the snoozy seaside town where he, Gillies and Joannou grew up. With just a hint of disdain, he stated, 'The rich people live up there.' A few years later, however, he lived right alongside them.

During 2000, the band spent their time off enjoying the spoils of several years' worth of hard slog. Joannou had bought a good-sized property on the NSW Central Coast, at McMasters Beach, the site of a former bed and breakfast, encompassing a main dwelling, a guesthouse and a studio, for a little over a million dollars. Gillies, who lived in a rented apartment in Merewether, had bought several small properties in and around Newcastle. Johns, meanwhile, had found a home in the stretch of Merewether known as 'millionaire's row' – his home is now worth somewhere near AUD$2 million. He also kept his smaller house by the beach.

But rock star chic it is not. It's almost as if Johns's anti-rock-star mindset has crept into his interior decorating. The spacious interior is decorated in a minimalist style: here a lampshade, there a Brett Whiteley print. There's a shining piano in his lounge room, on which he composed most of the band's fourth album, *Diorama,* during another long stretch spent alone with his dog. (Johns's composing on piano would have a huge impact on the band's next musical phase.) Next to the piano is a home entertainment centre, the kind so big you'd expect to see it in some multiscreen sports bar. Some of Johns's own art – a hobby he's pursued for years and a handy outlet when he's not writing music – is framed and scattered around the lounge room. The sun shimmers off a swimming pool, which looks pretty much unused. A telescope stands in an otherwise empty room. There's a home studio downstairs. The only real rock star trapping is a framed copy of Black Sabbath's *Paranoid* album, a gift from former girlfriend Aimee Osbourne – the only Osboume who refused to appear on their reality TV freak show – who gave it to him for his eighteenth birthday.

The view of the Pacific Ocean from Johns's deck is stunning, virtually uninterrupted. A queue of tankers can be spotted on the horizon, awaiting their call to enter the industrial harbour of Newcastle. On some nights, their horns are the only noise that cuts through the silence. Five minutes down the road, Johns's parents live in what was once a typically modest Merewether house, but now, post makeover, is a stylish two-storey suburban home, another stop along the Silverchair history tour.

Daniel Johns has no problem with Merewether's drowsiness. In fact, he's so comfortable with the solitude that he rarely left the suburb during 2000 and 2001, as he began piecing together the songs for *Diorama*, the band's fourth album. On a typical day, he'd have only Sweep for company; his relationship with Imbruglia was on hold as she was spending most of her time in the UK. His parents would phone, he'd say he was OK, he was working, don't worry. These days would fall into a familiar pattern: he'd drop Sweep at his parents' home; they'd walk his dog on the beach. Johns would go home, sit at his piano and continue working on his songs. But there was little of the darkness of early 1998, when he almost died. He was just lost in his songwriting – an obsession that led him, months later, to virtually live in the studio while the songs were recorded. Some nights during the writing it was just too much; there was music everywhere and Johns would wear earplugs to bed, because he 'could hear melodies in the cicadas outside'. Other nights he would put in an all-night stretch, wrestling with the kind of complex arrangements that would surprise some and shock many when *Diorama* was eventually released in April 2002.

One such session took place the night the sprawling 'Tuna in the Brine' was completed: 'I remember feeling so drained and so tired because I'd been thinking about all the parts for weeks,' Johns says.

When I finished it, it must be the feeling people get when they do intense meditation. My body felt really long, my spine felt really elongated; it was like I was on top of the world, looking down on everything. It was better than any drug.

Even though the rain was belting down, Johns (with his ever-present dog) went and stood outside, soaking himself in an effort to come down from this natural high. Then he headed back inside and stood in the shower 'and pretended I was still in the rain'. He finally crashed at about 6.30 in the morning.

Johns insisted at the time that this obsessive, hermitic behaviour was normal for him, almost expected. Although he didn't speak the actual words, he was clearly thinking back to the time prior to the making of *Neon Ballroom*. He had been in a worse way before, and his family were starting to accept this reclusiveness as part of his nature. 'They've seen me much worse,' he insisted. He knew he was a lucky man.

Silverchair only came up for air twice between their headlining spot at the 1999 Homebake Festival and the release of 'The Greatest View', *Diorama*'s first single, in February 2002. They appeared at Victoria's Falls Festival on New Year's Eve 2000 and then at the massive Rock in Rio three weeks later. It was offstage that most Silverchair activity happened during 2000, when they split, very publicly, from their label, Sony.

The split was a difficult one. While renegotiating their Sony contract, having now delivered the agreed three albums, Watson insisted the band be signed directly to Sony America for releases in the world outside of Australia. This would eliminate the label's requirement to pay a 'matrix royalty' back to Sony Australia. It would also give the label the incentive to work the band's records harder, particularly in North America, because profits would stay in-house. Watson felt Silverchair needed 'someone in Sony behind a desk in New York whose fortunes would rise and fall with that of the band'. But it was too big an ask; if the label agreed, they would have had to set up the same kind of deal for stars Ricky Martin (who was signed to Sony Latin America) and Celine Dion (signed to Sony Canada).

Unable to arrange a satisfactory deal with Sony, despite the willingness of the band to stay with the label on the right terms, Watson stitched up a lucrative deal with Atlantic in North America, as well as setting up his own boutique label, Eleven, in October 2000. The band's cheerleader at Atlantic was their then head of A&R, Kevin Williamson, who was sold on the band after catching one of their US dates in 1999. Williamson was an Atlantic veteran, who'd been with the label since 1990 and had worked on platinum-plus records for acts that ranged from pure pop bands to sensitive singer/strummers and hair-metal tragics. 'I was one of the only Atlantic A&R people on the west coast,' he explained to me, 'so I'd work on everything from Ratt to Winger, Jewel and the Cult, Queensryche.' Atlantic was appealing to Silverchair for a couple of reasons – the label had a history with such immortal rock acts as Led Zeppelin and AC/DC, and, in the words of John Watson, 'Their deal was very attractive in terms of guaranteed funds and other incentives.'

Eleven – which would also soon become the label of choice for Missy Higgins and Paul Mac – would release Silverchair's music in Australia, with manufacturing, distribution and publicity handled by EMI. The Atlantic deal – particularly in light of what would happen with *Diorama*, commercially, outside of Australia – was especially sweet. It was 'frontloaded', which essentially meant that the band would receive a hefty six-figure advance, regardless of the record's fortunes, whereas in Australia their deal was 'back-ended', which meant a higher royalty rate on sales. And because the album was funded by the US label, there were no recording costs to be offset against sales in Australia, New Zealand and South-East Asia. 'We've done better with this record than any other,' Watson admitted in 2003, which was quite a revelation, given that *Diorama* became their poorest-selling record, globally, by several hundred thousand copies, despite being their biggest seller at home. (As of April 2006, the album's US sales are a paltry 75,479, a commercial disaster by comparison with *Frogstomp*'s two million-plus.)

The band's departure from Sony also ended – temporarily – their relationship with John O'Donnell who, along with Watson, had launched the whole crazy trip in 1994, when they signed the band to Murmur. He was, understandably, gutted by their departure. 'It was heartbreaking,' he said. 'It was like walking away from mates. But I totally understood why they left; I would have done the same thing.' O'Donnell would leave Sony a little over a year after their star band, and in a happy return to the Silverchair family, he now heads EMI.

Sony retaliated against the break-up by releasing a two-CD greatest hits set in November 2000, which the band refused to help promote. (In 2002 Sony quietly released the *Silverchair: The Best of Volume 1* set, a repackaged single-CD version of the greatest hits set.) 'I have no qualms with the songs,' Joannou told *Rolling Stone*, when *The Best of: Volume 1* appeared, 'but it's nothing that Silverchair would have liked to do in their career. It's something you do when you're retired.'

The first Eleven release was an unexpected treat. Johns had developed a strong bond with Paul Mac, who'd played piano on *Neon Ballroom* and had remixed the song 'Freak'. They strengthened their rapport during 2000 when they collaborated on the experimental five-track *I Can't Believe It's Not Rock* EP, a reco0rd so deliberately underplayed that on release in December 2000 it was sold only via the Internet, with some of the proceeds going to charity.

Johns and Mac premiered a few of the songs with a performance on the ABC TV drama *Love Is a Four Letter Word*, an episode that was filmed not long after the EP's release and aired in April 2001. Mac played keyboards and Johns – decked out in porn-star shades and one of the most garish cardigans ever seen on the small screen – sang and played guitar, grinning madly. It didn't seem to matter that the performance wasn't live; they were both having a blast. The program's producer, Rosemary Blight, couldn't praise their performance enough. 'Daniel Johns was fantastic,' she gushed. 'He arrived with the brilliant Paul Mac, played great music, sent the crowd wild.' Johns rounded off a big day out by smiling for photos, signing autographs and playing soccer with the series' star, Peter Fenton, former frontman for indie rock band Crow (the same band that had lent Joannou their bass for the original 'Tomorrow' session). No one in the Sydney studio knew, however, what an emotional struggle it had been for Johns to get to this point.

A NEW TOMORROW

After the *Neon Ballroom* tour, Johns was determined to wean himself off the anti-depressants that had kept him going throughout 1998 and 1999. It was a tough process. Johns also returned to the therapist's couch, an experience he found 'uncomfortable', but more rewarding than in the past. 'All of a sudden,' he said, as his anti-depressant dependency waned, 'I started appreciating the ups, which I hadn't felt for such a long time.' It was around this period of recovery that Johns and Mac started to piece together *I Can't Believe It's Not Rock*. 'This was never a record we set out to make, 'Johns said on the EP's release. 'It happened by accident, but now that it's done, I really like it.'

(While all this was happening, Joannou was spending time with his girlfriend at the time, Sarah McLeod, who was six years older than him; they'd frequently be spotted at gigs in and around Sydney. Gillies, meanwhile, took a job at Sound World records in Hunter Street, Newcastle, stocking shelves and ringing up sales. Not used to the nine-to-five grind, he later said: 'I don't know how I lasted six months.')

The Mac/Johns partnership was an unlikely liaison. Before going gold with his 2001 solo album *3000 Feet High* – also released by Eleven – Sydneysider Mac was best known for his role with drug-guzzling dance duo Itch-E and Scratch-E. He left his mark on the local industry when, while collecting a Best Dance Artist ARIA in 1995, he publicly thanked Australia's ecstasy dealers. He's that kind of guy: funny, open and as affectionate as a headful of the 'love drug'. These are not the kind of traits you'd typically ascribe to Johns, who at the time was troubled, insular and cautious around everyone except those few people he believed didn't want a part of him. He didn't trust too many people, but he connected powerfully with Mac. As a teenager, Johns had seen Mac's legendary ARIAs speech, and made a decision on the spot. 'I fucking have to meet this guy.'

'I love the guy,' Johns told me, without hesitation.

Music is our middle ground but we have a really good friendship. There's something about when we play music together. It's great. He's really important to me. When I was writing *Diorama* a lot of people were really reserved about giving me an opinion but he stood up and said, 'Do it. It's a good thing.'

JEFF APTER

Their connection definitely ran deeper than just the music. When Johns was in his anti-depressant stupor after the *Neon Ballroom* world tour, he'd spend days with just Sweep for company, rarely leaving the house. His on-again, off-again relationship with Natalie Imbruglia wasn't happening. Even when he and Mac started work on I *Can't Believe It's Not Rock, Johns* still had days when he had to be prised from the couch.

The first part of the collaboration happened at Mac's home studio in the Blue Mountains, when Johns would travel down from Merewether to jam and hang out. There was one day, in particular, when Johns just couldn't face the trip to Mac's home: the idea of leaving his house and dealing with the drive simply freaked him out. Mac knew the solution. He jumped in his car, drove the two hours from his Blue Mountains home to Johns's spread in Newcastle and played chauffeur for the day. Their bond was formed.

Johns's psychological recovery moved up another gear when he agreed to play the Falls Festival and Rock in Rio. Both appearances were significant. Scotching the rumours that their Homebake finale was the end of the band, they agreed to ringing in 2001 at the Falls Festival, an annual alt-rockfest held at Lorne, a coastal town a couple of hours drive west of Melbourne. The festival stretched over two days – it now also encompasses both sides of Bass Strait – with the midnight New Year's Eve slot reserved for the headliner. As was their way, Joannou and Gillies arrived earlier on in the day, drifting through the crowd and checking out other bands on the bill, including Machine Gun Fellatio and the Vandals. Johns, however, arrived with just enough time to change and prepare himself for the set. Wearing a knee-length, designer-made, fully sequinned coat, even more extraordinary than the glittery shirt he sported during the *Neon Ballroom* tour, Johns led the band through a favourites-heavy set, including a slightly reworked 'Ana's Song' and 'Freak'. They also debuted two new songs planned for their fourth album, 'One Way Mule' and 'Hollywood'. 'It was great. We had a ball,' Joannou reported from backstage after the well-received set. By that time, Johns was well and truly out of there, but if he'd hung about, he would definitely have agreed.

The band's next public appearance, three weeks later, would be the biggest of their career. Silverchair hadn't toured South America since the craziness of 1996, but were invited back for a key spot on the Rock in

Rio Festival, the largest rock and roll gathering in the world, described by many as a cross between the Big Day Out, Woodstock and Britain's mammoth Glastonbury Festival, and then multiplied by ten. In fact, it had been the invitation to Rock in Rio that had motivated the band to play the Falls Festival. When the pitch was made to Johns by Watson – Gillies and Joannou, typically, were up for the one-offs – it was done speculatively. Johns had been the key instigator in the band's decision to take at least a year off. He was tired of touring, tired of playing live, and needed to get his head back together. But now, twelve months on from the millennium-closing Homebake gig, he felt sufficiently enthused to play the higher profile shows. Working with Mac had helped him rediscover the joy of making music. He was now up for returning to his Silver-life. And the money must have been very hard to resist.

Understanding the enormity of an invitation to Rock in Rio, Gillies was shocked by Johns's enthusiasm. 'I thought, "Holy fuck!",' he said. 'We'd just had this weird tour, things were a bit rocky, we weren't sure if we were going to stay together.' With renewed commitment, the band rented a space in Newcastle and put in six weeks of serious rehearsals. It was as though the tension surrounding the *Neon Ballroom* period had totally disappeared.

Established by Brazilian promoter Roberto Medina in 1985, Rock in Rio was far too ambitious an enterprise to hold annually. In fact, the 2001 event was only the third Rock in Rio. And it was coming at a particularly difficult time in rock festival history. Woodstock '99 was marred by riots, insufferable heat, violence and reports of rape in the moshpit. And Denmark's Roskilde Festival, where Silverchair had played in 1997, was still reeling from the fallout of the horrible surge during Pearl Jam's set in 2000, in which nine fans died. Even Australia's Big Day Out had paid a price, when sixteen-year-old Jessica Michalik died from a heart attack in January 2001 after being crushed during Limp Bizkit's show in Sydney.

The vibe at Rock in Rio, however, was uniformly positive. Sure, the Porta-Loos overflowed and most of the 250,000-per-day crowd – the event stretched for seven days in the midst of a predictably sizzling Brazilian summer – headbanged ankle-deep in the mud created by high pressure water hoses that regularly sprayed the crowds. But this was an angst-free, good-natured rock and roll celebration. Patronised by Brazilian teenagers starved of live (Western) rock bands, it was a massive success, and raised around US$1.5 million for local educational charities. As for the crowd, they spray-painted their hair every colour of the rainbow and flaunted T-shirts that screamed 'Fuck me I'm famous'. Inflatable sharks bounced around the massive moshpit like beach balls at a Grateful Dead show.

The stage itself was a monumental piece of engineering. Forty metres high and ninety metres wide, it was built from 200 tonnes of steel. The bizarre stage set was cheekily described by *Rolling Stone* as having been modelled 'after a spiny mollusc or a female-pleasuring device'. Oasis's Noel Gallagher passed pithy judgement on the stage setting, the massive crowd and the entire event when he roared to a journalist, 'It's actually fucking genius. It's the most disgusting, brilliant, outrageous thing I've seen in my life.'

The festival's first six days were a musical rollercoaster ride. Axl Rose proved that Guns 'n' Roses were both alive and kicking with a memorable set (although, true to temperamental character, he insisted a punter wearing a 'Fuck Guns 'n' Roses 'T-shirt be evicted). Rose even introduced into his band's Vegas rock act a samba outfit, who marched through the crowd while the Gunners played on. On subsequent nights, ageless grunge godfather Neil Young kicked out the jams, Foo Fighters did it for the moshpit, and Britney Spears was booed, loudly, when the image of an American flag appeared behind her during the song 'Lucky'. Silverchair were the penultimate act on the event's final night, proving just how big a drawcard they were south of the border. Only the Red Hot Chili Peppers – whose drummer, Chad Smith, revisited the good times of 1996 when he hooked up with Silverchair the night before – were billed above the Newcastle three.

On the band bus heading to the show, Joannou summed up the band's feelings: 'It's beyond being nervous,' he said.

> I mean, even 100,000 people is incomprehensible. I remember back to 1996 when we played the [Royal Sydney] Easter Show and that was like 25,000 people – and we were just there going, 'Wow.' So the prospect of over 250,000 just doesn't register.

The band's nerves were given another serious jangle when they arrived at the site and were told that there was a scheduling mistake: they didn't have two hours to showtime, but were due onstage in forty-five minutes. From backstage, Joannou took a peek at the crowd and returned with his verdict. 'Oh my God,' he told the rest of the band, 'this is ridiculous.' A week before, he'd been chilling out on his couch at home on the Central Coast. Now, 250,000 people were screaming for him and the band.

When they took the stage to a deafening roar, it was as if Johns's spangled coat had transformed him from Mr Introspection into the definitive rock star. The band opened their set with a blazing 'Israel's Son', Johns pulling off some wild rock moves. As the set progressed, the band mixed up the moods, playing the mellower 'Ana's Song' and 'Miss You Love' alongside the moshpit faves 'Pure Massacre' and 'Slave'. They also aired the new tracks 'Hollywood' and 'One Way Mule'. Because it was a one-off show, Johns seemed liberated; he had no concerns about playing the same songs for another crowd the next night, a similar freedom he would experience several years later at Sydney's WaveAid. He playfully thanked the crowd in Portuguese and even made a strange aside about being a friend of Ronaldo, the Brazilian soccer star which, naturally, no one believed. As the heat intensified, the water cannons were turned up, just a notch.

But that didn't stop a massive singalong during the opening verse of 'Anthem for the Year 2000'. It was so loud, in fact, that Johns stopped playing, clapping his hands above his head as 250,000 fans screamed his lyrics right back at him. The song had come to Johns in a dream about rocking a massive stadium crowd. Now that dream was coming to life before his stunned eyes.

The band closed the set with a screaming take on 'Freak', Joannou and Gillies bounding off stage as Johns drenched the audience in a spray of feedback. This time, post-gig, he didn't disappear; the three hung around for a time backstage with fans, posing for photos and scribbling autographs. Johns beamed. The band had played the biggest show of their lives. They'd even reconnected with *Frogstomp* producer Kevin Shirley, who mixed the band's live sound for the mammoth TV broadcast of the event (when he wasn't hanging out with Led Zep's Jimmy Page). 'That was great,' Shirley said of the band's set. 'It was an amazing gig; I thought they were fantastic, even it John Watson did seem to be mollycoddling them too much at the time.' When Johns headed back to their hotel, Joannou, Gillies and various members of the band's management and crew kicked on at a local strip club, where they witnessed the bizarre sight of a transvestite disrobing to Midnight Oil's 'Beds Are Burning'.

The next day, Johns's face was splashed all over the front page of the local newspaper, *O Globo*, which described their set as the 'surprise highlight of the day'. It left them wondering whether it was Silverchair or the Red Hot Chili Peppers who'd closed Rock in Rio III. Gillies summed it up when he declared: 'Rock in Rio was undoubtedly the most amazing experience we've ever had as a band. The crowd was incredible; I've never seen anything like it.' As for Johns, he was thankful that the lengthy flight home from Brazil gave him and his band-mates time to slowly return to earth. When he did, he remembered that he had a new album to write.

As cohesive as it would eventually sound, both thematically and musically, *Diorama* was an album with a false start. The lengthy, exhausting *Neon Ballroom* tour had wrapped in December 1999, and Johns had started writing new songs during 2000 and early 2001. But he felt dissatisfied with the music he was making; the songs seemed too easy, too familiar, full of the crashing riffs and heavy feelings that had marked the band's first two albums, *Frogstomp* and *Freak Show*, and to a lesser extent *Neon Ballroom*.

Johns's frustration reached a peak in February 2001, soon after returning from South America. He spent two virtually sleepless weeks walking Merewether beach and fretting about whether he'd ever move forward with his songwriting. At the end of this period of uncertainty, he made a big decision. 'He erased the two hours worth of material he'd recorded so far.' They just sounded too much like the last album,' he told me, when I covered the making of the album for *Rolling Stone*. 'I knew it was a risk, but I [also] knew if I kept them they'd be a safety net.'

Not surprisingly, the act was extremely liberating for Johns. And gradually, the songs for the album that was originally called *The Time Machine* started to take shape. (Guy Pearce, who, oddly enough, starred in the video for 'Across the Night', appeared in a film of the same name. Two weeks before the film's release, Watson found out about the coincidence and the album was changed to *Diorama*.) The elegant 'Luv Your Life', the sprawling 'Tuna in the Brine', the hook-heavy 'The Greatest View': these were all written after he'd scrubbed those early songs. Ignoring even his bandmates, Johns previewed the new tunes only to his brother, Heath, manager John Watson, and Paul Mac. 'Tomorrow' producer, Phil McKellar, who would soon reconnect with the band, was another of the chosen few to hear these songs-under-development.

Paul Mac might have developed a rapport with Johns during the creation of their own EP, but he wasn't quite ready for the shock of the songs Johns was preparing for *Diorama*. 'I didn't get it,' Mac laughed when I asked him how he reacted. 'Because he's not [musically] trained, here's this incredibly complicated stuff. I was going, "Fuck, what is this?"' Mac's new role was to act as musical translator, helping Johns get on paper the music he was hearing in his head. Later on, Mac also contributed several piano parts to the album.

Mac's surprise at the new material was shared by Joannou and Gillies. Prior to the recording that was planned to begin in April, Gillies and Joannou got a call from Johns to visit him at home. For Johns, there was a little of the same trepidation he had felt unveiling the *Neon Ballroom* songs, when Nick Launay acted as mediator. But this time around he was more assured. He lit a joint, sat down at his grand piano and played 'Tuna in the Brine' to the Silver-pair. As he recalled later, 'Ben said, "How the fuck are we going to remember that?" It was great.'

Pot had become a handy writing aid for Johns in this period of his life, as he would reveal to me:

> I smoked a lot of pot writing *Diorama,* but I don't consider our music pot music. Sometimes when I write I don't want any outside influences apart from my own thoughts, but sometimes I need to break through that self-conscious barrier and I smoke.

'We sat around and he played them one by one for me,' the ever-amiable Gillies recalled of these very early *Diorama* sessions, in September 2001.' He said things like, "This one sounds Beach Boys-y."' It was very cool.' Joannou made a neat understatement when he commented that 'some of the arrangements were quite complex.' Not only did Johns have the thumbs-up from Mac, his bandmates were on board with the new music he was writing.

It was just the encouragement he needed to keep going with these bold, cinematic pieces of music, songs that were the logical step forward from such *Neon Ballroom* tracks as 'Emotion Sickness' and 'Miss You Love'. But this time around there was a key difference – Johns wasn't digging into his heart of darkness for themes; instead he was opening up to the world around him. He wanted to make a hopeful, outward-looking album rather than another forty minutes of self-flagellation. It also helped that for the first time he was writing on piano and recording music on reliable home-recording gear (which Mac had helped install), instead of banging out demos on his guitar and recording them on cheap cassettes as he'd done in the past. Now he could experiment with vocal ideas and more complex arrangements before the band hit the studio proper. It was to have a major impact on *Diorama*.

Choosing a producer wasn't as easy for *Diorama* as for their first three albums. *Frogstomp*, *Freak Show* and *Neon Ballroom* were rock albums, in essence, so they needed a producer who could translate that raw rockin' energy to tape. Now the band needed someone different, someone who could understand where Johns was heading. This was an entirely different band to the rocking runts who blitzed the world with 'Tomorrow' six years earlier.

The band's new American label, Atlantic Records, proposed a shortlist of producers. Watson was keen for the band – especially Johns – to work with someone fresh, someone who would push him into the new directions his songwriting was taking. Launay wasn't on the shortlist, in part because he was too familiar to the band, but he listened to the demos, and put forward a couple of names as possible producers: Midnight Oil's Jim Moginie, who knew and understood the band and their work, having contributed various parts to *Neon Ballroom*; and, oddly, Brian May, the guitarist for Queen. The epic scope of these songs reminded Launay of Queen's *A Night at the Opera* and he felt that May would connect with that. Both were first-rate ideas, but not what Atlantic and the band had in mind. (Soon after, the reclusive May would record with American arena-rockers the Foo Fighters.)

American Michael Beinhorn, who'd worked with numetal giaiats Korn, as well as Soundgarden and the Red Hot Chili Peppers, was the first producer agreed on by the band and Atlantic. While the trio fine-tuned the songs in three months of rehearsals, after returning from Rock in Rio, they waited for Beinhorn to finish Korn's latest album, *Untouchables*. But as the Korn sessions dragged on, the Silverchair camp simply ran out of patience, and the deal fell through. In hindsight, this was fortunate, because Johns needed someone who could bring out what he would call the 'colours' and 'light' in his new songs; Beinhorn specialised in modern rock miserablists. Other contenders for the production job included Americans Bob Rock and Bob Ezrin, the latter a highly regarded veteran who'd produced masterly albums for Lou Reed and Alice Cooper.

The nod eventually went to Canadian-born, British-based David Bottrill, a bookish type with a shaved skull, glasses and a thoughtful nature. He'd produced albums by skilled metallers Tool, art-rockers King Crimson, baroque pop guy Peter Gabriel – even belter Toni Childs – so he'd proved his diversity. Bottrill's work with Tool proved he could handle heavy sounds, but his production work with Gabriel was just as impressive. The erstwhile Genesis frontman was a songwriter who shared Johns's anything-goes ambition.

Before disappearing into the studios, the trio spent some time at Mangrove Studios on the Central Coast during April, fine-tuning their home recordings with Phil McKellar. For the Sydney-based producer it was a sort of homecoming; he'd never really dropped off the Silverchair radar since producing the first version of 'Tomorrow' for *nomad*. It was further evidence of John Watson's insistence on keeping his friends close. 'Maybe I got the call,' McKellar figured, when I asked him about this in early 2006, 'because it's a close family; maybe they trusted me.' The way McKellar read the situation, the band needed someone who could work quickly. 'There was no real "producing" to be done,' he added. 'They just needed some decent sounding demos.'

As soon as he heard these new songs, McKellar, in his own words, was 'blown away'. He thought that 'Tuna in the Brine', in particular, was a stone-cold classic. 'Hearing those demos,' he recalled, 'I knew something magic was going to happen. I really liked the immediacy of the demos; I had shivers up my spine.' (Some of these demos would end up as B-sides of the various *Diorama* singles.) Although he's too much of a gentleman to say it out loud, I sensed that McKellar wasn't as excited by *Diorama*'s finished product.' But Daniel's such a talent,' he added, 'and these are journeys you have to take. But there was a certain fragility to those first demos.' ('They sound great, don't they?' commented Johns, when I raised the subject.) *Frogstomp* producer Kevin Shirley was another who was underwhelmed by *Diorama*. 'It was over-produced to the max,' he believed.

Johns, Watson and *Diorama* producer Bottrill first met in LA; not long after that, Bottrill had an interesting meeting with reps from Atlantic, including their head of A&R, Kevin Williamson. 'There was no secret about Daniel's grand plans [for the album],' Bottrill said to me, 'but they felt he'd still write the big rock hit. But he simply didn't want to do that.' Bottrill's previous exposure to Silverchair was fairly limited, although he did recall one incident that pointed out how much other players respected the band. During early sessions with Tool – a band as renowned for their prog–rock chops as their extreme attitudes towards sex and drugs – while they were recording their 1996 long-player *Aenima,* Bottrill asked guitarist Adam Jones what type of guitar sounds he was hoping to create. Without another word, Jones whipped out a copy of *Frogstomp*. 'Make me sound like that,' he told Bottrill.

Bottrill met up with Silverchair in June 2001, in the band's comfort zone of Newcastle. It was a strangely familiar environment for Bottrill, who'd grown up in the very blue-collar town of Hamilton, Ontario. ('But it doesn't have a beach,' he laughed when I asked about this.) Bottrill was quickly introduced to the harder edge of Newcastle after the first day of rehearsals, when he and Gillies hooked up for a drink in a nearby pub. They'd barely sipped their first beer when a fight erupted, with the brawlers spilling over the two of them.

Bottrill would convene with the band at 10.30 am each day for the next few weeks, and they worked through the new songs, plotted out their upcoming recordings, and then disappeared until the following day. It was the first time since they were teenagers that the band had made music in the morning. It wasn't done on a whim; Johns was making a very conscious effort not to replicate what he called the 'night orientated' vibe

A NEW TOMORROW

of *Neon Ballroom*. Instead, he wanted an album that was all about new sensations. Given that rock and roll is a world where nothing ever happens before lunchtime, at the earliest, playing before noon was definitely unfamiliar. 'I was trying to reverse things this time around,' Johns said, but added that 'it was really weird to play music' so early in the day.

'They're absolutely world class, without question,' Bottrill said of Silverchair, when I first spoke with him in September 2001.' Everybody in this band is of the highest quality I've ever worked with.' Bottrill was also impressed by the band's studio savvy. 'They knew what they were doing [in the studio],' he said.' They knew the process; it was no mystery to them.'

Once these rehearsals were wrapped – and after the band's first meeting with Kevin Williamson, who travelled to Newcastle to check in on his new signing – sessions for *Diorama* began in July at Sydney's Studio 301, the ground zero for most well-budgeted local recordings of the past ten years. (While Silverchair took over Studio One, the Whitlams and Midnight Oil were recording *Torch the Moon* and *Capricornia*, respectively, elsewhere in the complex.) Erecting the Silverchair table-tennis table was one of the first priorities for the band, as they settled into 301. As always, videographer Robert Hambling was everywhere, recording the making of the album for the 2002 DVD *Across the Night: The Creation of Diorama*. Engineer Anton Hagop was producer Bottrill's quietly spoken, super-efficient sidekick (and went on to win an ARIA for his work). Assistant engineer Matt 'Gizmo' Lovell, a Novocastrian who'd learned his trade at Sydney's Festival Studios alongside Kevin 'Caveman' Shirley, helped out on the technical side, and then, at the close of business each day, would document the day's events for the band's website. As Lovell would tell me, he was hired for various roles: to utilise his mastery of Pro Tools technology, to write the album diary and to be 'the vibe guy' in the studio. (During the more difficult moments of the *Neon Ballroom* sessions, Lovell's amiable, cut-the-crap attitude had helped alleviate some tension.)

Basic tracks were recorded during July and August. Paul Mac chimed in on piano. Jim Moginie, who'd played on seven of *Neon Ballroom*'s tracks, added some keyboard squiggles to 'The Greatest View' and 'One Way Mule' (the latter was the only song Johns had resurrected from the tape he'd scrapped earlier in the year). Bassist Joannou and drummer Gillies spent a lot of time playing ping-pong with Watson, but Daniel Johns rarely left the control room. He was absorbed in the making of this record.

Bottrill explained:

> This was absolutely Daniel's album and the band were happy about that. He really wanted to make this statement. Ben and Chris were curious as to how it would play out – they were happy to run with it. I'm not sure if they shared Daniel's vision, but there was no backroom bitching.

Bottrill also revealed that, even in these early stages of production, Johns knew exactly which songs on the album were better suited to a big production: he could hear where the orchestra belonged. Just like McKellar before him, Bottrill thought 'Tuna' was an 'epic'. 'My first reaction was, "What a great piece to work on." [And] that is the album, right there.'

In late September 2001, the band (plus Bottrill, his two engineers and Johns's dog, Sweep) had shifted camp to Mangrove Studios, the tranquil and very desirable musician's escape then owned by INXS bassist Garry Gary Beers. Here they started to experiment with some of the songs, adding extra texture to the basic recordings laid down at 301. Johns's mood was up – the songs were coming together almost as he had planned them in his head. The only interruption was when a crew visited from cable station Channel [V] to announce that the band had won their fifth consecutive Viewer's Choice award, even though they'd been the invisible men of rock during the past year. Johns, Gillies and Joannou laughed their way through the interview, which was aired at October's ARIA awards. 'We know other bands deserved it,' Johns mugged to the camera, 'but we're the 'Chair!'

By early October, the band was back in Sydney, at 301, confronting the most challenging – and costly – stage of the recording: the orchestration for six of the album's tracks. Once again, Johns co-composed the arrangements for three of these songs ('The Greatest View', 'World Upon Your Shoulders' and 'My Favourite Thing') with Larry Muhoberac, whose previous encounter with Johns was when the singer, in his green beanie, had lain on the floor shouting out the notes to *Neon Ballroom*'s 'Emotion Sickness'. After this came the real glittering prize: a fortnight with the legendary Van Dyke Parks, who penned the orchestral arrangements for 'Across the Night', 'Tuna in the Brine' and 'Luv Your Life', writing parts for strings, woodwind, brass, harp and percussion.

The sixty-something Parks – who Bottrill quickly figured was 'the campest straight man I've ever met' – is twenty-four-carat rock and roll royalty. Born in Atlanta but based in California, he collaborated with Beach Boy Brian Wilson on his great lost album, *Smile*, and is often cited as the man who steered Wilson away from the more commercially orientated Beach Boys, freeing his music while helping to mess up his mind. Parks also co-wrote the classic 'Heroes and Villains' (and the not-so-classic 'Vegetables').

Described as 'some mad cross of Stephen Sondheim, Burt Bacharach, Cole Porter and Randy Newman' and the 'cult figure of all cult figures', Parks has worked his sonic alchemist's trick on albums from the Byrds, Fiona Apple, Ry Cooder and U2. He's also spun some magic on his own hugely eccentric albums, recorded intermittendy when he wasn't working with others. These records included 1968's *Song Cycle* and 1984's *Jump!*, which was a bizarre attempt to mould a pop opera out of the Uncle Remus tales of Chandler Harris (complete with all their very un-PC dialect).

Avuncular and often downright hilarious, Parks is a studio master, but not so self-obsessed that he couldn't recognise a spark in Johns that he recalled from his own musical youth.

'I see all the musical qualities in him I heard and saw in Brian Wilson,' Parks told me, during the only interview he granted while in Australia.

> [Daniel's] an undefeated romantic; an informed optimist. I know there's a lot of dark meat on that bird but lurking in there is the voice of the human spirit. When I got the new material, I was astounded by the musicality, the lyrics, brimming with enthusiasm and a life force that guarantees this group as a continuing major force in music.

Or as *Rolling Stone*'s David Fricke put it, when I asked him about Parks:

> Van Dyke Parks doesn't work with clowns. He's got very high standards about music and musicality. The fact that he worked with them on *Diorama* is as much a tribute to what Daniel can do as a songwriter

and the band can do as players as the fact that Van Dyke Parks has eclectic tastes. He doesn't just take a job for the sake of taking a job.

(Typically, Parks would downplay this lofty praise, calling himself a 'whore' who makes his living in the whore's paradise that is Hollywood.)

Mind you, Parks almost didn't make the trip at all. When Johns said he was hearing lush, cinematic arrangements for many of these new songs, Watson had put forward Parks's name, but with a caveat. 'I think he's dead,' he told his star. (Parks found the anecdote so funny that he now sometimes signs off his emails as 'the recently deceased Van Dyke Parks'.) Johns wasn't familiar with Parks's work, but got very interested when Watson learned he was both alive and kicking (and still making music). Johns vividly recalls their first phone conversation: 'The first thing we heard was Van Dyke on the other end, playing the piano. I thought we were on hold before I realised. That was a good lesson: sometimes it's best to give yourself up musically rather than saying something.'

These phone conversations are hilariously documented on the *Across the Night* DVD, as Parks outlines his orchestral needs and dollar signs collect at the bottom of the screen. Even though the 9/11 terrorist attacks in New York delayed Parks's arrival by a fortnight, the connection between him and Johns was deep and true.

'I know a lot of talented guys, I've worked with them – I've almost made a career out of surrounding myself with talented people,' said Parks, in his unreasonably modest way, during a rare moment of downtime at Studio 301.

> I've been very fortunate. I'm a musical grunt in LA, I work in the TV and film industry. This offer came out of the ether; it was a blessing. When I looked into this work, immediately I wanted to weep. I thought the vocalist was in dead earnest; I liked that person, I wanted to know who he was. And this beat seeing David Crosby in a jacuzzi. This is someone I wanted to know.

Silverchair's early music had been implanted in Parks's mind, almost subliminally, because his children were big fans of the band's debut album, *Frogstomp*.

It was throbbing through the walls, especially when they had guests. I got curious about it, but could never have imagined that I would be fortunate enough to work on a project of theirs.

Parks recognised that the music Johns was now writing was far more advanced than the simple riff and roar that won over his children. He also recognised that development as a mark of the musically gifted:

All of the artists I like have a tendency to do that: to leave me in shock. The artist has a special faculty for pulling along his or her audience and with difficulty they move forward with them. It can get kind of dull if the artist rests on their laurels.

Johns would have loved more time to work with Parks, but they did conjure up some true musical magic in the two weeks they shared. The orchestrations are signature Van Dyke Parks: epic, sweeping and dramatic, full of rich sonic detail and golden melodies (possibly too much detail, because a lot of what was recorded was trimmed during the album's final mix). The best songs of Daniel Johns's life had been transformed into the band's best recordings and some of Parks's finest work. It said a lot about how rewarding it was for Johns to work with people he trusted and respected.

Bottrill was duly impressed by Parks's skills; he said that this fortnight was the 'highpoint' of his *Diorama* journey 'To watch him work the orchestra was brilliant,' Bottrill said. 'He was a comedian working a crowd and then he was a music professor.' Sometimes Parks would dumb down his act, swearing at the various players assembled in 301. 'He used profanity as a motivator,' Bottrill pointed out, 'as a wake-up call.'

But by early December, the mood surrounding *Diorama* had changed. Johns had been in Los Angeles for a fortnight, mixing the album with Bottrill. Throughout the making of the album, the band's American record label, Atlantic Records, had liked what they were hearing, but they still hadn't heard that one key song they felt would get the band airplay on the Rock and Modern Rock radio stations, the only radio formats that touched Silverchair in North America. Bottrill explained to me that Kevin Williamson was conflicted. 'I think personally he thought the music was amazing, but he was also under pressure from his label to extract another big hit from the band.' Atlantic's concerns reached a peak while Johns was absorbed with finishing the mix of the album.

But writing a song to order wasn't Johns's specialty, especially when he had almost finished work on Silverchair's most accomplished and detailed record. When I met him in LA, briefly, he was moody and sullen, clearly distracted by the demands of Atlantic. In the past he'd been shielded, wisely, by Watson, from many of the machinations of the record industry, but now he was coming face to face with the commercial expectations of a major label. This was a new and weird environment for him.

'That DVD [*Across the Night*] made out that we hated each other, but we didn't,' Johns insisted, when asked about his relationship with Williamson.

> We just weren't right, we weren't compatible. He was just doing his job and his job fucked with my head. He knew that Americans wouldn't buy that record, while I was eternally optimistic that if it's good enough they would.

Bottrill, for one, could see that Johns's heart simply wasn't in the idea of writing this 'contractual obligation' tune, even though he did have one more song under construction, and there had been some talk about rejigging 'The Greatest View' tor US radio. 'He'd made his statement,' Bottrill figured, 'and he had nothing left.' Eventually, a compromise was reached when Johns wrote the song 'Ramble', but this meant that he, Bottrill and the crew had to fly back to 301 in Sydney and reconvene with Gillies and Joannou to record the song. According to the band, it was the most extreme act of record company profligacy they'd ever witnessed. 'Ramble' was 'an arthritis-induced piece of shit,' according to its author. 'I hate it.' The last laugh was on the record company suits: this watered-down, by-the-numbers rocker ended up as a B-side for the 'Without You' single, even though Kevin Williamson thought it 'a good song'.

Further complicating an already uncomfortable scene was the increasing pain Johns was feeling in his knees, an early sign of the reactive arthritis that would soon leave him a virtual cripple. There were several contributing factors at work here: the stress brought on by both finishing the record and trying to pull a hit out of his backside, and the fact that his diet, although improved, still wasn't quite what a nutritionist would recommend. In fact, David Bottrill can only ever recall seeing Johns eat fruit throughout the months they spent together. 'He was starting to get these rashes,' Bottrill revealed, 'and I said to him, "Don't just eat the fruit plate!"' Although Bottrill insists that Johns was well enough to walk away from the studio when the mix was eventually completed, he could see that Johns's health was failing. 'He was getting tired more often – and a lot quicker.'

Johns was in the unfortunate position of being amongst the 6 per cent of Caucasian males – usually in their twenties – who, due to a certain type of blood tissue, are predisposed to reactive arthritis. (Another sufferer was Australian cricketer Michael Slater.) Similar to the over-all 'achiness' that you experience during a bout of influenza, but way more debilitating, the reactive arthritis 'bug' typically attacks the joints of the knees, ankles and/or toes, but can also affect skin and muscles. Because Johns's immune system had been weakened during his eating disorder, and due to his susceptible blood tissue type and high stress levels brought on by the album sessions, reactive arthritis hit him hard and fast.

There was, however, one highlight from their stay in LA. Johns, Bottrill, engineer Matt Lovell and Natalie Imbruglia had a chance meeting with U2's Bono in a club, and he invited them back to his suite at the Chateau Marmont, LA's premier rock and roll hotel. (This was the same site where the Red Hot Chili Peppers had recorded much of their *Californication* album, and John Belushi died of a massive drug overdose.) Bono asked what they were doing in town. Reluctantly, fearing that they'd be seen as abusing his hospitality, the Silverchair crew handed him a tape of the *Diorama* track 'Luv Your Life', which he then proceeded to play over and over again, to the increasing chagrin of his other guests, No Doubt singer Gwen Stefani and Smashing Pumpkin Billy Corgan, who, of course, had their own reasons for being in the company of the man from U2. Bono loved the song, later declaring: 'Swim to Australia to hear it if you have to.' His statement, ironically, would prove to be more accurate than even he could have imagined, given the album's rocky ride in North America.

The first music to be released from *Diorama* was the defiant single 'The Greatest View', a very clear statement from Johns about the new, positive state of both his mind and his music (if not his body). It debuted on Australian radio on 21 December 2001, the day after the video had been shot in Brisbane. When 'The Greatest View' was made available on www.chairpage.com before its official release, it rapidly became the most downloaded song in Australian music history. Ten thousand copies of the single were streamed, far outstripping the previous record holder, Paul Kelly, whose song 'Somewhere in the City' didn't even make it to a thousand downloads. It was another smart move on Silverchair's part – what better way to reconnect with your fans than by offering them a free song?

'The Greatest View' galloped into the Australian singles chart, debuting at Number One on 4 February. Its timing was perfect, because the band had just completed a live return as part of the 2002 Big Day Out. Almost three years had slipped by since the release of *Neon Ballroom*, and the rock public were Silverchair-hungry. The successful launch was a great relief for the band, given that they'd spent so much time out of the spotlight, and that during their period of reflection and recovery, Brisbane band Powderfinger had taken over as the country's favourite alternative rock band. Powderfinger's fourth album, *Odyssey Number Five*, sold 400,000 copies locally, a level Silverchair still haven't matched at home, and the band had scooped the ARIA awards in 2001. But their lush and tuneful songs didn't have that hint of obsessiveness heard in Johns's best songs, and their frontman, Bernard Fanning, despite owning a great, soulful voice, had none of Johns's enigmatic qualities.

In his first round of press for *Diorama*, Johns repeated the words 'light', 'energy' and 'positive' like a mantra, even as the pain in his knees – and soon everywhere else in his slight frame – increased. (Johns had only gotten through the short Big Day Out sets with the assistance of mega doses of painkillers.) 'The Greatest View' encapsulated Johns's new positivity; he described it to me as a song written for his parents, who have always watched over him, even when he was deep in depression at the end of the 1990s. But that may not be the only interpretation, given the serious time Johns had spent in therapy. When a song opens with the line 'You're the

A NEW TOMORROW

analyst', it wouldn't be a stretch to think some of his on-couch experiences influenced the lyric.

Gillies echoed Johns's thoughts on the record when it was released, even if he expressed it in simpler terms: 'We're really excited about it, it's really different,' he said.

> A lot of our stuff in the past has been kind of dark, so this is really quite uplifting. It's a happy album, which is cool. If we were a band that kept doing the same thing over and over we'd get bored shitless with it. That's when people start fighting and generally bands break up. That's an advantage we've had, that we've always done things differently.

'It's not a record that is born out of misery, it's a record that is born out of optimism,' producer Bottrill told the *Sun Herald* in January 2002, describing Johns as 'much more into the positive aspects of life now. Misery is easier than joy, I think, but ultimately joy is more satisfying,' and confessing, 'It's rare that you get to the end of a project and you're not sick of each other, but this was more like a relationship that I didn't want to end. I miss them all.' (Four years later, Bottrill was still immensely proud of the album. 'It's one of the greatest realisations of an artist's visions that I've been involved with.' He and Johns clearly stayed on good terms, because Bottrill made the VIP list for the Johns/Imbruglia nuptials. 'It was a great wedding,' the producer declared.)

A lot had changed since the teen-angst-by-numbers of their first two albums, or the heavy neuroses of *Neon Ballroom*. *Diorama* was a synthesis – and a refinement – of everything Silverchair had recorded over the past eight years. Johns readily admitted that the three songs featuring the band's trademark grunt ('OneWay Mule', 'The Lever' and 'Too Much of Not Enough') were included purely for the benefit of those long-term fans who had stuck with them since 1994. To Johns they were afterthoughts, songs that didn't 'fill any holes in my soul'. But it was one compromise he was willing to make. Commercial suicide was not a step that would thrill the band's management or US record company, who'd made a considerable financial investment in *Diorama*. Johns realised that his audience could only be coaxed along, step by step, into his new music, even if he wasn't willing to bend over for the suits at Atlantic when they asked for their hit.

'There's always an element of compromise,' Johns said.

> You can't deny that. It's always there when you've got people who've supported you and bought your albums and gone to your shows. You have to say, 'Here's a song for you.' It's for the loyal people. Hopefully the other songs will challenge them. It's hard for bands to make the transition and still be taken seriously. But we were fourteen and our fans were fourteen; we have to change. They've grown with our music, hopefully.

So while this trio of songs harked back to *Frogstomp* and *Freak Show*, such mood pieces as 'The Greatest View' and 'World Upon Your Shoulders' were natural steps forward from the rich melodies found on *Neon Ballroom's* 'Paint Pastel Princess' and 'Ana's Song (Open Fire)'. But even though Johns still had some very dark days – which were increasingly frequent as his reactive arthritis really began to take hold – he was pushing himself to generate a more positive, uplifting message with his songs. He was older, he was off anti-depressants, he was in love with Natalie Imbruglia – his occasional girlfriend since 1999, who was now becoming a stabilising influence in his life – and he was coming closer to realising the music he was hearing in his head. He didn't want to return from a lengthy break with *Neon Ballroom: the Sequel*.

While the combination of his music and words created more good vibrations than at any other point in the band's career, Johns's lyrics, when viewed in isolation, still made strange reading. But he was willing to defend them to the death. He stated that he preferred these lyrics to any others he'd written. 'It's really open to interpretation,' he accepted, 'but some of them are quite magical.' Sometimes, however, his 'feel good at any cost' message got lost in clunky prose. 'The Greatest View' opens with the couplet 'You're the analyst / The fungus in my milk', which was almost as peculiar as 'Tomorrow's 'There is no bathroom and there is no sink / The water out of the tap is very hard to drink.' And there was a spooky, though clearly unintended prescience in the very Beach Boys-like opening track, 'Across the Night', in which Johns sings that he 'hugged a man's arthritic shoulder'. However, his gently twisted sense of mirth burst through 'World Upon Your Shoulders', especially when he wailed: 'Violent, big and violent / Like a thing that's big, big – and violent.'

But few rock lyrics stand up to this kind of English Lit 101 analysis; it's the combination of voice and music and emotion and electricity that makes for the best rock music. And that's where *Diorama* succeeded. At its core it was a complex, musically and emotionally rich and challenging album. Its moods shifted between epic ('Tuna in the Brine', 'Luv Your Life'), aggressive ('OneWay Mule', 'The Lever') and uplifting ('My Favourite Thing', 'The Greatest View'). And *Diorama* closed with the simple piano-and-voice ballad 'After All These Years', which would become their set opener when the band eventually got back on the road. Though it may have sounded like a comedown on first listen, the song is actually a message of hope for Johns's future. He had endured a lot to get to this point of peace. 'After all these years / Forget about the troubled times,' he sings, as the record waltzes to its finish. And he meant every word.

In the commercial scheme of things, *Diorama* was going to be a tough sell. There was no obvious hit single, not a lot of trademark guitar crunch, and little of the fury that had marked the band's earlier work. The response to *Diorama* took a fairly predictable course: first reaction was surprise, but once the music sank in, few critics thought it less than praiseworthy (apart from the British, but by now that was to be expected). In my lead review in the April 2002 edition of Australian *Rolling Stone* I wrote that by 'going light on the antidepressant murkiness and heavy on surround-sound atmosphere, *Diorama* is one of the boldest statements ever made by an Australian rock band. Seriously.' It was granted a four-and-a-half star rating, almost a perfect score.

American *Rolling Stone* also gushed:

> Johns and company have become genuine artists on their own terms. Heavy orchestration, unpredictable melodic shifts and a whimsical pop sensibility give *Diorama* the sweeping feel of the work of Brian Wilson or Todd Rundgren.

The reputable *All Music Guide* seemed shocked that the band had made it through the 1990s and outlived grunge: 'Mostly this is a wonderful surprise from a band thought to have been finished in the late 1990s.' (The album had staying power, too. Producer Bottrill told me how almost every band he's since worked with have referred to the album as a 'classic'.)

There were naysayers, naturally. The British press had never thought much of *Frogstomp*, *Freak Show* or *Neon Ballroom*, nor did Silverchair sell many records in the UK, despite regular touring. Their European fanbase was on the continent, in Germany, France, Sweden and Holland, rather than the UK. The *NME* did its usual hatchet job on *Diorama*: 'They think they're making grand and mature musical statements,' they barked, 'but it just sounds like they're trying to impress their parents. Utter wank, but in a different way than before.' Canada had been a reliable market for the band – *Frogstomp* sold 204,000 copies there, *Freak Show* 183,000, *Neon Ballroom* 186,000.

But Kerry Gold, writing in the *Vancouver Sun*, wasn't sold on *Diorama* either:

> The album is a meandering, highly ambitious odyssey that more often fails than it succeeds. It's either bravery or arrogance that has driven Johns to think that he could ditch his formula for something that sounds at times like he's striving for Elton John in Disney mode.

It didn't help the band's commercial fortunes in Canada, either, when they tound themselves entangled in a spat between their North American parent label, Warner Bros, and HMV record stores, over wholesale prices. Nevertheless, 'The Greatest View' made the Canadian Top Five, and the album debuted in the Top 30. A few negative reviews and a business hitch didn't seem to hurt.

Silverchair had shaken off their Nirvana-in-pyjamas legacy with an album that displayed Johns's fast-developing songwriting gifts. The album debuted at Number One in Australia on 7 April, going platinum in two weeks. It also set a new record – Silverchair became the only Australian band to have four albums debut at Number One. Not even INXS or Midnight Oil had done that.

Diorama's overseas release and promotion, however, was as big as any drama during the band's rollercoaster ride of a career. The overseas release date was originally planned for July – preview shows scheduled for June in London and New York had sold out well in advance – but was rescheduled to 27 August 2002, after Johns was diagnosed with chronic reactive arthritis and cancelled all live appearances. It's a given in these times that you have to promote the hell out of an album, regardless of its merits, to rise above the hundreds of releases every week, but Johns was unable to do that. In fact, he couldn't even walk. Despite the favourable chart placings in Canada and Germany (the album was released in Europe on 29 July), *Diorama* limped into the US charts at Number Ninety-one and was gone within a fortnight. Without the band's physical presence to talk it up, *Diorama* sank there soon after, despite Atlantic's innovative promotion plan – web chats, free downloads and streannng of earlier live shows, all on the band's official website – designed to cope with Johns's illness. There was even talk of a limited theatrical release for the *Across the Night* DVD. None of this, however, generated the kind of sales that typically follow a tour.

David Bottrill, however, wasn't so sure that Atlantic had an adequate backup plan to help push the album:

> For me, it felt like the people who worked it had a specific plan, and then Daniel got sick, and they had no other ideas. Nowadays, it's really about short-term, big-money gain. There's no sense of [back] catalogue.

David Fricke perfectly summed up the fickle nature of the music industry, especially in America, when I asked him about the album's failure there:

> People don't measure the quality of their music or musical experience by quarterly earnings; corporations do that, not people. Because *Diorama* doesn't take off here in the first three months, it's like, 'Oh well, it's not happening.' But my take is that, 'Well, it's not happening for you now, but that doesn't mean it'll never happen.' To write them off now makes no sense. They'll come back. The problem is that people here think that the music industry is America. The measure of what you achieve is whether someone recognises you when you walk down the street in New York.

As for Johns himself, he didn't seem too concerned when we spoke in January 2003:

> I'm told it's not [dead], but I'm pretty confident it is. Everything's been contradictory. It's the only record I've made in my career that I'm really proud of and it's the only one that's failed in America. I think it's a good indication of where my head is and where the American public's head is.

Throughout much of 2002, however, Johns had little time to think about the downward turn in his band's commercial worth. He'd become a virtual cripple. After the Big Day Out dates and a few shows in New Zealand, Silverchair management had done everything they could to keep the band touring: they'd pushed back the start date for rehearsals to help Johns recover, and when that proved to be futile, they rehearsed without him, and even tried out a substitute guitarist, Dave Leslie, which would at least free Johns to simply focus on his vocals. Engineer Matt Lovell copied Johns's guitar parts onto tape and sent them to the former Baby Animals guitarist. (One of Johns's early heroes, Helmet guitarist Page Hamilton, had also expressed interest in standing in.) Julian Hamilton, who'd become the band's new keyboardist, and would go on to play almost fifty dates with the band, recalled how strange that particular experiment was. 'Rehearsing 'Chair songs with another guitarist playing Dan's part was very strange, let me tell you.'

'The start of the [world] tour was days away, and we still hadn't seen Dan,' Hamilton continued.

> We were learning the songs OK without him, and they were actually beginning to sound quite solid, but there was this uneasy feeling among the band and crew. No one was prepared to say it – but I'm sure everyone was thinking the same thing. Finally, on the last day of rehearsals, Bailey [Holloway, the head of the band's crew] picked up Dan and brought him in for the one and only run-through of the set we would get together.
>
> That's when it sunk in for most of us I think: there would be no tour. Dan looked terrible. He was thin and weak, he looked out of his

mind on painkillers. It was heartbreaking. He had a big smile and was pleased to see us, and we were stoked to see him – but we all knew there was something really wrong with him being there. He seemed really positive though: he was complimenting the band on how good it sounded; he was showing the guitarist how to negotiate some of the trickier guitar licks. But you could tell, as much as the guy wanted to play and get involved, he was just too sick.

Within a few days, Hamilton and the rest of the band and crew got the call they'd all been expecting: the tour was cancelled, and there was no clear idea as to whether it would even take place at all. The mood in camp Silverchair had never been darker; not only did they realise that the album was about to stiff overseas, but their star was in dangerously bad health. He would spend most of the year, often with the help of Imbruglia, searching, in both Australia and the USA, for the right type of therapy that would, literally, get him back on his feet. There were times when the pain he was feeling was so intense that he couldn't share a couch with another person; any movement would hit him with what felt like several thousand volts. He couldn't even take a shower, because the water pressure was simply too overwhelming.

When Johns was well enough to consider what he'd endured, he described the album and his subsequent physical meltdown as:

> the most emotionally turbulent time of my life – the best moment of my life, and the worst, in the course of one record. The best thing was having the confidence to do the kind of record I wanted to do – and having the funding to do that. Any other record, by this stage, I'd be looking back and going, 'Fuck, I don't like it any more.' And also the worst [was] being hospitalised, in pain every day for eight months, having the American record company first not wanting to release it [*Diorama*] and not get behind it because radio refused to play it. It's been fucking weird.

Johns was seriously understating the album's case. Even though his outlook, at the time of the album's writing, had been as dark as the days of *Neon Ballroom,* he'd mentally willed himself to create something positive and uplifting, only for his health to fall apart during the album's creation. It was a devastating kick in the pants, enough to make him wonder whether making music was worth all the pain. But, as his health slowly improved, he began to realise that the entire *Diorama* 'experience' was a bridge to far happier times. And by the end of 2002, at least in Australia, *Diorama,* like Johns, was back from the dead. By 20 December, the album had gone triple platinum (210,000 copies) and become the band's fastest-selling album in their home territory. And this was a record that seemed to have run out of steam. Although it shipped more than 100,000 copies – mainly to true believers – in its first week of release, it only sold 2000 copies over the next five months, as Johns's illness prevented the band spreading the word about *Diorama* either on stage or in the media.

Even years later, when we spoke in April 2006 about *Diorama*'s domestic success, Johns remained bewildered:

> That baffled me because it's such a musical record. I only ever expected music fans to either hate it or love it and didn't think anyone beyond that would hear it – which in America they didn't.

Six months after its release, record sales had received a second wind through some shrewd marketing and two key appearances. First there was Johns's reluctant 'comeback' performance at the 2002 ARIAs in October, where they collected five trophies, including those for Best Group and Best Rock Album. Johns, who was in the middle of his treatment at the time and unsure whether he should even be playing, was still struggling; I'd seen the band practise in a rehearsal space in suburban Alexandria a few days before the ceremony, and all he could physically manage was to play 'The Greatest View', over and over again, at ear-splitting volume. Due to his arthritis, Johns was having trouble bending his fingers to adequately cover the guitar parts; if they hadn't been playing so loud, I swear you could have heard him wince. It didn't matter on the night, though; the response the band received for their every award, and their live take on 'The Greatest View', was so overwhelming that it felt as though the Sydney Superdome might actually come crashing down on the crowd of fans and music biz players.

A NEW TOMORROW

Then there was the season-ending episode of *Rove Live,* one of the few outlets on commercial TV for local bands to force-feed several million people their new music. Aware of the wide audience for the program, and keen to steer the band's music towards an even larger audience, Watson struck up a deal with the show's producers for an entire program dedicated to the band.

It didn't seem to matter that the bulk of the show was lifted straight from the *Across the Night: The Creation of Diorama DVD*; the boost to album sales was remarkable, as Johns himself recognised afterwards:

> Since we were fourteen, we've been told [of] the importance and value of promotion, and we've gone 'Bullshit'. Now all we did was turn up on *Rove Live* and sell all these fucking records! I guess people are more liberal in their spending around Christmas. I've also bought a few thousand copies.

Not only had the band kept their loyal Silver-fans; mainstream Australia was also snapping up *Diorama* as commercial stations such as Nova FM put their songs into high rotation for the first time.

The album – which had been floundering well outside the Top 40 – raced back into the Top 10. Within days of the *Rove Live* airing, every major label, aware of the kick-start that *Diorama* had received, was calling the producers of the show suggesting a program dedicated to their own star of choice. A hefty TV advertising campaign and some high-profile Sunday news magazine stories – again, reaching a new audience for the band – didn't harm *Diorama*'s sales, either.

Silverchair were also, finally, about to get back on the road, even if their 2003 itinerary wasn't as exhaustive – or as exhausting – as their promo schedules for *Frogstomp* and *Freak Show*. But that didn't mean that Johns had scaled-down plans for the roadshow. 'Providing we have adequate financial support, I want to do something that's larger than life,' Johns said, as the band got back to rehearsals, 'that's visually surreal as well. It's going to be a sensory overload.'

With some handy advance warning from www.chairpage.com, tickets for all eleven 'Across the Night' Australian shows sold out on 4 December, the day they went on sale. Their first hometown show since they appeared as the Australian Silverchair Show in January 1999 sold out in a remarkable six minutes, turning over a useful AUD$167,750 in gross revenue. Tickets to the first Melbourne show were snapped up in nine minutes, generating another AUD$193,000. By February 2003, with Johns's health very much improved, additional shows were announced to meet the frenzied demand for tickets – these six extra shows were also sell-outs. Virtually all of the 7000 tickets for their Sydney Entertainment Centre show were sold on the first morning. (The band's two Sydney shows raised more than AUD$300,000 at the box office, while a single Perth show generated AUD$182,527, which, even after the taxman took his share, was still a handy little earner.) Then there was more chairpage-assisted action when 1000 pre-sale tickets were snapped up for their shows at New York's Bowery Ballroom in June. Extra dates were added to their short tours of the UK and South America, to meet demand. Silverchair may have spent most of 2000 and 2001 out of view by choice, and had 2002 ruined by Johns's arthritis, but the band's fans still needed them. Badly.

Just like the album that they were finally able to tour, there was an element of compromise to the 'Across the Night' shows. The shows would open with Johns alone on stage, seated at a small piano, noodling away at the sombre ballad 'After All These Years', a song more suited to the end of the night than the beginning. Often, he'd be decked out in a red velvet jacket, complete with ruffled sleeves, that looked like a leftover costume from the Beatles' *Sgt Pepper's* years. Then the first 'half' of the show would formally begin, when Gillies, Joannou, and keyboardists Hamilton and Stuart Hunter would join Johns and pour themselves into the heavy emotions of 'World Upon Your Shoulders'. The lavish stage setting, alive with retina-wrecking fluorescent lights and flickering video screens, would also burst into vivid life – it was almost as much a star of the show as the resurrected Silverchair.

The first of the night's two sets was Johns's chance to totally immerse himself in the 'new Silverchair', including such *Diorama* tracks as 'Tuna in the Brine', 'Luv Your Life' and 'Across the Night', numbers that were more reliant on melody and mood than the onstage muscle generated by the crack Silverchair engine room of Gillies and Joannou. They also threw reconstructed versions of older songs – 'Miss You Love', a devastating 'Paint Pastel Princess' and 'Steam Will Rise' – into the totally satisfying mix. Then the band headed backstage for a quick costume change, leaving audiences to sift through some of the more outrageous merchandise being flogged in the foyer between sets. Silverchair pyjamas, anyone?

But the band, and Johns in particular, understood the potential danger of alienating the true believers who'd stuck with them ever since they wandered out of The Loft back in 1994. So for the second half of their lengthy shows – well documented on the *Live From Faraway Stables* DVD, shot over their two-night stand at Newcastle in April – there was less emphasis on flashing lights and cinematic sounds, and way more grunt. And as the show turned for home, the stage was left to the three Novocastrian sonic soulmates, who riffed and roared their way through 'The Door', 'Freak' and 'Anthem for the Year 2000', leaving the full houses drenched in sweat and full of love for Silverchair. Finally Johns seemed comfortable in his role as accidental frontman; as the intricacies of the earlier songs were replaced by sheer noise thrills, he would turn his back to the audience and shake his skinny arse and scratch at his guitar like some kind of demented rock god, sometimes even humping his mountain of amplifiers or playing his axe with his teeth, while every female in the house screamed their lungs raw. Then Johns would spin around, flash a shy smile, and get back to rockin' business, as he and the band tore a hole in the sky with their furious closer, 'The Lever'.

Critics both at home and abroad heaped fulsome praise on the band and the shows. 'The "Across the Night" tour shows a totally different band from previous albums,' Robyn Doreian noted in *Rock Sound* magazine. 'It also becomes clear that this is only stage one of Johns's musical evolution, and that for the first time in a long time, the trio are enjoying playing together.' Under the headline 'Chairman Wow', the *New York Post*'s Dan Aquilante zeroed in on the reborn Daniel Johns, describing him as 'incredible'. 'If Silverchair play another NYC gig,' he declared, 'don't miss it.' Also amidst the heaving mass at their New York gig was long-time Silver-fan David Fricke, who covered the show for *Rolling Stone*. 'For Silverchair,' he announced, 'today is a lot more interesting than "Tomorrow".'

Even the virtually impossible-to-satisfy British were impressed by the shows, as the band plugged in at London's Shepherd's Bush Empire on 9 June, for the first of four sold-out nights.

Covering the show for hard rock rag *Kerrang!*, writer Essi Berelian was another who noticed how much joy Johns was deriving from playing rock god for an hour or so:

> Johns indulges shamelessly in rock star posing and hip wiggling, like some Elvis-besotted teen miming in front of his bedroom mirror; bassist Chris Joannou stomps dementedly on the spot [and] drummer Ben Gillies somehow manages to keep time without losing his pork pie hat.

What the local critics didn't realise was that they could have been witnessing the final shows of Silverchair. Neither Johns, Gillies nor Joannou had any idea what was next for the band, and breaking up was as possible as anything else.

Johns told me in 2006:

> It wasn't a big secret that we were contemplating that being the end, but we didn't want to solidify it, because we didn't know what we wanted to do, or whether we'd be crying after six months because we missed each other. So we tried to make those Shepherd's Bush shows killer. Even the British critics liked them, which might have been the right time to get out! But I knew after that I wanted to do a whole new project, which became the Dissociatives, that would take my mind off the pressure I was feeling at that stage.

Looking on with shock and awe sidestage at Shepherd's Bush was Natalie Imbruglia, now a familiar face in the world of Silverchair. Sucking on a lollipop – a post-arthritis Johns had also recently developed a sweet tooth – Imbruglia was electrified by the sweet noise her beau and his pals were creating. 'It was amazing,' she whooped after the show. 'The crowd was amazing.' Also in the midst of the Silver-scrum was *Diorama* producer David Bottrill, who was intrigued as to how the band would reconfigure their latest album for the stage. He, too, was impressed by the spectacle. 'He's a real star,' Bottrill said of Johns, 'and the show was a good representation of the album.'

The last of the Shepherd's Bush shows marked the end of the road for *Diorama*. Despite the heavy praise heaped on their US shows – and the wild scramble for tickets to their LA gig, which sold out in record time – the charts proved Johns right, and their fourth album died a hasty death in North America, thereby ending their relationship with Atlantic. Even though the poor US numbers shocked him, Johns actually found this failure liberating.

'We all feel incredibly lucky,' he said when the band was preparing itself for their fifth album.

> We're not sitting here going, 'Damn, *Diorama* didn't sell in the States.' I really think it was for the creative good of myself and the benefit of the band that it wasn't a massive success overseas. It made us realise that we're not dependent on commercial success to be happy with our stuff.

But Johns had other more pressing matters in mind during 2003 as the band headed off to their different corners of the planet after the obligatory end-of-tour knees-up: not only was he planning an A-list wedding that would drive the paparazzi crazy – Imbruglia had accepted his marriage proposal in January 2003 – but he was set to shock his fans by forming a new band. The whispers started up once again; maybe it really was all over for Silverchair this time.

* * *

The Label Guy: An interview with Kevin Williamson

Kevin Williamson was the A&R Director at Atlantic Records who signed Silverchair in the hope of them recording a 'big rock album'. Instead, they delivered the cinematic masterpiece *Diorama*, which sold almost 500,000 fewer copies in the USA than either *Neon Ballroom* or *Freak Show*. He is now the head of A&R at Maverick Records, but insists that there is no connection between his move and *Diorama*'s commercial disaster in the USA.

Prior to signing the band, how aware were you of Silverchair and their musical roots?
I was spending a lot of time in Seattle. I became friends with Stone Gossard from Pearl Jam and when their singer from Mother Love Bone died, I was helping them look for a new singer when they found Eddie [Vedder]. I was at their first show at the Off-Ramp – and you could tell right away that that was the end of that. I didn't really end up signing anyone you'd consider a grunge band, per se; I continued working with more mainstream rock bands. But I loved the sound, definitely. I was always going up there [Seattle], looking for bands. I'd also heard about Silverchair, heard about how young they were, heard some of the songs and thought, 'Wow, these guys have tons of talent at such a young age – someone in that band knows how to write a great song.'

What happened next?
The first time I was asked whether I was interested in the band was through their attorney, Jill Berliner. I was interested in the band but didn't know to what degree, because I hadn't seen them live yet. The first time I saw them play was in San Luis Obispo, a college town about an hour north of Santa Barbara. They were opening for Blink-182. I was just floored. My jaw hit the floor. They put on one of the best rock shows I'd ever seen, period. That iced it for us; we immediately wanted to do the deal, we knew we were watching something great. And Daniel, who I met afterwards, was a really intriguing individual to sit and talk with; you felt like you wanted to be involved with someone who was on such a high level and had such sheer music talent. At first we thought he was a little standoffish, but I don't blame him; he'd just gotten off stage and there were two Atlantic execs on a bus with him.

Were you aware of their Sony experience?
We were. I think there was some unhappiness from their side about how certain things were handled, but it really wasn't my concern. I just saw something that I thought we could probably do better at the time. Not to say they didn't do a good job, because everybody around the world knows who Silverchair is, but every relationship has its problems and they were ready for a change.

Were there also other labels in the hunt to sign the band?
I can't remember who was also interested or who John [Watson] was talking to. But my whole thing was to just win. If I can't remember who was involved, I either didn't think they were a threat or felt that we were showing our best hand and I felt confident that we were going to get this thing.

Can you outline the offer you made to the band?
I can't remember the specifics. I think it was a good offer; a very well-structured deal that had a lot of incentive built into it and a lot of sharing involved if the record was successful. They could have probably got more money elsewhere but to their credit they told us what they wanted and were stand-up guys and we gave them what they wanted. It was a good deal for them and for us, but it wasn't in the stratosphere.

Did you have to sell the band to your bosses at Atlantic?
Craig Kallman, the president of Atlantic, knew about the band and thought Daniel was a star and thought that we could do a better job moving his career along. We knew that there was a little backlash towards the grunge scene and that the sound was dying. But in talking to Daniel we knew that he wasn't going to make another grunge record; instead he was going to do what naturally came out of him. When someone like that says he wants to push the envelope, you know it's going to be interesting.

How soon after signing did you hear the new songs? And how did you respond?
Right away. He started sending in songs; 'Tuna in the Brine' was one of the first. To be honest, that was one of the songs that was the most experimental, in my opinion, and it did make us all take a step back and go, 'How are we going to sell this? How are we going to get this on the radio?' We immediately started having these conversations. But at the same time I think Daniel knew that he had to let it all out and then sit back and evaluate it. That's the agreement we came to when we first sat down in the studio. I kept pushing him to at least give me a couple of songs we could get on the radio and he kept telling me that he knew what he was going after and that I should trust him. One day in the studio we looked at each

other, shook hands and said, 'I'll trust you if you trust me.' We never had any fights or anything like that; it was always constructive conversation. But I can't say that I knew exactly what was coming; as they were laying it down, Daniel would hear things and they would try them out.

Can you outline what Atlantic expectations were?
Atlantic is a major record company that likes to sell records. Initially we were expecting a record that sounded more like *Neon Ballroom* and continued on with their more harder-edged sound, the more straightforward, radio-structured side of Silverchair. Initially we were expecting that and pushed for some of those songs to end up on the record. And there are – 'Greatest View', 'World Upon Your Shoulders' and several other songs on the record are very radio-friendly. We were very happy when we started hearing stuff like that.

In your opinion, was David Bottrill the right producer for the album?
I think for the record Daniel wanted to make, David was one of the few guys who could have gone in there and made that record. It wasn't easy. David's a very patient producer who is very visual, as I think Daniel is. They were two people who could sit together and talk to each other and visualise what the final product should sound like. I think Daniel trusted David and vice versa.

Did you suggest a lot of changes to the original material?
I consider myself very hands-on. Some bands are very self-contained and I don't have much to do. But in Daniel's case, because I was the record company guy, I had to push for the more single-sounding songs on the record. On the DVD [*Across the Night: The Making of Diorama*] you can see that we had that dialogue. To Daniel's credit, he sat and listened. Some artists don't want to hear it. That's where I was most involved, going through the material and tightening it up with David and Daniel. Daniel['s response] was no worse than any of my other artists, although I may have had some who have been better. But in pre-production, if I had an idea, they'd play it. If it worked, they kept it. I said to them, 'I'll have ten ideas and nine of them might suck.' But

Daniel is the true genius behind all this; I'm just the guy sitting back, looking on, like the basketball coach.

Were you aware of Johns's uncertainty towards recording these songs as Silverchair?
It's no secret that before *Diorama* Daniel wasn't sure what he wanted to do. He had a lot of thoughts and ideas that he needed to get out at that point in his life and sometimes they can be very personal. I've made solo records with artists that have been in bands. Daniel was struggling with whether or not he wanted that to happen as Silverchair or as Daniel Johns. But we didn't sign him as a solo artist and our goal was to keep the [Silverchair] brand name moving forward. But I don't know if that was part of his decision, but he did the right thing. I think they're even closer as friends because of that. And I think the world of Chris and Ben; they're amazing musicians.

Was Van Dyke Parks the right choice for the arrangements? Did he blow out the budget?
Once I clearly started to see what Daniel's vision was, I thought it was a great idea. He's one of the most well-known and talented arrangers there are, bar none, and an inspirational person to be around. He's a ball of fire, too.

It was a great call on Daniel's part and I think they did an amazing job together. He's not the cheapest guy on the planet but you get what you pay for. It was more than we would want to spend, but when we found out he loved the music, we weren't going to stand in the way of that. We were glad to be in a position where we could afford him, let me put it that way.

You visited Australia twice during the making of the record: was the record heading in the direction you thought it would?
After the second visit, when they were recording at [Sydney's Studio] 301, that's when I came in and listened to some stuff. There weren't any huge surprises or what I would consider disappointments. We were still wondering whether we had the lead-off radio song and subsequently when they came to mix, I asked Daniel to write another song. And he did; it ['Ramble'] was a good song. But to Daniel's credit, he gave it his best shot and he didn't like it. I thought we had some really strong material on the

record already. There was just this slight gap I was trying to bridge, to bring his old fans to this new sound. You don't want to lose your old fan base and I think this was Daniel's biggest dilemma – he had to get all these feelings off his chest. You can't damage the integrity of that effort by putting something on the record that everyone would know is there purely because it sounded like something from the past and it would get on the radio. That was the end of that; we moved on and finished mixing the record.

How did your colleagues at Atlantic respond to the finished LP?
I think they all loved it. I think, at first, it takes a few listens. Anyone who is a true fan of that record knows they're listening to something great but need a few listens to get their head around it. And to me that's the sign of a great record. There were so many things Daniel brought into this record, it's such a theatrical presentation, that when you were in the studio, you were listening to the soundtrack to several movies all rolled up in one great record. It's a great compilation of a lot of emotions he was going through at the time and it takes a genius to get those songs out and not sacrifice his beliefs. But, yeah, we knew it was going to be something of a battle [to sell]. My feelings, and the feelings that I was trying to get across to the company, was that there are always transitions in long-term careers and there are always going to be records that may be not so successful but act as a bridge between two phases in an artist's career. It has to happen. My feeling was that it was an amazing piece of work that people are going to respect. And if that sets us up for another four or five records out of him, then so be it. We as a record company have to stand by our talented artists and allow them to have a home. My belief and Atlantic's belief was that Daniel was one of those artists and he'd made a record that people will be listening to for years to come. I'm still surprised by how many young bands come up to me and want to talk about the making of that record.

Was 'The Greatest View' the right single for US radio?
I think people really liked that song. I think what hurt us is that Daniel got sick and we couldn't bring him over to do any shows. A lot of people still hadn't seen this guy and met him, and these were the things that made me sign him and the band. To lose that hurt us; our goal was to bring him in

here and win fans and radio people over, bring them to the live show, meet him and watch them play. We wanted to change the way people thought about Silverchair.

How long did you have, realistically, to make the record succeed commercially?
We had six months at the most; we were trying to get one of the tracks off the ground and then hope to get Daniel on the road, or we were in trouble. But that turned out to be a tough thing that he got.

[In an odd footnote, Andrew McMahon, the leader of another Williamson signing called Jack's Mannequin, finished an album, *Everything in Transit,* and then came down with leukaemia, but has since recovered enough to start playing live.]

Was there any consideration given to not releasing Diorama *in the USA until Johns recovered?*
We were all – including management – trying to make the right decision. What do we do? It scared everybody. We were down the road already; all the gears were moving and the decision was to move forward and hope that Daniel would get better soon. We talked about all that, but our hopes were that we'd get the record out and he'd get better, which didn't happen.

Was the record partly to blame for his sickness?
I think he put so much effort into the record that it played a role in him getting sick. I'm no doctor, but I seem to remember that a lot of his illness was stress-related.

What were Atlantic's commercial expectations for Diorama*?*
I think gold [500,000 copies] was our hope; that was our goal. I think that if we had Daniel here we could have done that and that would have been fine.

Chapter Eight
FREE DISSOCIATION

Andrew Denton: 'I think you're enjoying life now. Would I be right?'
Daniel Johns: 'Yeah, definitely, I love life. It's the best thing in the world.'
Denton, 2004

For much of their relationship, Daniel Johns and Natalie Imbruglia have lived liked gypsies, bouncing between homes in Sydney, Newcastle and London. 'It's a weird lifestyle,' Johns once explained to me, 'but pretty exciting as well. Like anything in life, it has its advantages and disadvantages.' But Johns was especially partial to the time he and Imbruglia spent at her palatial home near Windsor. Here, Johns was, in his own words, 'Captain Nobody'. There were no photographers parked outside his window, hoping for a chance snap of him, nor were there any lost and lonely teens camped on the front lawn, dreaming of exchanging just one word – a look, even – with Daniel from Silverchair. He'd had enough of this in Newcastle when the band first exploded, yet even as recently as the time of recording *Diorama* in Sydney in 2002 there'd been a collection of hopefuls camped outside the studio most days, hoping for a chance encounter with Johns.

It wasn't as easy for Imbruglia, of course, whose fame in the UK even eclipsed her partner's at home. This meant that Johns was required to do most of the menial things in the outside world, as he explained in his 2004 interview with Andrew Denton. 'I've been in shopping lines in Windsor [where Natalie lives in the UK],' he laughed, 'because I have to go buy the groceries. I'm just Captain Nobody over there.' Johns had established a relationship, of sorts, with 'my fellow sixty- to eighty-year-olds ... that I only see at [local shop] Waitrose.' There was one local in particular whom Johns had befriended, 'this guy that has this amazing hat and cane ... I would kill for it.' Johns greeted him as 'old mate'; the usual reply was, 'Hello, my Australian friend.'

In fact, Johns embraced the English knack for eccentricity – Captain Nobody, as it turned out, was just the beginning. While in Windsor, where he now spent six months of each year, Johns rechristened himself one Sir Whilliam Hathaway (the extra 'h' was his idea), an 'English statesman/poet', according to Johns.

He took to doing the shopping in three-piece suits while holding a cane, even though he no longer depended on one to get around.

Johns revealed:

This is a concept I've been working on for a couple of years, but apparently he's a prose writer from the 1800s, who also had something to do with the mass selling of gin, back when it was the workers' drink. I ask people to call me Whilliam. I'm not trying to run away from myself; I just like people to call me that.

Soon after, Johns would insist that his Dissociatives band-mates refer to him strictly as Sir Whilliam; or Will, in lighter moments.

As much as Johns enjoyed the freedom of a totally new persona, he also knew that a prying paparazzo lens was never too far away, because he'd sometimes hear the words: 'I think that's Natalie Imbruglia's [partner].' It was then that he'd jump in his car and head home.

Shopping – and life as Sir Whilliam – were not the only tasks that soaked up Johns's time while living in the UK, however. At the end of the Silverchair tour in June, he'd put in a call to his old pal Paul Mac and invited him over to tinker about in the basement studio that Johns had set up in Imbruglia's home. Over two weeks that Johns would later recall were part of 'a beautiful English summer', the Dissociatives were born.

Ever since their collaboration on *I Can't Believe It's Not Rock* and Mac's increased involvement with *Neon Ballroom* and *Diorama*, Johns had planned to work again with the piano man, who was now also his label-mate at Eleven. Johns had been kicking around the idea since early 2003, when I spoke to him while he was in New York. When I raised the subject of Mac, Johns was emphatic: something new was going to come out of their musical relationship. 'But it's not going to be called *I Can't Believe It's Not Rock*,' he said.

Johns then explained their different motivations for *I Can't Believe*, which smacked of a side project indulgence:

> For Paul, he felt like he'd needed to express himself artistically again after writing a very mainstream pop/dance record [*3000 Feet High*, which was released in July 2002 and would sell more than 35,000 copies]. For me, I was getting back into writing again and I felt like I needed a catalyst. [But] next time it's going to be an actual album.

And that's exactly what they started to create as they hid themselves away in Imbruglia's basement.

Said Johns:

> It was never about, you know, 'I want to create a band to step up to the Silverchair mantle and take over the world.' It was just about creating a band that had a completely different set of rules – without expectations. We were baffled by how many people liked it, because we wrote and recorded all of it in two weeks [which was all the time Mac had to spare].

Taking a cue from the White Stripes, Johns and Mac shut themselves away in the basement of Imbruglia's Windsor mansion – dubbed 'Nat's Palace' by the Sleepy Jackson's Luke Steele, a close friend and songwriting partner of Johns's – and worked out some ground rules for the Dissociatives.

Johns admitted:

> We'd been talking about it for months and months. We just wanted to get ourselves in a dark, confined space, with all our own gear – a little computer, a microphone, a compressor and eight different

instruments, which was all we were allowed to use. Every single track we had to make sound different and interesting using these eight instruments. It was a test. We were adamant that the best creativity comes from restriction; when the possibilities aren't endless. Especially after *Diorama*, where we had some fucking money.

Although the musical magic they made was several light years away from Silverchair's electrified rock, the Dissociatives was a natural extension of Johns's increased involvement with Silverchair's writing and production. He wrote all the lyrics for the album's eleven songs – except, of course, for the breezy instrumental 'Lifting the Veil from the Braille', where Johns whistled while he worked – and recorded almost every note of the music with Mac during those two weeks in the basement. The dynamic duo also produced, recorded and mixed the album of cool, clean, digital-age pop, which had more in common with such continental acts as Air and Phoenix than it did with anything in Silverchair's back pages. There was a little outside input, mainly from drummer Kim Moyes who, along with Julian Hamilton and James Hazelwood, would later make up the Dissociatives live ensemble. The 'Surreal for the Kids' choir added their voice to several tracks, while Imbruglia sang on 'Thinking in Reverse'. (Johns would repay the favour by co-writing the track 'Satisfied' for Imbruglia's 2005 album, *Counting Down the Days*. 'It was very liberating,' Johns told me. 'I just went, "Right, I'm going to write a pop song for someone else."')

Having recorded all the music in Imbruglia's 'dark' basement, Johns and Mac then shifted base to Johns's home studio at his house in Merewether – aka 'Merry Wether Forever' studios – where they cut all of Johns's vocals. As the album's liner notes attest, the final 'digital swamps, crackle and pop' was added at Stereogamous Studios in Sydney. By the time a formal statement – which simply read, 'Meet the Dissociatives' – was released to the media on 11 December 2003, the album was done and dusted, and a video for the lead single, 'Somewhere Down the Barrel', had been shot by animator James Hackett, who was best known for his work on the opening credits for *Enough Rope with Andrew Denton*. (The eye-popping, part-animated, part-sort-of-live action video for 'Barrel' would later win an ARIA.) The single was scheduled for a February 2004 release, with their self-titled album set to follow two months later.

Not surprisingly, this announcement generated another round of whispers about the uncertain future of Silverchair, and Johns and Mac gave the rumour mill a further nudge when they insisted that the band was 'more than just a side project'. But as usual, the eternally restless Johns had little time to answer questions about where next for the 'Chair, because he was moving on again. Now he had a wedding to organise.

When Johns and Imbruglia announced their engagement in January 2003, I asked Johns what the commitment meant for him. After all, most rock stars don't necessarily conform to the more 'normal' aspects of society, and marriage seemed like an odd move for a restless guy such as Johns. 'It's awesome, really good,' he told me. 'It solidifies commitment and I think that's pretty important if you want stability – and that's basically what everyone wants. [But] I haven't thought about having children or becoming an adult.' At that stage, all Johns knew was that the wedding would take place in Australia, 'maybe in my backyard'. He even jokingly suggested that they could tie the knot at Newcastle landmark, Fort Scratchley. 'To scare off the paparazzi,' Johns figured, 'we could . . . point the cannons at them.'

But Johns's wedding proposal revealed a rarely-seen side of the man: he was a romantic. When he proposed, Johns and Imbruglia were surrounded by 300 pink and yellow roses, and the hefty platinum and diamond ring that he gave Imbruglia was from upscale jeweller Craig Leonard. Now he had to piece together an equally romantic wedding, and somehow also stop the snappers from spoiling the party.

The Fort Scratchley idea, of course, was just a ruse, but everyone involved with organising the A-list wedding did an exceptional job of keeping the venue a secret, as New Year's Eve 2003 rolled around. Throughout the week leading up to the wedding, virtually every rag and mag in the country speculated on just where the nuptials would be held. Even the guests, which included the families of Johns and Imbruglia; Silver-pals Ben Gillies and Chris Joannou; plus Paul Mac; Julian Hamilton; Eleven's John Watson and Melissa Chenery; as well as producer David Bottrill; piano virtuoso David Helfgott and his wife, Gillian, and actor Guy Pearce, had no idea where the gig was to be held.

The instructions on the wedding invitations were simple: the sixty guests were told to pack enough clothes for three days in a warm climate. They were also supplied with air tickets to Cairns. Upon arrival, they assembled and were then transported by bus to a secluded beachside stretch just outside Port Douglas's very upscale Thala Beach Lodge, a five star 'nature lodge' where the nightly room rates run close to $500. A specially built marquee had been set up for the occasion, in a tranquil clearing between the beach – part of a two-kilometre stretch of pristine coastline – and the resort.

Despite the tropical heat, Johns was resplendent in a vintage pale blue suit, a variation on the formal garb he'd been wearing during the opening halt of most Silverchair shows during 2003. Imbruglia's outfit was more sophisticated; she wore a V-necked silk chiffon wedding dress with a handkerchief hem from designer Monique Lhuillie, plus a Kaviar and Kind necklace and high heels – sand be damned – by Jimmy Choo. After a breakfast banquet the formal ceremony took place, followed by a DJ set from Paul Mac who, despite his strong bonds with the groom, still had to sing (or spin discs, to be precise) for his supper. Johns, however, had spelled this out to Mac beforehand. 'I told him, "Paul, if you want free accomm, you have to do something."'

Like many grooms, Johns recalls that the day went by in a blur of handshakes and toasts. 'I didn't get a chance to enjoy it, I was just so busy,' he said. 'It was beautiful, but it was just "Shake hands, shake hands, thanks for coming, thanks for coming."'

Interestingly, rather than call on his rock and roll pals to plug in and supply the music for the day, Johns (with a little help from his and Imbruglia's PR manager for the event, John Scott, and wedding producer Marcus Francisco) took a far more sophisticated approach. An eighteen-piece ensemble – including four percussionists, a five-piece string section and five men on horns – breezed their way through a selection of classical and world music tunes, which included such melodies as 'Crystal Silence' by Chick Corea, Tito Puente's 'Oya Como Va' and 'Ran Kan Kan', Dave Holland's 'Conference of the Birds' and 'Afro Blue' from Mongo Santamaria. Clearly, both Johns and Imbruglia had come a long way from their down-home, working-class roots. During one of his few quiet moments during the day, Johns took time out to adjourn for a few drinks with some old friends, and check out the band. He was impressed. 'Some of the musos we had were killer, playing sambas and things like that. I took away a couple of ideas.'

Not surprisingly, the couple had been offered serious dollars by the tabloid weeklies for exclusive access to their wedding snaps, an offer that had been taken up by such other celeb couples as Danielle Spencer and Russell Crowe and Bec Cartwright and Lleyton Hewitt. Johns and Imbruglia, however, had other plans. Although one unauthorised photographer did guess the right venue, and a helicopter buzzed the wedding during the actual ceremony, security managed to keep a tight lid on the event. At one point during the day, the guests arranged themselves in some kind of orderly fashion, and the one invited photographer, Adrienne Overall, who'd been shooting the band since the days of *Frogstomp*, took the money shot, which she immediately downloaded to her computer. The newlyweds agreed that any media outlet could buy the snap, but it would cost $5000 per usage, with the money going to the couple's charity of choice (which they chose not to reveal).

The few invitees that I've spoken to were full of praise for the big day. Julian Hamilton described it as 'lovely'; David Bottrill said it was 'great, apart from the helicopter'; David Helfgott felt it was 'beautiful'. Johns's mood was captured precisely by Andrew Denton, when they spoke a few months later. After asking about his relationship with Imbruglia, Denton said, 'I think you're enjoying life now. Would I be right?' 'Yeah, definitely, I love life,' Johns replied without hesitation. 'It's the best thing in the world.'

A post-honeymoon Johns would maintain his upbeat mood when the Australian public were given a sneak preview of the first Dissociatives single, 'Somewhere Down the Barrel', on 6 February The song was streamed on the EMI website three days later and would finally be available in the stores on 8 March. By early March, the highly hummable, keyboard-powered track would be one of the five most played tracks on Australian radio.

'It's probably the purest music that I've ever come up with,' Johns admitted, when asked about the Dissociatives.

> The idea of collaborating [wasn't] appealing to me until I realised the close musical connection I had with Paul. There's something about

two people with equal passion for something that really makes magic happen.

There was more than one partnership at work with the Dissociatives. James Hackett's excellent trilogy of inter-related videos, part animation, part live action photography, for 'Somewhere Down the Barrel', 'Young Man, Old Man' and 'Horror with Eyeballs' would go a long way towards establishing the Dissociatives' day-glo identity. Hackett had been approached by Melissa Chenery at Eleven on the strength of his work on the Denton show and ABC's Fly TV, a clip he'd directed for the band Bumblebeez, and an unsuccessful pitch that he'd made for a domestic violence campaign. He'd learnt the animation trade in London, where he worked on graphics for a variety of projects, including U2's Popmart tour. His style, which would be given full and colourful life in the three Dissociatives clips, was a curious whirlpool of influences, drawing from sources as diverse as film director Terry Gilliam, Japanese Manga comics, the recent videos from 'virtual' pop band Gorillaz and the films of Tim Burton. He would modestly refer to his work as 'cute experiments in broadcast design'.

Johns recalled:

We saw his show reel and what he was doing was what we were thinking: distorted imagery and something almost cartoonish, but not in a Gorillaz way. So we did what he already does and pushed it even further. We wanted surreal stories and all about the band. We saved the world a couple of times, because that was our job!

Hackett was hired to produce a Dissociatives 'package' – two videos (which was later extended to three), plus artwork for the band's album, their numerous singles and their 2004 tour. Budgets for each of the videos was set at a modest AUD$35,000. For 'Barrel', he spent three days in a Sydney studio with Mac and Johns, where he simply asked them to assume a variety of poses which, with the assistance of numerous computer programs, would make up the 'action' components of the videos. By the time of the third clip, for 'Horror with Eyeballs', Hackett only needed the pair for one day because, as he told me, 'we had lots of leftover body parts' which were simply recycled. Johns did bring along a guitar for the first shoot, but that was little more than a prop.

Johns and Mac didn't have a lot of creative involvement with the first video; they were sufficiently taken with Hackett's idiosyncratic vision to simply let him do his thing. By the time of the second clip they became more actively involved. 'After they saw the first one,' said Hackett, 'they understood what could be done.' Johns, in particular, grabbed the chance to mess with the 'serious young insect' persona he assumed for most Silverchair clips. By the end of 'Young Man, Old Man', Johns had morphed into a bearded hillbilly farmer, slapping out hand jive on his back porch. It was hardly 'Ana's Song'. According to Hackett, 'Daniel was right up for the idea' of destroying his Silverchair identity.

It was also Johns who suggested the idea of strapping on a pair of overalls for the guitar solo that closes 'Young Man, Old Man', a solo that Johns rates among his personal favourites. And, as any Guns 'n' Roses fan would attest, the backdrop for that solo was an irreverent 'loan' from their blockbuster clip for the song 'November Rain' – yet another Johns suggestion. Of the many highlights in the three videos – Johns and Mac doing battle with robot wasps in 'Barrel', the unlikely sight of Mac operating a combine harvester in 'Young Man' and the Gothic overtones of 'Horror with Eyeballs' – this was the perfect Dissociatives moment: it was clever, tuneful and wilfully perverse. Johns, however, rated the 'Horror with Eyeballs' clip as his favourite document of the Dissociatives era. 'I love that clip, I think it's the funniest, darkest clip ever. All those dismembered limbs, and there's Paul on his deathbed, smoking a cigarette.'

Despite the radical difference in musical style to anything Johns had recorded before – or maybe because of that 180 degree shift – critics gushed with praise for both 'Barrel' and the self-titled *Dissociatives* album, which dropped in early April and would go on to sell 60,000 copies locally. Australian *Rolling Stone,* long-time Daniel Johns advocates, gave the album a four star rating. 'Music unlike anything ever produced by an Australian act,' they boldly declared. 'A pop/rock record for the ages to be placed alongside your Beatles and Beach Boys discs.' But it wasn't as though the venerable rock rag was going it alone; virtually every review of the Dissociatives music was awash with praise. Writing in the *West Australian,* seasoned rock writer Michael Dwyer was sold. 'This is an album that's hard not to love,' he stated. *The Australian*'s veteran music writer, Iain Sheddon, was even more impressed by the album.'[It's] a beautiful work that will undoubtedly rattle the doors of Album of the Year come ARIAs time . . . '[It's] stomping, brooding, anthemic and incredibly poppy.' *Daily Telegraph* columnist Kathy McCabe called the album 'a masterpiece which can rightfully claim its place beside the great albums of our times.' The Dissociatives were compared to everyone from the Beatles to the Buggies, Radiohead to Brian Eno. Just over a year later, when the album was picked up for distribution in the UK, Germany, France, Belgium, Sweden and Switzerland, mostly strong regions for Silverchair in the past, the reviews were equally uplifting. *Mojo* declared that 'The Dissociatives lose touch with reality in gorgeous fashion', while Q magazine even likened the band to Antipodean pop treasures Crowded House, going on to say how the album was 'smart and brave in equal measures'.

Though few musicians admit to even reading their press, Johns revealed that the favourable response to the Dissociatives album, both critically and commercially, came as a huge relief. What he found even more gratifying was the realisation that he could be playful on record and get away with it.

According to Johns:

It was good for everyone involved with me, that record. It made me so much happier to know that people would still accept my music if I wasn't slitting my wrists.

And these reviews weren't blowing smoke; there really was a lot to like about the Dissociatives. They were refreshingly unfettered by the expectations of Johns's day job – he had told me more than once that he has felt like a 'prisoner' of Silverchair over the years – allowing the obligatory guitar crunch and heavy emotions to be relegated to the background, as washes of synths and a heavily processed mix of voices, bass and drums led the way. And despite some worryingly bleak song titles, such as 'Horror with Eyeballs' and 'Young Man, Old Man', Johns's lyrical mood was overwhelmingly bright and upbeat, proving that his *Diorama* mindset wasn't some post-anti-depressant aberration. As mentioned elsewhere, Johns was so damned chipper that he whistled his way through the irresistibly breezy 'Lifting the Veil from the Braille', acting on a suggestion from Mac. And in the stark, wistful ballad 'Forever and a Day', Johns and Mac crafted a valentine to Johns's soulmate, Natalie Imbruglia. He may have purged his emotions in the past, but Johns had never been bold enough to croon such lines as: 'A thousand sunshines on rainbows / I don't see nothing if I don't see you.'

When we exchanged emails in 2004, Johns was slightly coy when I asked him if the song was a straight-out love song for his wife. 'It could certainly be a love song,' he cagily replied. But the truth was in the track; it was a heart-aching standout on an album with more highs than a Woodstock reunion. As for Mac, he was more taken by such urgent, tearaway tracks as 'Thinking in Reverse', where he attacked the keys with all the ferocity of his playing on *Neoti Ballroom* and *Diorama*. Mac informed me that this was the one song he was truly looking forward to playing live, 'as it gives me a chance to have an old-fashioned bash on the piano.'

Forming a touring band for the Dissociatives was easy; all Johns and Mac had to do was sign up most of the players on the album (including Julian Hamilton and drummer Kim Moyes, plus new recruit, bassist James Haselwood). When their June/July Australian tour was announced – with Little Birdy, a band of Perth hopefuls signed to John Watson's label, Eleven, opening each show, along with the electro-pop Presets, whose members included the hard-working Moyes and Hamilton – the concerns about Silverchair's future increased. But Johns's work with the Dissociatives didn't bother Chris Joannou, for one, who would frequently check in on the album's progress. He seemed genuinely interested in the direction of Johns's new music. Yet a comment Johns made at the time of the tour announcement suggested he was having way more fun with his fellow Dissociatives than he was with the outfit that made him a star. 'I'm really looking forward to this tour, which is not something I'd usually say,' Johns understated.

Johns wasn't kidding when he said that this was an uncharacteristic statement. Little more than twelve months earlier he had given me the full rundown of why he was so reluctant to get on the road. 'I just get bored really quickly,' he said. Johns, at least initially, had no such concerns with the upcoming Dissociatives itinerary: they were only scheduled to play fifteen dates over a month, beginning in Hobart on 8 June and working their way through most capitals, plus such regional centres as Tweed Heads, Coffs Harbour and their hometown of Newcastle. The venues were more intimate than those Silverchair had filled on their 2003 tour – in Sydney the Dissociatives played two nights at the cosy Enmore Theatre, rather than the cavernous Entertainment Centre bunker – while their sets were shorter, concentrating on the album and a few whimsical covers, including Johns's gravelly-voiced take on Tom Waits's 'Coin' Out West', a song he'd always planned to cover.

'Funnily enough,' keyboardist Julian Hamilton admitted to me, 'that was probably the most enjoyable song for me to play in the whole show.' As for Johns, he loved singing it, but quickly learned that his throat wasn't necessarily built for the tune. 'It didn't hurt to sing; by that stage I was pretty loose, in more ways than one. But for the next hour I'd stop and clear my throat and go, "Tom Waits is getting to me."' As for the rest of the Dissociatives setlist, there were definitely no Silverchair songs. As Hamilton pointed out to me, Silverchair and the Dissociatives were 'completely different bands: different music, different people, very different dynamic'.

One thing that didn't change dramatically was the make-up of the crowd at each of the shows. The same screaming teens that had treated the 'Across the Night' shows like some kind of second coming were there in numbers during the Dissociatives tour. And they were in equally strong voice. Julian Hamilton confirmed this when I asked him about the crowds at each gig. 'It was the same mental 'Chair fans at all the Dissos's shows,' he reported. 'The 'Chair fans certainly are a special bunch,' he added. 'Every tour we do, there are always a group of kids who are at every show, every airport, every hotel. They must spend so much money following the guys around.'

Hamilton was among the many people who were reluctant to use the term 'side project' when discussing the Dissociatives. To him, it was every bit as vital as Silverchair – or any of his own projects, such as Prop and the Presets, for that matter.

'I generally don't like the term "side project",' he told me.

It seems to imply that just because a musical project doesn't sell as many records, or doesn't get as many 'bums on seats' as an artist's 'main project', then it is somehow less important to the artist or, as the name suggests, it is just something worth pursuing on the side. In that respect, the Dissos was definitely more than a side project to Dan and Paul. They seemed to put as much love and energy into that project as they would The Paul Mac Experience or Silverchair.

However, Hamilton went to some lengths to point out that it wasn't all strictly business on the Dissociatives tour. Drummer Kim Moyes had mentioned to me that Johns's love of pot meant that he 'smoked harder than Snoop Dogg', and Hamilton had no reason to doubt this, saying:

It's not my recreational drug of choice, but there sure was a lot of it around on that Oz tour, let me tell you! The secondary smoke coming from Dan's joints in the tour bus got me pretty stoned.

Later on, Johns would freely admit that he was stoned for pretty much the entire two-year life of the Dissociatives.

During the Dissociatives period I was excessive. I remember all of it, and fondly, but I was trying to break something in my brain [with pot] and I think I did. I'm not smoking as much now.

(However, in early 2006, when Silverchair were readying demos for their fifth album in an inner-city Sydney studio, a colleague caught up with Johns for several hours and failed to recall a single moment when the Silver-star didn't have a lit joint in hand.)

Hamilton had seen Johns at his worst, physically. During the brief New Zealand Silverchair tour of January 2002, he recalled how Johns 'seemed to be in quite bad shape . . . He wasn't coming out for drinks after the shows, he wouldn't go swimming with us. He pretty much stayed to himself.' But the singer's mood was decidedly more upbeat on the Dissociatives tour of 2004. According to Hamilton, the band – including

Johns – spent 'heaps' of time together. 'We had many a night out on the town here and overseas,' Hamilton said.

The lead-up to the tour, in a promotional sense, couldn't have been better: Mac and Johns beamed from the cover of the June 2004 issue of *Rolling Stone*, and the pair co-programmed ABC TV's *Rage*, focusing purely on videos that had some kind of animal reference. Their playlist included the Muppets, the Beatles' 'I Am the Walrus', Sleepy Jackson, Radiohead, Mercury Rev, Pink Floyd's wigged-out 'Set the Controls for the Heart of the Sun', Spinal Tap and Kenny Rogers, while their contribution segued into a hefty set of Silverchair and Paul Mac clips. The band then performed 'Somewhere Down the Barrel' on *Rove Live*, while the night before their tour began, Johns opened up in his far-reaching, occasionally clumsy interview with Andrew Denton, and then plugged in with the band to sing 'Horror with Eyeballs'. It was the perfect set-up for a tour that received the same kind of critical thumbs-up as their album, which had debuted in the Australian charts at Number Twelve.

Covering the Dissociatives' Sydney shows, street press mag *Brag* likened them to American psychedelic minstrels the Flaming Lips, currently one of the hottest live tickets on the planet. *Drum Media* was equally effusive, praising the band's 'almost bizarre but amazing performance'. (Johns had taken to playing some shows wearing aviator sunglasses missing one lens, which did add an odd twist to the onstage overload of flashing lights, images and swirling sounds.) Other street press mags were all over the gigs; *dB*'s critic claimed it was 'easily one of the best shows I've seen in the last couple of years,' while *Beat* declared that the Dissociatives were 'grand and surprising'. But *Rave* magazine topped the list for smart observations. 'The Dissociatives preset their controls for the heart of the sun,' they wrote, 'with their happy, psychedelic pop.'

Mind you, there were one or two hitches along the way to psychedelic bliss. Good business at the box office meant that additional shows were added in such far-flung spots as Tamworth, Blacktown, Port Macquarie, Byron Bay and Warrnambool, which made the tour's itinerary far more expansive than any Silverchair road-trip since the time of their Summer Freak Shows. But two weeks in, Johns's voice started to show signs of wear. The band reached Sawtell, on the NSW north coast, for a show on 22 June, and went as far as setting up and sound-checking, when it became painfully clear that Johns simply had no voice left. The show was cancelled. The next night the band moved on to Brisbane, where they managed to get through their set, but Johns admitted from the stage that they'd also considered cancelling that gig right up until showtime. Johns took a trip to the local rock doctor immediately afterwards, who advised him to blow out the next couple of shows and let his voice recover, which he did.

But with one exception, there was little of the drama, both physical and psychological, that had plagued Daniel Johns's life on the road in the past. Killing time before their gig at rural Warrnambool, the band soaked up a few hours at the local pub. But as the word got around that 'Daniel from Silverchair' was in the house, an unfriendly vibe started to build as a crowd grew around the band. Eventually, Paul Mac took the sensible step of driving Johns back to their motel. For a few brief moments, Johns was reliving the worst moments of Silverchair, when his celebrity eliminated any chance of a normal life. But in the main, just like their album, the Dissociatives tour was a good time, pretty much all the time. Paul Mac summed it up neatly after they played their final date at Byron's Splendour in the Grass festival, and readied a DVD, *Sydney Circa 2004slash08*, for release.

'The Dissociatives tour was really special,' he stated. 'Hopefully this DVD will allow people who missed the gigs to get a sense of how much fun they were.' To make the package complete, the trio of James Hackett-directed videos – for 'Somewhere Down the Barrel', 'Young Man, Old Man' and 'Horror with Eyeballs' – were added to the DVD, rounding off footage of the band's wildly received set at Sydney's Enmore Theatre. Johns's Silverchair bandmates, Claris Joannou and Ben Gillies, were in that crowd, cheering him on.

As it turned out, the Dissociatives Australian tour was really only the first part of Johns's post-Silverchair odyssey. In mid September, the nominations for the 2004 ARIAs were revealed, and the Dissociatives had scooped the pool, making the shortlist for Best Pop Release, Best Group, Album of the Year, Producer of the Year (a particularly sweet nomination for the Johns/Mac team), Best Cover Art and Best Video (James Hackett was nominated for the latter two gongs). Even though the band would only claim the 'minor' awards for Cover Art and Video, these half dozen nominations proved to anyone who dared ask that the Dissociatives were way more than some mere 'side project'. A. subsequent APRA Award nomination, for Song of the Year, only served to strengthen that. (Their Eleven label-mate, Missy Higgins, would win that trophy for her watery hit 'Scar'.) James Hackett would also go on to claim an AVMA Video of the Year award for 'Somewhere Down the Barrel', at the inaugural Australian MTV Awards, held at Luna Park. Backstage, before the band's performance, a clearly chuffed Daniel Johns worked on his sweet tooth, wandering around with a handful of lollipops. 'Dannii Minogue didn't quite know what to make of it,' Julian Hamilton laughed.

By this time, Silverchair had already made their triumphant, shirtless return at the WaveAid fundraiser a month earlier. The sheer energy and electricity of their performance quickly killed off any suggestions that the band had simply run out of steam, or that Johns was more interested in his life as a Dissociative.

But even though Johns had begun to think seriously about the next Silverchair LP as soon as their WaveAid set was through, the Dissociatives still had touring commitments, playing shows in Europe and the UK during 2005, supporting their album's release in Europe, the UK and North America. To Johns, those shows were not just the best that the Dissociatives would play, but they were some of the best sets of his life. 'We were in these packed little clubs and we were just going to town, doing these wacky, Frank Zappa-inspired gigs.'

That run of shows also reminded Johns of the differences between playing with the garage-raw rockers of Silverchair and the more schooled Dissociatives.

> I'm really inspired by playing with guys who have formal training. I feel so lucky to have worked with those guys. With Silverchair, I show Chris how the bass goes, then do the same with Ben and then say, 'Right, just make this sound good.' With the Dissociatives, they'd go, 'Right, that's an A-minor inflection there,' and I'm like, 'Wow, don't overwhelm me with details!'

At the end of the Dissociatives European tour, the rest of the band took the time to check out Natalie Imbruglia's basement, where the core of the album had been recorded. Julian Hamilton was actually a guest of Imbruglia's for a couple of weeks but, sadly, found that the basement had been stripped of any musical equipment. 'There was nothing that hinted at past album glories,' he revealed.

Come August 2005, Paul Mac announced that he had been spending the past few months working on tunes for the second Paul Mac Experience album, *Panic Room,* prior to an appearance at the annual Homebake festival. This was the first time Daniel Johns had seen Mac play outside of either Silverchair or the Dissociatives.

So it wasn't just Daniel Johns who was moving on; Mac had other musical plans.

Hamilton and Moyes's outfit, the Presets, meanwhile, were gaining considerable attention for their wicked electro-pop album, *Beams,* to which Johns contributed a co-write and played guitar. 'I guess you could say he's had an influence on our sound,' Hamilton admitted, when I asked about this collaboration, '[but] I'd like to think that working with us influences Daniel as much as he influences us.' The Presets were also in demand in Europe, where they toured in early 2006, and were one of ten acts hand-picked by Absolut vodka to put their own spin on Lenny Kravitz's track 'Breathe', the soundtrack to the Absolut Kravitz music project. At the launch at Sydney's Australian Technology Park in late February 2006, Johns and Mac looked on like proud parents as the Presets tore a hole in 'Breathe' before a crowd of music and fashion scenesters. All this activity meant that Hamilton had to pass, reluctantly, on touring with Silverchair for their handful of dates in March and April 2006.

As for Ben Gillies and Chris Joannou, they'd clearly spent enough time on the sidelines watching Daniel Johns reinvent himself as a psychedelic pop star. They had their own musical projects to pursue. Joannou had obviously been putting his home studio to good use, because he signed up as co-producer for White Stripes-influenced duo the Mess Hall. Joannou shared production credits with engineer Matt Lovell, who had helped out in the studio with the past three Silverchair albums, as well as working on chart-topping albums from Melbourne pop/rock moodists Something for Kate (and maintaining a daily log on www.chairpage.com during the creation of *Diorama*). (Lovell had actually been living in the guest house at Joannou's McMasters Beach house for several months, so his relationship with Joannou ran much deeper than the studio.) The pair's first co-production was a single for singer/songwriter Josh Pyke.

Melburnians the Mess Hall had been peddling their dirty blues since 2001, playing hundreds of shows all across the country. By the time they came off the road to record their debut EP, *Feeling Sideways*, with Joannou and Lovell, they had fine-tuned their sound to the point where their co-producers simply had to capture the pair's mad energy on tape. The lead track, 'Lock and Load', whose 'cocaine / cocaine' chant hinted at the Queen of the Stone Age's toxic 'Feel Good Hit of the Summer', was adopted like some long-lost stepchild by Triple J, who put the song into high rotation upon its release in 2003.

Joannou and Lovell used the same uncluttered approach to recording the duo's debut album, *Notes From the Ceiling*, over a fortnight at Byron Bay's Rocking Horse studio. The LP came out in June 2005. They may not have had to add much in the way of studio polish, but Joannou still received a surprise Best Producer ARIA nomination, although, just as with Johns's Dissociatives, he didn't win the gold on the night. (However, in a stuff-up worthy of *Yes, Minister*, Lovell did win the ARIA for Best Engineer despite not rating a nomination for Best Producer, even though he co-produced the record with Joannou.) But the project was ample proof that Joannou wasn't content with being known simply as 'Chris from Silverchair'. 'Chris is awesome in the studio,' said Lovell. 'He's got a good head for music.'

As for Ben Gillies, he took the lead from Johns and formed a new band. Just like the Dissociatives, Tambalane was worlds away from the music made by Silverchair. Gillies's relationship with Tambalane co-songwriter, guitarist and singer, Wes Carr, was a creative marriage of convenience. During this lengthy stretch of Silverchair inactivity, Gillies and his partner had moved from Newcastle to Bondi; Adelaide-born Carr, meanwhile, had been living in Sydney for a few years, after being expelled from an Adelaide high school in 1998. So, for starters, they happened to be in the same city at the same time, were both looking for work and were both signed to Sony Publishing. Carr had been playing and writing for a few years when he met John Watson, who had briefly worked with him with the view of possibly making a record (which didn't happen). Gillies, who'd not contributed any songs to the past two Silverchair albums, was still writing music. Prior to meeting Gillies, Carr cut a self-funded EP, which he flogged after his solo gigs. During a few of these shows Gillies looked on from the crowd, chewing over whether he could write with Carr.

When I asked Daniel Johns about his rejection of any Silverchair input from Gillies, he explained that he and his old schoolmate were heading in completely different songwriting directions.

Johns confessed:

> To keep this band working, I had these conceptual ideas [*Neon Ballroom* and *Diorama*] that I had to do by myself. I can't share them with people. I wanted ... to be totally selfish with that. Ben was cool with that. He just said that he loves playing in this band, and I guess he must like the songs that I write. I'm sure that he's writing at home.

Several years later, Gillies finally had the chance to flex some creative muscle.

During their first song writing session, sparks flew between Carr and Gillies. They sketched out a couple of songs during that initial meeting and over the next few months wrote somewhere between thirty and forty tunes, which were demoed and shortlisted for a proposed Tambalane album. Even at this early stage, Gillies fully understood the usefulness of the band for both him and Carr. 'Tambalane helps him break the shackles of being a one-man-folk-band in a smoky pub just as it helps me break the shackles of Silverchair,' he figured, reasonably enough.

John Watson took on the role of managing Tambalane, a band that was rounded out by bassist Greg Royal and keyboardist Gerard Masters. Keeping with his policy of helping out those who had been loyal to Silverchair over the years, Watson sent their demos to 'Tomorrow' producer Phil McKellar, who immediately liked what he heard. He thought Carr had an 'amazing voice' and that the Carr/Gillies twosome was 'a great teaming'. 'They were awesome demos,' McKellar told me. The veteran producer was equally impressed by the sonic quality of the demos; Gillies had become a Pro Tools master, and it showed in these polished recordings.

McKellar recognised that, just like the Dissociatives, Tambalane had the potential to be more than some side project dalliance on the part of Gillies. Before they started recording at Sydney's Megaphon studios, he met the pair in a pub, and slipped them a copy of the John Lennon DVD, *Gimme Some Truth: The Making of Imagine*, a priceless document of an album in creation. He also gave them a copy of *The Best of Badfinger*. 'Great songs, great sounds,' McKellar explained to me. 'That's what I wanted to achieve.' While in the studio – the album was recorded in twenty days and mixed over ten – McKellar also exposed the pair to DVDs of the peerless UK Classic Albums series, making sure they checked out the making of Fleetwood Mac's *Rumours*. These were prime motivational tools for Tambalane.

The self-titled Tambalane record featured a dozen Carr/Gillies cowrites and was released independently in August 2005. Anyone who was surprised how far Johns had strayed from Silverchair with the Dissociatives was in for another shock: clearly inspired by the pristine pop that McKellar had exposed them to, Gillies and Carr had written an album of high-grade, grown-up, melodic rock and roll, with hints of the type of tunes you'd only hear on a radio tuned to the early 1970s. There was none of the heavy-metal thunder that Gillies had brought to *Frogstomp* and *Freak Show*. In fact, there were even hints of the pomp rock of Queen in such songs as 'Become', while 'Livin' on the Upside' hinted at the rock and raunch of the Black Crowes, Bon Jovi echoed through 'Skywalk', and the swampy blues of Creedence Clearwater Revival left their mark during 'Jungle'. They may have lacked a distinctive voice of their own, but Tambalane was some sort of eight-legged human jukebox.

Yet despite a residency at Sydney's Annandale Hotel, some Triple J airplay, and a belated lease on life when their track 'Free' was picked up for a Foxtel Commonwealth Games ad, the *Tambalane* album failed to connect with a larger audience, and the band broke up. Months later, McKellar, for one, was still scratching his head about the LP's lack of recognition: 'The album achieved exactly what their goals were – I'm dumbfounded that it's gone unheard.'

John Watson hinted at some disharmony within the Tambalane ranks. 'There ended up being a bit of friction there,' he mentioned in an email, 'so I think it's something [that Gillies is] not keen to revisit in any depth.' Gillies, however, was typically sanguine when I asked him where Tambalane went wrong. 'There was a bit of a power struggle [between me and Carr] towards the end,' he said.

Gillies did, however, undergo a handy crash course in life within an indie band during his time with Tambalane: he was responsible for finding people to help with promotion and distribution, tasks he had never had to undertake as part of Silverchair.

Speaking several months down the line, Gillies compared Tambalane's lack of chemistry with the magic that happens when Silverchair plugs in.

> 'That was one thing Tambalane made me realise,' he told *Rolling Stone*. It's just that thing that sets bands apart, that certain something you can't really put your finger on. You can't replicate it with a bunch of guys you call up and go, 'Let's have a session.'

By the time the members of Tambalane went their separate ways, Gillies was well and truly set to return to Silverchair. He and Joannou had just received a call from Johns, who had been spending another northern summer in the UK with Imbruglia, balancing his time between songwriting, fulfilling his chosen role as Captain Nobody and taking in intermittent bursts of English sunshine. Daniel Johns was about to make his bandmates an offer they'd be foolish to refuse: he wanted to make another Silverchair album.

* * *

The Engine Room: An Interview with Ben Gillies and Chris Joannou

Since the days of *Neon Ballroom*, Silverchair has felt increasingly like the Daniel Johns Band. However, bassist Chris Joannou and drummer Ben Gillies have always been an integral part of the Silver-machine. And with their latest album, *Young Modern*, in the can, they're looking forward to a future where, as Gillies says, 'You put us in a room with any of the top ten bands in the world, [and] we could take them.'

How different is the new four-piece Silverchair to the 'big band' of Diorama?
Ben Gillies: It's definitely a different vibe; it's more back to being a rock band. It's been really good, a lot of fun.

Chris Joannou: It's a completely different feel with this record. The last one wasn't exactly smooth sailing.

Are there standouts amongst the songs for Young Modern *– and how different will this record sound from* Diorama?
CJ: Collectively, they're all pretty exciting to play. New stuff is always good. They're definitely a lot rawer. 'Straight Lines' is really fun to play live; people think at the start it's a ballad and then it grows and grows. You can see people get right into it. It's an epic.

BG: It'll have flavours of *Diorama,* but it won't be quite as polished, or quite the onslaught that *Diorama* was. I think it'll be like splashes of things here and there, rather than being bombarded. And there's a sense of looseness about the new songs, definitely. With the new record we're trying to capture the feeling of it, rather than make it perfect. And that approach is now rippling back through our older songs when we play live.

Did you have any concerns about working with Nick Launay again?
CJ: I think both parties have changed dramatically since we last worked together. Nick has been living in LA and has found a new lease of life; his enthusiasm is incredible. He works himself into the ground.

BG: I think now it's not so much like the band and the producer. I think we're all more confident. His producing was kind of heavy in the past, but now, for capturing that magic and pulling good sounds out of us, he's perfect for this band and this record. And I think six takes is maximum; if you can't get it in six, move on. We have the confidence and knowledge to know, now, when something isn't working.

CJ: And trust me, you don't have that spark by the twentieth take.

Are the three of you still coming from the same place, musically speaking?
BG: We had a night out recently where we had a few drinks together and a few laughs and I wrote down this great list of records that those guys have that I don't. [Nick Cave's] *Abattoir Blues* was one of those. The Rapture, too, and the Necks. The really good one we've been listening to is Brian Eno and David Byrne, *My Life in the Bush of Ghosts*. They sit on these fucking unbelievable grooves forever.

CJ: It was good to hang out, talking music, shooting the shit. It's good to find out what other people are getting into.

Are you comfortable with the band's new sense of independence?
BG: The only people looking over our shoulder are the people in our inner circle, but even they know the deal. And Dan has been very cool about not being regimented with what he wants; he's been very open to everyone. And everyone's been saying things that they genuinely think could make it better, rather than out of pure ego. It's such a good way to work.

CJ: It just feels a lot more comfortable in the band than it has for a while.

How do you look back on the experience with Atlantic, especially the recording of a song on the demand of the label?
BG: For a B-side ['Ramble'], that was just fucking nuts. But you could see where the guy [Kevin Williamson] was coming from, that it sounded different to what we've done in the past, and he wanted the 'rock song'. But I thought 'Greatest View' was the perfect song for America. In the start, they approached us in typical record company style, giving us all the Led Zeppelin studio recordings. They always love you at the start. But I couldn't work it out; if they were smart, and listened to all three records up to then, they should have seen that we were going to go further out there. They were being a bit naïve thinking we were going to do the same thing. But we've always had weird experiences with record companies overseas. Even on *Freak Show* they were adamant that 'Abuse Me' was the first single and it was such a fucking mistake. Record companies aren't always right.

CJ: That was pretty silly. And the guy pretty much telling Daniel that he needed to go away and write the first single, that's enough to send anyone insane. I reckon they were in damage control from the time they first heard Daniel's demo for 'Tuna in the Brine'. That was the most out there Daniel song I'd ever heard.

What's your take on Sir Whilliam, Daniel's new persona?
BG: It's been funny; Daniel and I have been staying together and we've had a couple of nights out – my girlfriend's in Newcastle and Natalie's overseas, so we've had a few conversations about knowing when he should turn it on and turn it off. He's got it down to a fine art.

Is there an explanation for the band's more relaxed approach on stage?
CJ: Half way through the *Diorama* tour, I reckon it changed. There was a German show where a bottle of Kashaza and a bottle of vodka went, even before we went on. I don't know how it happened. It would have to be the worst show we've ever done, but at the time we thought it was great. I think that was the night we'd discovered the boundary of where we could push it.

BG: There were a couple of nights where we were blind on stage and somehow pulled it off.

Yet you spoke about being nervous at the Gaelic Club show in March 2006.
CJ: I was bloody nervous; it was pretty nerve-racking. There was a sense of feeling comfortable because you know most of the people in the crowd, but at the same time you're going, 'Oh shit, they're going to be the biggest critics.'

BG: There's something about those small shows that's just electrifying on stage. With the bigger shows you have to project so much more, and that sucks up so much energy. It's so much more exciting to have the people right there, in your face. I think it's so much easier for us to connect with each other in those smaller gigs – it's like in *Ghost-busters* where they're trying to cross the streams; this is us trying to cross the streams.

Would you say you've learned something about the band from your shows in 2006?
BG: I think one of the special things about this band is our musical rapport; I think there's something almost telepathic about it. We all know where we're going to push and pull, we all know the groove we're shooting for. With all our past records, we've always gone in with an idea of recording live and then we've done the rhythm track and decided to revert to a traditional approach. And we've realised that got rid of that initial connection between the three of us when we play. This time, being older and having a little more control, we've decided, 'This is it, this is how it's going to be.' You hope you can capture that special moment.

CJ: Even for the demos of the new album, you can see that whole idea. We did eleven songs in three days; we did eleven rhythm tracks in one day. You can really feel the spark, the energy. To scrap all that and start again doesn't seem right.

Was Wave A id a turning point for Silverchair's future?
CJ: We had those few days of rehearsal beforehand, but it wasn't until we played – in fact, after the gig – that we went, 'Holy shit, how much fun was that?' It probably wasn't the greatest show we've ever played, but the energy after that show was amazing.

BG: I was less nervous at Rock in Rio than Wave Aid. I was fucking nervous that day. But it was incredible, the whole day. It would have to be in the top five moments of my life. It was just incredible.

Did you sense that Diorama *could have been the end for the band?*
CJ: I thought, well, it could be a year, it could be five years before we do anything again. Dan was doing the Dissociatives thing and we knew it could at least be a couple of years before Silverchair would even talk about making another record. You have to do something with your time, so I started working with Matt [Lovell]. I really enjoyed the Dissociatives; Dan and Paul have a special kind of musical relationship that really works on

a number of levels. And I was really surprised when I heard the record; I didn't expect it to be so pop-based. I expected it to be a lot weirder.

BG: To be honest, over the years, even after *Freak Show* and *Neon Ballroom*, we've always taken time off after the record and didn't really know where we were going to go. But I always knew in the back of my head that none of us were going to let Silverchair go; it's always the kind of thing where you know – especially after everything that happened with *Diorama* – that you need some time to step back. You have to have a long hard think about keeping the band going.

What did you take away from your Tambalane project, while Silverchair was on hold?
BG: The whole Tambalane experience, for me, was a godsend, even though at the end, the singer, Wes, and I were both on different pages; it was going in a direction I didn't want it to go. In the future, if I have any new music, I'm just going to put it up on the Internet for free. That's all I want. But I learned fucking truckloads about the music industry, things like budgets and so on. Because we were independent we had to get our own radio guy, our own publicist, and find out how much we had to pay them. It was a good experience, and I do like the record, although in hindsight I'd do things a lot differently, but it really made me appreciate being the drummer in Silverchair. John Watson has always said that Silverchair has a musical connection that he's never seen before. And I think Daniel feels the same thing. After the Tambalane thing I went, 'Fuck, he's right again.'

CJ: It's like a marriage.

Do you think you're in good shape for what will be two full years of Silverchair?
CJ: Yeah. I think there's a pretty conscious design to lock out a couple of years and really go for it.

BG: We've really decided to put in the time. In Australia we have a pretty solid base, but overseas it's been a long time since we've really been on the scene, this time around we know that we're going to have to work hard. We're buzzing now; all the ingredients are right. And if we didn't get through that *Diorama* experience, we wouldn't be buzzing so much now. I honestly believe that if you put us in a room with any of the top ten bands in the world, we could take them. It's not arrogance, either.

Chapter Nine

A NEW TOMORROW

> You don't want anything from *Frogstomp* anymore,
> do you, mate? You've just seen the future.
> Daniel Johns to heckler, Gaelic Club, Sydney, March 2006

It didn't take long for the 2006 version of Silverchair to reveal a totally new side of their collective nature: pragmatism. Having been dropped by Atlantic after the underwhelming US sales of *Diorama*, they were label-less outside Australia. In the early months of the new year they had to find the perfect way to reintroduce themselves to their loyal audience, and at the same time raise the necessary cash to record their fifth album. Unless they were willing to dip into their own savings, the band had to generate approximately AUD$500,000 – somewhere close to the *Diorama* budget – and figured that the best way to do this was to get back to the road. But rather than play a series of one-nighters, which were liable to mess with their leader's mind and body, they agreed to a trio of large-scale events: the Rock-It Festival, held at Joondalup in Western Australia on 19 March; the Clipsal 500 car race in Adelaide on 24 March – 'the greatest motorsport festival on Earth', according to its promoters, which must have had boundless appeal to the car-loving men of Silverchair – and the Great Escape, a festival held over the Easter weekend in Sydney, where they were to share the Friday night bill on 14 April with Icelandic guitarchitects Sigur Rós.

Yet in spite of their big-ticket comeback, Silverchair's first public show since January 2005's WaveAid couldn't have been any more low-key. Billing themselves as Short Elvis, the tag they used as schoolkids when their set list consisted of 'The Elephant Rap' and little more, they announced a 'secret show' at Sydney's Gaelic Club on 16 March. It had the same exclusive feel The Australian Silverchair Show had in Newcastle's Cambridge Hotel way back at the beginning of the *Neon Ballroom* tour.

The few hundred tickets that were available to the public were, not surprisingly, snapped up within hours of the show's announcement on www.chairpage.com in early March. The rest of the crowd of 700 comprised true believers hand-picked for the guest list by Eleven's Melissa Chenery, which explained the high proportion of media in the crowd. (It was another smart move by Chenery, an integral part of the Eleven/Silverchair machine since 1996.) At a glance I spotted writers and photographers from *Rolling Stone*, *J Mag*, *The Australian*, the *Telegraph* and more, standing armpit-to-armpit alongside the usual industry players and eager punters. Well before the doors opened at 7.30, the queue snaked for several hundred metres along inner city Devonshire Street, with punters eager to get a rare close-up view of the band. To Watson, it must have felt like their first US shows way back in 1995, just as 'Tomorrow' exploded. There was a tangible excitement to the gig, which clearly spilled over to the four guys on stage.

After a quick 'hello', the newly stripped-back four-piece Silverchair: Johns, Gillies, Joannou and Paul Mac – who had just signed on for a two-year commitment to the band – moved swiftly into a new track. With a working title of 'If You Keep Losing Sleep', the song had a relentless funkiness that brought to mind Californicators the Red Hot Chili Peppers. And the band's on-stage dress sense also hinted at the funky punks: Johns wore a sleeveless vest, which he discarded after a few songs, while Gillies didn't even bother with a shirt, playing the entire set topless, a la most of the Chili Peppers, a group of reprobates who don't appear to actually own shirts. Joannou was more circumspect in a regulation top, sleeves rolled up, ready for business. As for Mac, he sported a top that read 'Yoko Ono', his self-effacing joke about his role as the man who keeps dragging Johns away from the band for their own pet projects. (A few weeks later, Johns explained to me that Mac had called him before the show to get his approval. Johns thought it was a great idea, adding that 'it had to be better than a T-shirt that read Linda [McCartney] or Courtney [Love].')

But rather than use the Gaelic Club gig as a chance to road test new songs only, the quartet offered up a 'greatest hits' set, of sorts. Johns good-naturedly fended off frequent requests from the moshpit for songs from *Frogstomp*, but did deliver such 'oldies' as 'The Door', 'Emotion Sickness', 'Pink Pastel Princess', 'Ana's Song' and a hefty serving of *Diorama* tracks – 'Tuna in the Brine', 'Across the Night', 'The Greatest View', and the usual set-closing 'The Lever'. These were intermingled with a handful of new tunes-under-development, which included 'Sleep All Day', 'Mind Reader' and 'Straight Lines', the aforementioned blend of U2's 'With Or Without You' – a reference that Johns loved – and Coldplay's 'Clocks' (which he wasn't so mad about). The most accessible of the new tunes, 'Straight Lines' had hit written all over it.

When the *Frogstomp* requests kept coming at the Gaelic Club, Johns tore into another new song, and then observed: 'You don't want anything from *Frogstomp* anymore, do you, mate? You've just seen the future.' And it clearly didn't matter that the band were a tad rusty at times; when Joannou fluffed the opening bass line from 'Across the Night', Johns simply stopped, smiled at his old pal, and told the faithful: 'It's OK, it's just a rehearsal – and you didn't pay full price, anyway.'

Johns had never been more gracious or playful on stage, frequently thanking the crowd for simply showing up. He even requested that someone buy him a vodka tonic, which hastily appeared on stage from somewhere deep in the moshpit. The garrulous Johns also passed his judgement on Surry Hills, the sleazy-but-chic Sydney inner-city suburb where the Gaelic Club is situated: 'Eez good,' Johns slurred, 'I like.' At one point he even warned the audience about one of the more furious-paced new songs, as if he was performing some kind of rock and roll community service. 'This'll hit you like a truck,' he grinned. And it did.

Gillies, however, admitted that he felt more nervous prior to the Gaelic Club show than he did before plugging in at such mega-shows as WaveAid or Rock In Rio. 'I was scared shitless,' he confessed, 'because we knew everyone in the crowd and were worried they'd be judging us.'

Yet for the first time in more than ten years of playing live, Johns seemed completely comfortable on stage. Maybe it had something to do with the two-year-long pot binge he underwent while with the Dissociatives, or perhaps married life had mellowed him. Maybe it was because he had relaxed his attitude towards onstage drinking. (A few weeks later, at the Great Escape, he stumbled drunkenly about the stage, swigging heartily from a bottle of bourbon during the band's set.) Whatever the reason for Johns's newfound onstage freedom, it was infectious: Silverchair have never smiled so much. 'I just walked onstage at the Gaelic Club and immediately felt comfortable,' Johns told me, when I caught up with him during pre-production for the band's fifth album.

The night was a huge success, a near flawless way of informing both the paying public and the media that 2006 would be the year of the 'Chair. Oddly enough, it was also the first time that Paul 'Yoko' Mac had played live with the band (unless you considered his cameo with Silverchair at the 2002 ARIAs a 'live' performance), despite his considerable input to their past two albums and the Dissociatives LP. 'We didn't want to throw him in the deep end, you know,' Johns explained.' You know, "There's 20,000 people out there, Paul, don't fuck up."'

The Gaelic Club gig felt more like a formal rehearsal than a serious, pre-tour showcase. Despite the huge scale of the shows they were about to play – they drew a crowd of 20,000 in Perth, almost 40,000 at the Clipsal race and around 10,000 in Sydney – and the pressure of getting back into the studio to make a worthy follow-up to *Diorama*, the band seemed remarkably relaxed. They threw themselves into each song, irrespective of whether it was a new track or something from their now sizeable back catalogue, with all the glee of a quartet fresh out of the garage. Long into the night, well after the show had ended, Ben Gillies – now wearing a shirt – mingled with the hundred or so punters who stuck around after the gig, beaming a smile through his lengthy mane of hair and droopy, pimp-worthy moustache. His smile said it all: Silverchair were most definitely back in the building.

There had been plenty of advance warning of the band's 'proper' return, prior to their Gaelic Club show. On 18 November 2005, a press release entitled 'Back in the Chair' clogged in-boxes all around the country, as EMI and Eleven confirmed what most media already knew: Silverchair were working together again, still buoyed by their WaveAid performance several months earlier.

The release proclaimed:

> Silverchair have confirmed rumours that they are currently making music together in regional NSW. The band has also announced that they plan to record a new album and do at least a few gigs during 2006 . . . Providing all goes well with these very select dates the band will then start recording their new album around next May. It will probably be released in late 2006 or early 2007 and more extensive touring is pencilled [in for] thereafter.

And no official Silverchair announcement was complete without at least one denial: 'Since 2003 Silverchair have denied several inaccurate media reports which claimed that the band had split up,' snapped the final sentence.' This announcement will hopefully put that issue to rest.'

Of course, Silverchair's return to the stage and the studio wasn't that simple. Even though the trio rediscovered their mojo at WaveAid, Johns had returned to the UK soon after with plans for another non-Chair project, in this case a solo album. And he did more than consider the idea; by the middle of 2005 he had spent time writing songs with both Julian Hamilton and Luke Steele, the dreamer who led the band Sleepy Jackson. Steele had impressed Johns during a few support dates on the 'Across the Night' tour, and had become a close pal. These collaborations were destined, at least at the time they were written, for Johns's solo LP. (Three co-writes with Hamilton would end up on the Silverchair album, while the Steele co-writes were kept aside for a collaboration that he and Johns intend to pursue once the Silverchair album is done.) Hamilton who, as a formally trained musician, approached his craft in a totally different way to the unschooled Johns – 'my background is based in theory, in rules, in patterns; Dan has no real formal training in music' – was amazed by Johns's winning way with melody.

'We've been doing some writing together recently,' Hamilton mentioned to me mid 2005, 'and he would start singing these amazing melodies. I'm like, "Far out, I'm sitting next to Brian Wilson."' According to Hamilton, Johns possessed what he liked to call the 'sunshine' – the only other songwriter he'd encountered with a similar gift was none other than Luke Steele.

As Hamilton explained:

When you hear a song and the melodies and chords alone make you feel so positive – that's the sunshine. Listen to the chorus in 'Ana's Song' or 'World Upon Your Shoulders' or 'Greatest View' and it's easy to understand what I'm talking about. Dan's definitely got the sunshine, and it's something us trained writers and players would kill to have. Plus, he makes it seem so effortless. Don't get me wrong, I'm sure he has days when he battles with his music and doubts his writing, but when he's on fire, he really burns.

As these new songs began to come together during the UK summer of 2005, Johns was having second thoughts about going solo. His mind flashed back to WaveAid and the sheer noise thrills that he, Gillies and Joannou felt when they turned the SCG into a seething, sweating mass of bodies. 'I started writing this "solo album"', Johns said, 'then, as usual, I got about eight songs in and started missing Ben and Chris.' While still in the UK, Johns put in a call to Gillies and Joannou, floating the idea of using the songs he'd already written – alone and with others – for the fifth Silverchair album. His bandmates couldn't agree quickly enough, even though Gillies, despite his songwriting rebirth with Tambalane, was still left out of the creative process. Gillies wouldn't admit it publicly, but it must have stung him to look on as Johns teamed up with others – Paul Mac, Julian Hamilton, Luke Steele – rather than suggesting they try writing together again. As Gillies knew all too well, even a lone songwriting credit on a Silverchair album guaranteed handsome royalties.

Just prior to Christmas 2005, Johns returned to Oz. He, Gillies and Joannou rented a house (two houses, actually) in the Hunter Valley, near the NSW central coast, and entered a period of personal and musical rejuvenation.

Johns told *Rolling Stone*:

We just went to a little farm in the bush, and just lived and breathed and played music. [We] got back together, got to know each other again. It was great.

The Hunter Valley jams gave the band enough confidence to start recording demos of the new songs early in 2006. The trio worked in a few different studios, including Sydney's 301, where they had recorded most of *Diorama,* and Big Jesus Burger Studios, a facility in inner city Surry Hills. The latter studio was flooded with loads of natural light that poured through a skylight, which didn't sit too well with Silverchair. Despite their daylight experiments on *Diorama*, they were still more comfortable recording in the dark. So they booked the studio at night and worked during the graveyard shift. (It said plenty about Silverchair's intentions with the new record that they recorded demos in studios designed for proper album sessions. They weren't messing around.)

Roughly twenty new songs were rehearsed (Johns had stockpiled double that many), and about a dozen had been recorded as demos by March 2006, as the band readied themselves for their aforementioned brief return to playing live.

Even at this early stage, Johns had clear plans as to how the album would differ from its predecessor:

> If *Diorama* was like a painting, this is more like a sculpture. It's not going to sound professional or nice. I'm really proud of *Diorama*, but this one I'd like to make more dirge-y and swollen and infected. Some of this album is heavy, but not like heavy rock; it's not Wolfmother. It's more angular and heavy in terms of the emotion; [there'll be] a lot of Kraftwerk-inspired zone-out, done by a rock band. I want it to be sprawling and unpredictable. If people like it, they like it. I know I'm going to like it.

When I raised the subject of new sensations, Johns cited such albums as Talking Heads's *Remain in Light* and Brian Eno's *Here Come the Warm Jets* as key influences on the new Silverchair LP, *Young Modern*. Both were benchmark records in terms of cutting-edge production; the former was one of the first examples of a Western band embracing world music flavours.

But Johns also had other music dancing around in his head, as he explained to me when I asked him what to expect with the next album:

> Imagine The Band combined with elements of Kraftwerk and the Rapture and things like Talking Heads and Brian Eno, but really organic. [There'll be] swirling electronica and epic, cinematic soundscapes. There are still songs, though. It's not an art concept.

By April 2006, just as the band entered three weeks of pre-production at Sydney's Stagedoor studio – working in a rehearsal space they dubbed the 'Human Nature Room', due to its wall-to-wall mirrors, perfect for checking out your dance moves – Johns had finished the lyrics for the Hamilton co-writes.

It was the type of new twist that kept the short-attention-spanned Johns interested in making music with Silverchair.

> Julian's music, to me, didn't feel like it needed metaphorical confusion. It just needed really good lyrics instead of merely interesting ones. I've really started getting interested in words; in the past, I've not given a shit. I've never gone, 'Right, what am I writing about?' I've just written and hoped for the best. And there are probably five songs on this record where I've had something to communicate to people that I wanted to get through.

This was a big admission to make, especially for someone whose lyrics have often been scrutinised to within a punctuation mark of their life, and who has readily talked up the conceptual themes in Silverchair's work. (Need proof? *Neon Ballroom*'s liner notes read: 'Album Concept By Daniel Johns.')

Even at this early stage in the album's evolution, Johns could spot recurring themes in his lyrics, although he was reluctant to discuss them in great detail. But many of his new songs had come to him during a restless few nights, when he wandered about 'Nat's Castle', unable to sleep.

'It was a real "Across the Night" experience,' he said, referring to the epic night of songwriting (and showering) that led to the completion of *Diorama*'s centrepiece.

I didn't realise what I was writing about until I'd finished. Some of the lyrics are deliberately vague, whereas some are the most direct I've ever written. I'm really getting into the idea of trying to communicate to people who don't want to hear [Silverchair], as opposed to the music fans.

Nick Launay sensed a similar change in Johns's lyrical focus:

I think he sometimes gets inspired to write about a particular thing that has happened, or a feeling he has, and then turns it into meaning something else. I think that, as with many great songs, they will mean a different thing to different people. There are three songs about sleeping on this record ... I think he has been experimenting with not doing much of that!

Rather than write on the piano, which had been his weapon of choice of *Diorama*, Johns had now gone back to composing on the guitar. 'I really rediscovered my love of the guitar,' he said, a point proved beyond doubt by his amped-up performances during the band's brief live return in 2006. As unremarkable as this seems – Silverchair is a rock and roll band, after all – it's worth taking into account that only two years earlier Johns had virtually hung up his six-string. When Matt Lovell was working on Sarah MacLeod's *Beauty Was a Tiger* LP, he approached Johns about borrowing some guitars. Lovell found Johns's axes in storage, untouched, gathering dust and rust in equal proportions.

As for other inspirations, Johns was citing such arthouse flicks as *Memento* and *Pulp Fiction*; he was searching for some sort of narrative flow with the new LP. 'There's a lot of inter-relationship between songs,' he said. 'I want to cut stuff up, really cut it to pieces and put verses from one song into another, that type of thing.' And for the first time in a long time, Johns wrote while listening to other music. In the past he'd disappear into his own headspace, fearful of copying anything he was listening to at the time, and would only re-engage with the outside world when a sketch was done. As it turned out, one of these soundtracks to his new songwriting would also help Johns choose the producer for the fifth Silverchair album.

Johns was completely mad for Nick Cave and the Bad Seeds's latest two-album set, *Abattoir Blues/The Lyre of Orpheus*. 'It blew my mind to pieces,' he said. Once he recovered, Johns asked himself, 'Who the fuck produced that?' It turned out to be none other than Nick Launay, the expat Brit who had worked the controls for *Freak Show* and *Neon Ballroom* and who had gone 'egging' with the band back when they used to hoon around Newcastle in search of likely targets. 'I didn't consider many others for this record,' Johns said to me, as the band neared the end of their three weeks of pre-production in Sydney and started packing their bags for recording sessions that would take them from California's Laurel Canyon to the UK and Prague and then back to LA for the final mix.' Fortunately, it was someone I knew.' And Launay's reputation for perfectionism – he had often requested twenty or more takes of individual parts during sessions for *Freak Show* and *Neon Ballroom* – was no longer a concern for the band, as Ben Gillies explained to me. 'We're more mature now as people and as musicians,' he said, 'and we now know when to say, "That's enough". And we will.'

There was an explanation for their studio globetrotting while making the new record: Johns felt it was essential that at least some of the album be recorded in the same country where the songs were written. Sadly, the band had to scrap plans to record in London's Abbey Road – at roughly AUD$4000 per day, it was simply too expensive – even though Johns had written much of the album under the guise of Sir Whilliam Hathaway, his imaginary English 'statesmaia/poet' persona. If only he had access to some of Sir Whilliam's money, he might have been able to live out the dream of recording in the Old Dart. In the end, they opted for a cheaper UK studio.

Unlike earlier albums, where major label needs and Johns's fragile health had made for tough times in the studio, the only hitch during the making of *Young Modern* was of the band's design. It had been agreed that Launay would mix the record, as well as co-produce with Johns, but after four mixes were completed by September, Johns took a week's break and decided that he simply wasn't satisfied with the results. Citing the old classic 'musical differences', Johns fired a disappointed and slightly bewildered Launay (though he still retained his co-producer's credit). David Bottrill, Johns's right-hand man during *Diorama,* was put on hold to do the mix, which delayed the album's release until early 2007. If nothing else, this insistence on getting it absolutely right proved that this record truly belonged to Johns and the band. Everyone else was a hired hand.

As for their choice of California's Laurel Canyon, it was almost as rich in musical history as the famed Abbey Road, and it was also the preferred working home of LA-based Launay. Van Dyke Parks – who worked his magic on three *Young Modern* tracks, recorded in a studio-converted school where Albert Einstein once taught in Prague – had even written a pair of songs in honour of this legendary hideaway for musicians and other artists, on his surreal 1968 album *Song Cycle*. Only a short drive from Hollywood, yet sufficiently removed from La-La Land to keep your head clear, in its heyday during the late 1960s and early 1970s, Laurel Canyon had been to the LA muso scene what Woodstock once was to Bob Dylan, The Band and co. only a few years earlier: a musical Mecca. Frank Zappa, Joni Mitchell, Neil Young, Randy Newman and innumerable other music-makers had gravitated to 'the Canyon'. In the words of writer Barney Hoskyns, the bucolic spot presented the 'perfect antidote to urban stress and pollution'. More recently, uber-producer Rick Rubin had turned the former Laurel Canyon mansion of illusionist Harry Houdini into an idyllic studio-cum-playhouse. Among the many albums he produced there was the Red Hot Chili Peppers's career-making *Blood Sugar Sex Magik*. Silverchair were making a wise choice; Laurel Canyon oozed musical history and inspiration.

Ben and Chris took advantage of their new surrounding and, according to Launay, 'trained like athletes to play the best imaginable'. Their regime involved an 8 am start followed by a long run or hike in the Hollywood Hills.

It was also abundantly clear that Johns's post-*Diorama* experiences with the Dissociatives, and his other collaborations, had opened him up to a whole new planet of sound. He was now healthy and happily coupled; his life was as good as it had ever been. He dismissed a Sydney newspaper report that he and Imbruglia were experiencing trouble in paradise with a simple: 'Those things give me the shits. We heard about it and just went, "Who is this source?" Time will tell if our marriage is on the rocks.' Admittedly, their marriage could hardly be considered typical – Johns spends much of his time either on the road or locked away in a dark studio, while Imbruglia, in her role as the face of L'Oreal, is on call to attend product launches and parties virtually anywhere on the globe, often without her husband. But Johns had found something that closely resembled domestic harmony. This meant that he no longer had to look into his heart of darkness for inspiration, as he had during the grim days of *Freak Show* and *Neon Ballroom*. Instead he was soaking up new grooves from the people who surrounded him (and the one persona that he had created for his own amusement). Joannou and Gillies were essentially the same likeable blokes from 'Newie', just far worldlier – the BMW-driving Gillies had even developed a taste for Grange Hermitage. But Johns was a totally different person from the diffident teenager who glared at the world and snarled, 'Yeah, I'm a freak of nature' or taunted them with the lines, 'Come on, abuse me more, I like it.'

Julian Hamilton was one of those close enough to Johns to see the radical change he had undergone over the past few years:

> Sometimes I'll see a press photo or a billboard with him on it, looking all sad and troubled, and I'll have a laugh, because that's not the Dan that I know at all. He's just a regular guy. I think that most musicians are – despite the hype and spin and press photos, we're all just regular people.

Diorama producer David Bottrill also felt that there was a vast difference between the media-created image of Johns and the real man:

> He's a pretty unique character and his nationality has a lot to do with it. He's a happy Australian character, very warm, very welcoming, who had to spend a lot of his early years hiding away, protecting his privacy.

Bottrill cited Johns's strong ties with his family as a key reason why he hasn't lost himself in self-indulgence, or fallen victim to the dreaded 'lead singer syndrome'. 'He's a musician who can do what he wants, who's free of the trappings of rock stardom and fame.'

And the band could throw themselves into their fifth album safe in the knowledge that no other Australian band was in such a fortunate position. Silverchair were no longer dependent on a major label to bankroll their recordings, knowing as they did that they had the audience willing to pay to see them and thereby generate the necessary dollars whenever they felt the need to get back in the studio. This freedom also eliminated the possibility of another Kevin Williamson/'Ramble' experience: the only people passing judgement on Silverchair's new sounds were the band themselves and the few insiders who were exposed to the songs-in-progress. And rather than sign an overseas deal before cutting their fifth album, they had decided to sit down with US labels only when the record was done.

For a band seeking creative freedom and an all-round sense of autonomy, it was a flawless arrangement. Launay gave their new LP some truly high praise, describing it as 'more thematic than *Neon Ballroom*; it's quite conceptual. It's one of the most extravagant undertakings by any band in the world, more on par with "Bohemian Rhapsody", for example.' Having lived through the type of inner-band tension, commercial pressures and creative uncertainty that would kill most groups stone dead, not to mention Johns's own private horrors, the Silver-trio had now hit upon a design for survival that seemed to work.

After five albums, millions of record sales, hundreds of shows and several near break-ups, Silverchair were finally comfortable in their own skins, and were heading into a bold future, boundless in opportunity.

Johns summed it up neatly when I asked him about Silverchair circa 2006:

Now I feel relaxed, but I used to feel scared out of my head – all the time. Even on the *Diorama* tour I was so scared of fucking up and [having] people think I was shit. I'm still scared of people thinking I'm shit, but I'm quietly confident in what we're doing. [And] if you don't like what we're doing, well, you just don't get it.

* * *

Young Modern: An interview with Daniel Johns

It was early October 2006 when the phone rang. The man at the other end of the line announced himself as 'Whilliam' (with an 'h', of course). It took a minute to sink in; it was Daniel Johns, in Sir Whilliam Hathaway mode, back in the country briefly prior to the mixing of the band's fifth album. On the couch at home in Merewether, he spoke candidly about his aborted musical (really only a three-day experiment), *Young Modern's* 'medieval' influence, the song that changed his life, parenthood and the band's seemingly boundless future.

Would you say that the recording of Young Modern has stuck pretty much to the script?
Ah, it's had its twists and turns. We keep trying to explore different ways to do things and usually revert to the original concept, but occasionally something good happens. It's part of the luxury of having the confidence to do it how you want it to be and hope it's good. But it sounds great; we're really happy with it at the moment.

Can you tell me why you decided not to have Nick Launay mix the LP?
Listening to the mixes, I thought that more could be brought to the tracks considering what we put down. And I thought that David [Bottrill] worked so well last time, even with the complex tracks, that it'd be nice to work together again.

Is this part of your new role as lord of the Silverchair manor, making key decisions without a major label dictating the terms?
Yeah, I think so. I just felt like if it's not right and it doesn't give you goosebumps and doesn't inspire you in the way it once did, then you have to take back the reins and bring it back to what you had in mind. It's no longer up to anyone else to ensure it's good; it's up to me.

Do you enjoy being your own boss?
It's pretty good. [Nervous laugh] Now I feel more confident with what I want to do with music. If there are too many people involved, sometimes it can steer in the wrong direction and sometimes it takes a while to realise you're driving down the wrong freeway. We were fortunate in that we were in a situation that we could stop. It's the first record where we haven't had the pressure to rush it out. It's been so long that I wanted to make sure that this one is right.

Was there any tension in the studio?
Everyone has changed [since *Neon Ballroom*]; we were really relaxed around each other. It was more a case of when it's working we'll keep working together – and it worked for a really long time. But [sacking Launay] wasn't like some disaster; we just wanted to remix it and go with someone else. We both had a different role that we brought to production, and I was really happy with what we achieved. It was just that we had all this great stuff and I didn't want to crash the train. It was more my wanting to make sure that everything was right before we committed everything to tape for life. It's about wanting to make things really human and at the same time really unnatural.

You mentioned everyone from the Rapture to Kraftwerk as reference points for your new music: is it still that diverse?
Yeah, I think so. It doesn't sound like them but the approach to the music making is similar. There's some stuff that thinks a bit like Kraftwerk's *Autobahn,* where you can be crazy and go on this wild rampage and let everyone come with you. There'll be some headphone moments, too. Right now we're trying to make it more palatable; we're taking [The Beatles'] White Album style of production, where every instrument has its moment.

Does the album have a centrepiece, a la Diorama's *'Tuna in the Brine'?*
This record has a lot more facets than *Diorama* did; *Diorama* had two significant sides to it. I was trying to write something like the White Album but more condensed; I don't think one song encapsulates it. But I think 'If You Keep Losing Sleep' has a lot to do with the writing of the record. It was originally intended to be for a musical that was a tribute to sleep, but I cut that short. [Laughs] Yeah, songs for the sleepless. I feel like if you listen to, or write music all day, there's still reverb in your ears and your head. That can stop you from sleeping.

Does the process of recording an album feel like living in a vacuum, cut off from the real world?
Yeah, definitely. I feel a bit strange at the moment because we've been working so long on the record. It does feel like you're living in some kind of bubble. Sometimes you've washed so much that the suds are making

the surface area slippery so you can't actually find your feet. It's definitely a reluctant feeling, but once you're there you get used to it. There's a lot of stuff to think about with an album; you don't want to fuck it up.

Is it the same for Ben and Chris?
Once they've done their thing I take the reins and go where I want to go with the record. I feel really lucky that they've trusted me in the way they do. For all they know I could be sitting here making it absolutely mental, but they have enough trust to step away and say, 'Do your thing.'

How would you describe their roles in the studio, away from playing?
I think Ben plays the chilled-out role; he's the guy in the corner. People can't stop looking at his moustache and then off you go, there's some joke about Mexicana or something. Whenever you ask a question and you want a comical comeback, Chris is your man. He's like the Bill Hicks of the band, the Australian equivalent, crossed with a little Dame Edna.

Speaking of comics, how did it feel to work with Van Dyke Parks again?
It was so good, this time especially, having kind of known him longer and stayed friends with him. We had complete trust for each other and went for it. We had a great time in Prague, just hanging out and making music. It was important to take the tapes overseas and let them travel, take them somewhere exotic for a while and let them get a bit of . . . *air*. It was good to go to Eastern Europe and live in a different -world for a week. It felt like we were starting from a different perspective by the time we got back [to LA]. I'd never been there before, but I loved it; it's an amazing city. I got into the romance of the whole deal.

Van Dyke worked on three tracks: are there signature moments?
It's hard to describe some of the tracks because they've still got these grand gestures of orchestral madness, but the tracks are not the ones you'd expect to hear strings on, for the majority. It's a little bit more funky but still classic Van Dyke Parks. He really read into the vision of the album and got into what I wanted to achieve. He was spot on. And the whole presence of Van Dyke Parks, whenever you're with him, is hard to digest.

He's an astounding guy – he's achieved so much yet he's still the hippest guy I've ever met. You walk away and go, 'Man, *he's got it down*! We did three tracks together, but we also did celeste and harpsichord for other tracks. I don't know, I think the record might get a bit medieval. Every time I hear a harpsichord I start thinking about knights, but that might just be me.

Is it true that Van Dyke helped you name the album?
The first time I ever thought [*Young Modern*] was a great album title was when I called Van Dyke and talked about going out to dinner and he said, 'I'll see you there, Young Modern.' I thought, 'Yeah, that's a cool title.' Still to this day he calls me Young Modern. The only reason it's the title of a track is that I wanted to have the words 'young modern' in a lyric. I think the song is going to end up being called 'Young Modern Station'.

Will there be any of Diorama's *lushness on the new record?*
Yeah, there's definitely sentimental and romantic elements to this record, but it doesn't dwell so much on the same thing as the last record. We just tried to make something that sounds fresh and natural and sounds more like a band.

Sentimental? Are you talking about power ballads?
Ballads is such a weird word. To me it always reminds me of [Poison's] 'Every Rose Has Its Thorn'. To me, that's a ballad. There are definitely softer elements, but we tried to make them feel like The Band or Neil Young or something else that we really loved.

What about lyrical themes? Diorama *was very conceptual.*
There're a lot of repetitive themes and lines, but I think these lyrics are a bit more straightforward than the last Silverchair batch of lyrics. I was trying to be more literal and take the [listener's] concentration away from trying to figure out the lyrics and actually hear the music a lot better. You don't have to figure out puzzles. I guess that the goal with this record was to make it sound like a band playing together and take the influence of the music that I've enjoyed over the past couple of years and roll it into

this ball that encapsulates what we've done and what we want to do in the future. It's like a catapult this record; wherever we land is the catalyst for the next batch of stuff that we do.

Regardless, are you prepared for the scrutiny that is usually given to your lyrics?
There are some that people might take the wrong way, but I've always liked that about lyrics; I like to keep myself as uninformed as the listener as to what the song is about. Sometimes I want to write a song about two things and I combine them both, in a way that makes it feel as though it's one very broad thing. But I'm so sick about talking about my lyrics; it really does my head in.

Have you stayed in shape throughout this album's recording?
Yeah, I'm pretty healthy. I was making sure that I didn't stop eating or anything. I always get really obsessive-compulsive about things when I'm making a record. I get really unreliable. I think these things might be grating on people, but I get obsessed. I get a one-track mind and can't see that much reason because I know what I want the music to be like. But the potential of music, that's what gives you that internal pressure. You know that people would be so much happier if you get that perfect thing, if you make something truly special. It's not a disaster if you don't, but you can make something special, if you really push the boundaries of what you're 'supposed' to do.

With Diorama *you were forced to write a single; is there a radio-friendly song amongst the new tracks?*
I'm definitely conscious of it but I wasn't writing for it. But when those moments happened I would go, 'Oh fuck, that one comes in at under four minutes, it doesn't have a tempo change and it sounds pretty catchy to me. I think we have a single.' That was a lot better than sitting down and trying to write a single. I think, ultimately, we were trying to make something like a big U2 record.

Was this the largest budget you've ever had at your disposal?

If I was a betting man, I think it's the biggest budget we've had for a record, but now it's well and truly gone. I think this is the record that I've felt the most responsibility but also felt the least amount of external pressure. It doesn't feel like there's anyone on the outside pounding down on me.

Are you prepared for the long haul of promoting the album when it's done?
I want to make sure that this band is amazing, and the only way to do that is play more than you preferably would. I'd like to play a whole batch of shows and see how we can get the band to sound and really get in touch with that. Then maybe the next record will be even more live sounding.

Will you stick with the four-piece line-up?
For me it really worked with Julian [Hamilton] and now it really works with Paul [Mac]. Playing as a four piece is something I really like, and it has a really different quality that I like. The invitation is definitely there for Paul to keep playing, but I'm not sure anyone wants to put themselves through what we will probably be doing. Some people prefer not to do that. [Laughs]

Is Natalie OK with the idea of you being away for so long?
She's all right. She's known me long enough to understand.

Did you ever track down the so-called 'source' of the tabloid story suggesting you had marital problems?
Those things always slide over so quick. Everyone knows they're a load of shit after the first read. It's not like I have people coming up to me and saying, 'I hear you two are having trouble.' They last tor two weeks maximum; you just have to wait for them to blow over.

Were you tempted to write a song about it?
[Firmly] No way.

Do you ever check out your earlier music and think about how far you've progressed?

I don't really listen to the older stuff that much. When I do I smile and think it's novel and all that. But to me it's like a whole different band. To me, that's like the first band I was in with Ben and Chris, and we've now moved on to a different band. There was definitely a point where we changed bands as well, where we felt like we were no longer young kids in school trying to sound like our heroes. I think it was *Neon Ballroom*, I think that was definitely the start where I went, 'Hang on, now we're 17 or 18 and we should be playing more than the music we love. We should really write something significant.'

Was there one key song?
I think 'Emotion Sickness', in the sense of having a vision that was bigger than a rock and roll band and that we pulled off and didn't feel wrong about it. It was a catalyst for a lot of things I've done since. I don't feel any shame about anything I've written in the past, but 'Emotion Sickness' was one where I went, 'Oh fuck, cool, I can pull it off. Next time I'm really going to hone in on that idea and make it bigger and better.' I think that was the song that a lot of the stuff on *Diorama* was modelled on bettering.

Do you ever think about your days in The Loft and wonder how the hell you got to this point?
I never envisaged it any other way. Even when I was 12, I thought, 'All right, I'm a musician now, that's what I do.' I never thought about any other option from the moment I first started playing guitar. So I sort of expected all this, to always be playing music; there was never another option. I never enjoyed anything else so much as to devote my life to it. If it wasn't music, I was going to try and win the lottery.

Do you consider yourself fortunate?
I definitely feel lucky to be in a position at 27 to be making a record where you have the reins and have control over what you're doing. That's a blessed position to be in; I'd never take that for granted. I definitely feel lucky.

Can you predict the future of Silverchair?

I would love to make two or three more records with Silverchair, at least. This to me feels like we're starting something new, so it would be nice to see what would happen in another five years. I haven't discussed it with the other guys, it's all mental telepathy, but we can all feel the *vibe,* man.

Do you have a thicker skin these days?
You can stab me in my heart and I'll bounce back like some resilient fish. I don't get very affected by other people any more.

Have you and Natalie ever discussed being parents?
I've heard nothing but good reports [about having children], I'm not scared of it, but I don't want to do it yet. I'm not having kids until I'm about 70, and Natalie's happy with that. [Laughs] I've got no problem with the concept, I think it's very cool, but I have a few more years of exploring the benefits of not having to get up early. That's a good 50 per cent of how my brain works – and that's a big thing to give up. I need those extra hours in the morning.

SILVERCHAIR DISCOGRAPHY

Albums (Australia)

Release date	High point	Weeks in chart	
27/03/95	1	86	*Frogstomp*
03/02/97	1	67	*Freak Show*
08/03/99	1	64	*Neon Ballroom*
13/11/00	16	85	*Best Of Volume 1* (CD + DVD)
31/03/02	1	50	*Diorama*
21/10/02	60	21	*Silverchair – The Best of Volume 1*
17/12/02	N/A		*Rarities 1994 – 1999*

Albums (USA)

	High point	Weeks in chart
Frogstomp	9	48
Freak Show	12	20
Neon Ballroom	50	30
Diorama	91	2

Singles/EPs (Australia)

Release date	High point	Weeks in chart	
16/09/94	1	45	Tomorrow (EP)
13/01/95	2	22	Pure Massacre (S)
12/04/95	11	15	Israel's Son (S)

Release date	High point	Weeks in chart	
19/06/95	28	14	Shade (S)
13/11/95	N/A		Findaway (fan club only)
13/01/97	1	15	Freak (S)
24/03/97	9	29	Abuse Me (S)
30/06/97	5	21	Cemetery (S)
06/10/97	25	21	The Door (S)
15/02/99	3	35	Anthem for the Year 2000 (S)
10/05/99	14	25	Ana's Song (Open Fire) (S)
06/09/99 ·	17	31	Miss You Love (S)
Late 1999	N/A		Paint Pastel Princess (fan club only)
28/01/02	3	33	The Greatest View (S)
13/05/02	8	43	Without You
02/09/02	20	27	LuvYour Life
31/03/03	24	N/A	Across the Night

Singles (USA)

	High point	Weeks in chart
Tomorrow	1	26
Pure Massacre	12	16
Israel's Son	39	1
Abuse Me	4	16
Freak	25	7
Anthem for the Year 2000	15	13
Ana's Song	28	9
The Greatest View	DNC*	N/A

(* Did Not Chart)

Collections
1997	*Freak Box* (Freak Show Singles Box Set and interviews)
2002	*Diorama Singles Box Set*

DVDs
2000	*Emotion Pictures*
2000	*Best Of Volume 1: Complete Videology DVD*
2002	*Across the Night :The Making of Diorama*
2003	*Across the Night DVD single*
2004	*Live From Faraway Stables*

Soundtracks, Compilations etc.

Year	Track	Album/Film
1995	Stoned	*Mall Rats*
1996	Blind	*The Cable Guy*
1996	Surfin' Bird	*MOM, Vol 1: Music For Our Mother Ocean*
1996	Madman	*Tonnage, Vol 2*
1997	Spawn	*Spawn*
1998	Untitled	*Godzilla*
1998	Freak	*Head On (Remix for Us Rejects)*
1998	Freak	*Triple J Hottest 100, Vol 5*
1999	London's Burning	*Burning London, The Clash Tribute*
1999	Freak	*Shockwave*
1999	Freak	*Much at Edgefest*
1999	Anthem for the Year 2000	*WBCN Naked 2000*
2000	Punk Song #2	*Scary Movie*
2002	Anthem for the Year 2000	*Total Rock*

(Australia chart figures courtesy of ARIA; US chart figures courtesy of www.billboard.com)

Printed in Great Britain
by Amazon.co.uk, Ltd.,
Marston Gate.